W9-APX-315

Showdown

Showdown

How the Outlaws, Hells Angels and Cops
Fought for Control of the Streets

Jerry Langton

John Wiley & Sons Canada, Ltd.

Library and Archives Canada Cataloguing in Publication

Langton, Jerry, 1965–

   Showdown : how the Outlaws, Hells Angels and cops fought for control of the streets / Jerry Langton.

ISBN 978-0-470-67763-6

   1. Outlaws (Gang).   2. Hells Angels.   3. Parente, Mario.
4. Motorcycle gangs—Ontario.   I. Title.

HV6491.C32O5 2010a   364.1'0609713   C2010-901907-5

Production Credits
Cover design: Diana Sullada
Interior design: Michael Chan
Interior layout: Thomson Digital
Illustrations: Tonia Cowan
Printer: Solisco-Tri-Graphic Printing Ltd
Cover image credits: © Johner Photography/Veer, ©iStockphoto.com/shipov, ©iStockphoto.com/gaffera, ©iStockphoto.com/DuxX

Editorial Credits
Executive Editor: Don Loney
Production Editor: Pauline Ricablanca

John Wiley & Sons Canada, Ltd.
6045 Freemont Blvd.
Mississauga, Ontario
L5R 4J3

Printed in Canada

1 2 3 4 5 TRI 14 13 12 11 10

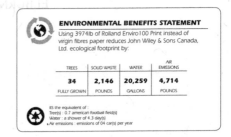

ENVIRONMENTAL BENEFITS STATEMENT
Using 3974lb of Rolland Enviro100 Print instead of virgin fibres paper reduces John Wiley & Sons Canada, Ltd. ecological footprint by:

TREES	SOLID WASTE	WATER	AIR EMISSIONS
34	2,146	20,259	4,714
FULLY GROWN	POUNDS	GALLONS	POUNDS

Its the equivalent of :
Tree(s) : 0.7 american football field(s)
Water : a shower of 4.3 day(s)
Air emissions : emissions of 04 car(s) per year

Contents

Introduction

"I'm really sorry I have to miss our ball game tonight," I told my nine-year-old son. "I have to take a biker out to dinner."

Aware of what I do to make a living, that made perfect sense to him. For as long as my son could remember, his dad had been an author who wrote about crime, particularly bikers. Actually, he thought it was pretty cool. Immediately, he asked me if the biker had ever killed anyone. Yes, I told him, he had.

So I called up Nick, my assistant coach, to take over the game for me, and made plans to meet one of the most important and influential figures in the history of Canadian outlaw motorcycle gangs.

It had all started with an e-mail about a week earlier. It read: "I've got your next bestseller."

Ever since I started writing books, I've gotten a lot of e-mails like that, so I was prepared to ignore it. I didn't recognize the name of the person who sent it, so I was within a second of hitting the delete button when I read further and saw that the person in question was promising to get me in contact with Mario "The Wop" Parente. That really caught my eye.

If the subject of my first book — super-secretive and incredibly powerful former Hells Angels national president Walter

Stadnick — represents the Holy Grail of Canadian bikers from a reporter's standpoint, Parente is at least the Ark of the Covenant.

While Stadnick's Hells Angels were building a coast-to-coast organization that dominated the drug and vice trades from Halifax to Vancouver, they were, for the most part, stopped at the Ontario line.

While it was well established and common knowledge that Ontario is by far the most lucrative market in Canada for organized crime, Hells Angels just couldn't make anything substantial happen there for a very long time. After fighting and winning two bloody wars to conquer Quebec's underworld, leaving hundreds of people — some of them totally innocent, one of them an 11-year-old boy — dead, they swept through B.C., Alberta, Manitoba, Saskatchewan and the Atlantic provinces with relative ease. But, even after that, the mighty Hells Angels couldn't do a thing in Ontario.

According to many people on every side of the situation, the main reason was Parente. He grew up in the same place as Stadnick — my own hometown; a decaying former industrial hub called Hamilton, Ontario — and they weren't very far apart in age. They both became bikers in high school. In fact, they even sort of ran together in the 1970s when Parente was a member of Satan's Choice, and Stadnick was in charge of a gang called the Wild Ones who worked off and on for the Choice, among others. Stadnick, according to many sources, desperately wanted to become a member of the Choice (or any other major gang), but they wouldn't have him.

It wasn't because he wasn't a good biker. He was tough and smart and — from what I've been told repeatedly — extremely talented at selling drugs. But he had one serious shortcoming in the eyes of Satan's Choice. He was just five-foot-four. Because of his height, or lack of it, lots of people — bikers, cops, Mafia, media — disrespected him. And they totally underestimated him.

But few who knew Parente withheld their respect. He's not really tall, but he's rock solid. While nobody has ever tracked down a legitimate job held down by Stadnick (and I have spent many hours trying), Parente had worked in construction and welding and regularly served as a bouncer at some of Hamilton's most notorious bars and strip joints. It was a profession that put him head-to-head with Hamilton's street toughs and members of such esteemed local organizations as the Ball-Peen Hammer Boys. And he always came out on top.

The dude was, indeed, hardcore. He'd taken a bullet for the club and had more than once fired one. In a city and a province (and a country for that matter) in which bikers were eclipsing the traditional Italian and Irish Mafias for organized crime supremacy, Parente held considerable sway. And when the Outlaws — the oldest and second-most powerful motorcycle gang in the United States — came north to expand, they spoke with him.

The Hamilton Chapter of Satan's Choice became the Outlaws, and Parente was their president. The affiliation with the giant American organization only added to his power.

And it's not like Stadnick disappeared, either. Eschewed by the Ontario bikers, he was, ironically, accepted by the more powerful, more established Hells Angels in Quebec. Despite his size and utter lack of French-language skills, he was so well liked by them, that he eventually became the Hells Angels' national president — a post far above the dreams of the hardscrabble Hamilton bikers who wouldn't let him into their clubs.

And he did it, some say, without firing a shot or even throwing a punch. While it's unlikely that Stadnick rose to such prominence in the world of outlaw bikers completely without violence (and a great deal of evidence contradicts that theory), there is consensus among bikers and cops alike that he was extraordinarily nonviolent for a biker chieftain. He managed to build a Hells Angels empire stretching from Vancouver Island to Halifax with very little bloodshed. And he stayed well under the radar while doing it. Rarely arrested and never convicted of anything worse than a traffic ticket during his reign, he refused to speak to the media and was monosyllabic with the police, never giving them anything they could use against him or anyone else.

He was a new kind of biker — national president as stoic, secretive, outlaw CEO. Stadnick built the Canadian Hells Angels as a giant corporation with mergers, acquisitions and the occasional hostile takeover. He had strategic alliances, franchises, branch offices and even subsidiaries.

But he was stopped in Ontario. The Ontario bikers — an uneasy alliance between the Outlaws, the Para-Dice Riders, the Vagabonds, what remained of Satan's Choice after the Hamilton merger and others — knew Stadnick had his eyes on their province. Not only was it Canada's richest market for drugs and vice, it was where he was from. Imagine how galling it must have been for him to control a mighty nationwide criminal organization, but not be able to walk the streets of his own hometown without bodyguards. It was so bad for him that, when he was in hospital in Hamilton recovering from severe burns received in a motorcycle accident, Hells Angels actually sought and received police protection for him. Significantly, even though Parente was behind bars at the time, his name came up in a phone conversation between Stadnick's common-law wife and police.

And that's how it stood for many years: Hells Angels reigning basically unopposed — after putting down the Rock Machine rebellion in Quebec — throughout Canada. Except Ontario. While the Outlaws stood at the top of a multi-headed monster that ruled that richest and most desirable of provinces.

But things changed. And years later, I'm taking Parente out for a bite to get his side of the story.

I make the plans with Luther, the guy who e-mailed me in the first place. He suggests we meet in Burlington. Since they both live east of Hamilton and I'm in downtown Toronto, Luther says they are "meeting me half way." I tell him I'm looking forward to it. He describes a restaurant located opposite the gas station across from Spencer Smith Park. He can't remember the name, but his directions are succinct. I know the area well. My wife's from Burlington, and we were married in a church about three blocks away from the restaurant. I ask how I'll recognize them. "Well, I'm about six-foot-four ..." says Luther.

In the days before the meeting, some of my friends joked about how dangerous they thought the whole thing was. I laughed it off, pointing out that Parente would have no reason to want to harm me. But when I got stuck in traffic, I was careful to call Luther to let him know I'd be a couple of minutes late. Certainly wouldn't want to be rude. Luther laughed and said it'd be fine.

Some creative highway driving got me there before them. There are actually two restaurants at the place Luther described, but one's kind of a cafeteria, so I ignored it. I looked inside the better place. I waited out front. Ten minutes passed. I called my brother; he kept me loose. I looked over my shoulder and saw two big, tough-looking guys sitting at a table on the patio outside the cafeteria.

"Luther?" I asked the huge guy. He shook my hand and grinned. It was a sincere smile. He introduced me to Mario, but called him Mike. I wasn't surprised. Before the meeting, I called up veteran Hamilton biker cop Sergeant John Harris and asked him about meeting up with Parente. He told me: "If you want to get on his good side, call him Mike; he hates being called Mario."

Okay, so he's Mike. Cool. They complained to me about waiting for a waitress. I pointed out that they could wait all they like, but no waitress would ever come out of the cafeteria. We agreed to go to the nicer restaurant next door.

We sat. There was silence. I gestured at Parente's ball cap. "Redskins fan?" I asked him.

He nodded.

"Why?" I asked. "Jack Kent Cooke?" It was a strange gambit, but over the years I have met three people from Hamilton who became Washington fans because Cooke, their longtime owner, was a self-made billionaire from their hometown.

Mario laughed. "Nah, it goes back to John Riggins and those guys." I noted that the only guy he mentioned was the NFL's last great white halfback, and that he mispronounced the name Riggins "Reagan." I told him I'm a Colts fan. He said that's an easy pick because they always win. I told him that I've been a Colts fan for more than 30 years and had seen my share of 1–15 and 2–14 seasons. He commiserated. I was beginning to like him already.

When he took his hat off, I finally got a good look at Parente. His face kind of looked like Joe Pesci's, and he gave off a similar but far less unctuous vibe. He had very dark brown eyes that indicated a depth of intelligence. His head was shaved, but he had a thick, short, whitish-gray beard that started at his cheekbones.

It was augmented by a longer, thicker Fu Man-chu mustache of the same color. The line of his nose was an elongated *S*, indicating multiple breakages. I looked closely at both of his eyes, because I had heard he'd been stabbed in one of them, but couldn't see any permanent damage.

He talked with his hands like gangsters do in movies. It was very hard not to be charmed by his mixture of wit, bonhomie and strident speech.

He wasn't tall, maybe six-foot, but he was clearly strong. He was thick all over. He later told me that was because there's nothing much else to do in prison aside from lift weights.

While Parente looked like he'd wandered off *The Sopranos* lot, Luther appeared as Scottish as his last name indicates (although he later told me he's of Irish descent). He looked bigger than he said he was and had a great deal of natural muscle. He had long, wavy reddish-brown hair and a more thoughtful face than I normally associate with bikers. Aside from the tattoos, he looked more like people I know in the music business than the bikers I've interviewed. He didn't say much — this was clearly Parente's show — but enjoyed a laugh and indicated there was a deep backstory to him.

They were nervous about ordering. I told them not to worry, that an interested TV producer would be paying for dinner. To get the ball rolling, I ordered a pint of Stella Artois, Parente got a Coors Light, Luther, significantly, had a coffee. I ordered bruschetta for the table and a pizza before thinking that it might offend a guy named Mario "The Wop" who'd rather be called Mike.

He ordered a pizza, too. He flirted a little with the young, plain-looking waitress. Luther claimed not to be hungry, but I insisted. He said he'd have a slice. Confused, the waitress said they only serve whole pizzas. He demurred and said he'd share Parente's.

Before we started talking, Parente put his hand on my notebook. Clearly he didn't want me to write anything down. That was fine with me. I have a great memory.

For the next four hours, Parente talked. And he was fascinating. A charismatic guy who really knows how to tell a story, he told me what it's like to be a biker, what it's like to do time and what it's like to shoot someone. He told me things I didn't know about Stadnick and some of the cops, lawyers and bikers I had interviewed. To my surprise, he didn't dodge a single question, and he told me quite frankly how it felt to kill another man.

For a reporter, it was a gold mine. I knew he wasn't going to say anything to incriminate himself or libel anyone else, but I also knew that he'd provide an unprecedented look inside Canadian outlaw biker gangs.

He asked me what I intended to write. I told him that my thesis was that Stadnick's Hells Angels were doing everything they could to build a national empire and that the biggest obstacle to moving into Ontario was Parente and his Outlaws, but that politics and law enforcement and other factors had changed all that. He smiled and said that was actually pretty accurate.

There was a couple at the table next to us. She was about 25 and wearing less than the weather demanded. Parente had already commented on her appearance in frank terms. She was with a neatly dressed, well-coiffed man in his late 50s, maybe 60. It had been obvious that she was listening to our conversation and, now that she'd had a few drinks, she'd finally gathered the courage to talk to us.

Looking right at Parente, she gestured at her date and said as a curly blonde lock fell between her eyes: "You probably don't know this, but he's the best criminal lawyer in Hamilton."

Without missing a beat, Parente looked him up and down and asked him: "Oh yeah? What's your name?"

The guy, looking and sounding rather pompous, told him.

Parente chuckled. "I've heard of you; but you're not the best." Then he returned to our conversation.

Chapter 1
Death of a Godfather

A man lay in a pool of his own blood on a Hamilton sidewalk struggling for breath. It was May 31, 1997. His death was the start of a revolution that decided who was in charge of organized crime in Ontario.

He wasn't a Hells Angel or an Outlaw. And he certainly wasn't a Loner or Para-Dice Rider or anything like that. He wasn't a biker at all, and neither was the man who killed him.

No, he was John "Johnny Pops" Papalia. He was the Godfather of the Hamilton Mafia, and the primary source of cocaine and other drugs — as well as a mastermind of prostitution, loan-sharking and other products delivered via organized crime — in Southern Ontario.

Born in 1921 to a Calabrian family in Hamilton, Papalia dropped out of school at 13, so he could get into the family

John "Johnny Pops" Papalia

business — organized crime. His father, Antonio, was one of a close-knit group of Italians in Hamilton that ran liquor into the U.S. during prohibition (the same men smuggled liquor *into* Canada during its own, earlier era of prohibition). "I grew up in the '30s, and you'd see a guy who couldn't read or write but who had a car and was putting food on the table," Johnny said proudly. "He was a bootlegger, and you looked up to him." Antonio was also a prime suspect in the assassination of Rocco Perri, Hamilton's first Godfather.

John Papalia developed an even more profound mistrust of authority than you'd expect, even from someone who spent their whole life involved in organized crime. It happened when his beloved father was confined at an internment camp during World War II. His crime was being a prominent Italian. Johnny is said to have taken it hard.

With prohibition long over in both countries and most of the Hamilton Mafia veterans and leaders involuntarily working in Northern Ontario, Johnny did what he could to get by. That generally meant burglaries. He was so successful at it that he started a prosperous fencing operation in an abandoned ice warehouse at the corner of Railway and Mulberry Streets, across the road from where he lived with his mother, Rosie, whose cousins had been involved with Perri's business. Papalia was not a big man — maybe five-foot-eight and slight — but he had a reputation for extreme violence, and was rarely messed with.

He was first arrested in 1945 for a burglary, but he didn't see any real jail time until 1947, when he was caught running an illegal gambling house in his warehouse. Inside, he met a successful Toronto heroin dealer named Harvey Chernick (who, in turn, was being supplied by Sicilian Antonio Sylvestro). In the almost two years they were behind bars together, Chernick taught him the trade and hooked him up with suppliers.

Almost as soon he started selling heroin, Johnny got caught. A cop spotted him making a deal in front of Toronto's busy Union Station and took him in. But Papalia was, above all, resourceful. At his trial, he told the judge that he wasn't selling a drug, but buying one. In the days before sophisticated forensics, he convinced the judge that the white power he had wasn't heroin, but a patent medicine cooked up by a friend. It was the only thing, he said, that helped relieve the pain of his syphilis.

The judge — apparently believing nobody would admit in a public forum to having syphilis unless he really had it — bought the story and gave him two years less a day if he promised to see a doctor when he was released.

Papalia did his time and was rewarded for keeping his mouth shut with an apprenticeship in Montreal with some friends of Sylvestro's — Luigi Greco and Carmine Galante. Both were big-time mobsters, who had met with the likes of Lucky Luciano and had strong ties with the Manhattan-based Bonanno crime family. In fact, Galante had been Joseph Bonanno's personal driver and had been sent to Montreal by him specifically in an attempt to dominate the city's drug trade.

After he had learned the ropes, Papalia went back to Hamilton where he bought a taxi company on the city's heavily Italian James Street North. The cops believed that the cabs were just a front for a gambling ring. When one of the drivers, Tony Coposodi, was executed with two bullets to the back of the head, suspicions that the bootlegger's boy was up to no good increased.

Throughout the '50s, Papalia played the part of the area God-father with great gusto. He had big, fancy cars, wore expensive suits, squired around lots of pretty women and always carried at least $1,000 in cash with him. He always liked to flash what he called "reds and browns" ($50 and $100 bills) wherever he went.

He had protection-racket money coming in from Montreal and extortion-racket money and gambling-house money coming in from Toronto, in addition to what he made in Hamilton. Although he had many slices of many different pies there, the bulk of his money came from an ingenious loan-sharking scheme. He would lend money to anyone, especially business owners. They would agree to pay back $6 for every $5 borrowed. If it wasn't repaid in a week, every $5 of the new balance would require a $6 repayment the following week. Few could afford this outrageous 1,040 percent annual interest. Traditionally when a debtor defaults to the Mafia, they take what they can from him and then kill or severely injure him. And there's little doubt that Papalia and his men did plenty of that, but he gave some business owners another option. They could just put in his vending machines — he had since set up a company at his old Railway Street headquarters called Monarch Vending Machines — with all the profits going back to him. Of course, the debt wouldn't be forgiven, just some of the interest knocked off. It was incredibly lucrative — because much of what they sold in the vending machines was stolen through truck hijackings or warehouse burglaries — and it even gave him the veneer of a legitimate business.

Papalia made the big time in 1959. He was the only Canadian invited to a meeting in New York that set up what was later to be known as "the French Connection." Joe Valachi, the minor-league gangster who later turned world-famous informant, was in attendance and testified that he knew of Papalia as a capo (boss) who ran much of Southern Ontario under the auspices of the Buffalo-based Magaddino Family.

The plan was to source high-grade heroin from the Middle East, funnel it through France and then ship it to New York, the distribution point for North America.

Papalia worked extensively with the Sicilian Agueci brothers until 1961, when Vito Agueci was arrested and the Magaddinos had Alberto Agueci murdered. But that didn't slow Papalia down. He found new European connections — including Sicilians working out of France — to keep the heroin supply steady. And he understood that it was just business. There were no hard feelings between him and the Magaddinos over the dismissal of the Aguecis.

Back home, Papalia became a victim of his own ambition. For years he had been involved in an extortion racket with a group of mostly Jewish bar owners, but he decided he wanted it all. One man, Max Bluestein, refused to play ball, so Papalia and his men showed up at his Yonge Street jazz club, the Town Tavern. When Bluestein exited the bar, Papalia and his men beat him nearly to death with a metal pipe. No less a celebrity than Pierre Berton referred to it as a "semi-execution," and made it the focus of a personal anti-organized crime campaign in his newspaper column.

But not a single one of the literally hundreds of people who witnessed the beating outside the popular nightclub on the country's busiest stretch of pavement came forward to testify against Papalia. Even Bluestein claimed not to know who did it to him.

But a marked increase of police raids on his and his associates' businesses convinced Papalia — or, more likely his boss, Magaddino — that he should turn himself in. He got 18 months.

After almost a year in prison, Papalia was indicted by the Americans for his involvement in the French Connection. As he was being led to the airplane to take him south of the border, a couple of reporters caught his eye. "I'm being kidnapped! Help me!" he screamed at them. "They're taking me someplace I don't want to go!"

Indeed they were. Papalia was sentenced to ten years in a West Pennsylvania prison. But, just as he had convinced a Toronto judge he needed heroin for his syphilis, Papalia fooled the U.S. Justice Department into thinking he had tuberculosis. They let him out after less than five years on compassionate grounds. When a group of American reporters met him at the gate on his release, he refused to talk with them, claiming not to be important enough to warrant their time. "Look, fellows, I'm a sick man," he told them. "I'm not even a spit in the ocean; I'm a nothing."

Back in Hamilton, he was greeted with a big party and great a show of fealty from his old crew. But he also received some bad news. While Papalia was in prison, the Magaddinos had turned over some of his interests in Toronto to his much-hated rival from Woodbridge, Paul Volpe. It enraged Johnny Pops. Not only was Volpe young and loud-mouthed, representing the new generation of gangsters Papalia had no use for, but he also freely admitted to having a homosexual relationship when he was younger. Papalia considered him to be an absolute abomination.

Humiliated over the ascension of Volpe, Papalia met with acting Ontario boss Giacomo Luppino (also from Hamilton) to see if he could get his Toronto businesses back. He didn't, but he appeared to have a new job.

On June 6, 1969, police saw Papalia visit Luppino at a restaurant on College Street in Toronto. The next day, the bullet-riddled body of Filippo Vendemini was discovered in the parking lot behind his small Bloor Street West shoe store. When his wife, Giuseppina, found him, her screaming was so loud that a couple of neighbors called police to report a woman was being assaulted.

The police determined that the former extortionist and smuggler was said to have owed money to the wrong people. Under questioning, Giuseppina (who was pregnant with the couple's sixth child) provided little of value other than the fact that Filippo had been on the phone frequently with a man named Vincenzo. And she described a man she'd seen him with the day before he died.

The police soon tracked down Vincenzo Sicari, a Montreal pizzeria owner who had worked for Salvatore "Sammy" Triumbari, an extortionist whose murder two years earlier had gone unsolved. Sicari told them that he and Vendemini had gone to Hamilton to visit a mutual friend. Then Vendemini drove him to Toronto International Airport. The next thing he heard, Vendemini was dead.

On July 28, 1969, Papalia was again seen with Luppino in Toronto. Later that day, Sicari's body was found in the same neighborhood as Vendemini's.

It was at about this time that many started referring to Papalia as "the Enforcer" in reverent tones. Although respected by everyone who knew him, Papalia was far from well liked. He had a habit of stealing his friends' wives and girlfriends and then dumping them. He had little tolerance for young wannabes and would viciously taunt and punish them for minor mistakes and transgressions. "We had to respect him because of his role," said one Hamilton man who worked with him. "But he got on everybody's nerves."

Over the years, Papalia maintained his control over Hamilton and most of Southern Ontario, but his interests in Toronto dwindled as Volpe's star rose. Papalia ruled Hamilton like a sultan, establishing the Gold Key Club in the mid-1970s. No storefront hole where old men would quietly sip espressos, this ostentatious nightclub boasted a luxurious lounge, private rooms and an elaborate discotheque. Only members and their guests — usually dates and local celebrities — could get in. "There wasn't actually any gold key," said Sergeant John Harris of the Hamilton police.

"They used a password that changed from time to time, just like in gangster movies."

It had a huge illuminated sign that hung over Main Street. Across Wentworth Avenue was Cathedral High School, where the next generation of members was expected to come from. And across Main was a 24-hour coffee shop. There was always at least one cop in the front window. "Nobody ever went in or out of there without us knowing about it," one retired cop who pulled Gold Key duty told me. "We knew who they all were, but they didn't care."

Not everyone in the Gold Key Club could trace their roots back to Sicily or Calabria. A lot of non-Italians worked at the club or with the members. Papalia himself married a woman of Irish descent he met at the club. Shirley Ryce was a bartender there when she caught Johnny's eye. A tall blonde, her dad had been a bookie with close ties to Papalia's sphere of influence.

He declared bankruptcy in 1982, but somehow managed to be chauffeured around town and show off his still-thick wad of bills. Things got immeasurably better for him on November 13, 1983 when Paul Volpe's body was found curled up in the trunk of his wife's BMW in a long-term parking lot at the Toronto airport. With him out of the way, and Luppino a doddering 84-year-old, the Magaddinos had no choice but to put Papalia in charge of Ontario.

He expanded everywhere. A joint task force arrested 10 men in Toronto's Greektown on Danforth Avenue, including two they knew were friends of Papalia's, in December 1985. But they couldn't get anything to stick to Johnny Pops. "Yeah, I know the people they charged — they're friends of mine," he told a reporter. "But that doesn't mean I was involved; I wasn't, because I wouldn't have anything to do with Greeks — I don't like them, I don't like their restaurants, I don't like their food."

Well into the '90s, Papalia was the undisputed Godfather in Hamilton, especially after Luppino died in 1987. He owned an entire city block among his vast real estate holdings. His companies were the biggest vending-machine and liquor-dispensing equipment firms in Canada. He made millions, and laughed about it in the media.

But eventually ill health — particularly his troublesome gallstones — did what his enemies and law enforcement never could, it slowed him down. The old man didn't get out much after about 1994 or so. He'd make the short trip from his easy chair in his 14th-floor Market Street penthouse apartment to the black leather couch at Monarch Vending. At the penthouse, he spent most of his time in his big leather chair watching old movies on his big-screen TV. And at the business, he generally chatted with the old guard or dozed off. He lived that way until the day he was shot and killed on the way to Monarch from his home.

At the time, some speculated that he was suffering from the early stages of Alzheimer's. But everybody still did what the old man said. And one of his rules was that his men were never to deal with the Hells Angels. He'd seen what they'd done in Montreal, and he didn't trust them. And it was probably that pronouncement that kept Hells Angels out of Ontario for so very long. While Hells Angels could probably have taken on the Outlaws and every other biker gang in the province, they would not have picked a fight with Papalia and his boys. Because then they'd also be looking at war with the Magaddinos, Cotronis, Violis, Musitanos and potentially even the Rizzutos. It was not a good plan.

And, although it would have been in their best interest to do so, the Hells Angels did not kill Papalia.

It was one his own. Sort of. Papalia and his old friend Dominic Musitano both operated out of headquarters on Railway Street. Compared to Papalia, who by this time ruled all of Ontario and answered only to the Magaddinos, the Musitanos were small-time. "They were not at the same level of Papalia," said Canadian organized-crime expert Antonio Nicaso. "For many years, the Musitano family lived in the shadow of Papalia."

Their relationship was grudging at best, with paranoid, willful Papalia not always trusting the short-tempered and secretive Musitano. And they had one consistent bone of contention — whom they'd hire.

Johnny was dead set against bikers of any stripe, but Dominic (and his brother Antonio) used them all the time for all kinds of jobs. They sold his coke, they bombed businesses that fell behind in their payments and they made witnesses' minds change about testifying.

Dominic, the only potential threat among the Italians to Papalia's power structure, suffered a massive coronary in 1985, and his ability to lead diminished consistently until he died of a stroke in 1991. Antonio, also known as Tony, didn't have Dominic's leadership ability and, in any case, he wasn't able to act in any significant way with so many parole restrictions stemming from convictions for conspiracy to commit murder, six bombings, two attempted bombings and two arsons.

So the Musitanos' business fell to Dominic's two sons: Pasquale (better known as Pat) and Angelo (better known as Ang). They represented a different breed; they were, according to many who knew them, North American kids who learned about the Mafia from movies and TV, rather than from the old Sicilian or Calabrian traditions. "They were totally different in terms of character than Papalia; he always tried to keep a low profile — he was a very old-fashioned boss in that sense," said Nicaso. "They are the new face of organized crime — they like to show off."

Both Ang, who was a heavy man, and Pat, who was truly obese, liked to wear expensive tailor-made suits and lots and lots of jewelry. And they liked to, as one cop told me, "play at being gangsters." They got in contact with a lowlife named Kenny Murdock. They had known him since they were both young children because he used to drive their dad around. They also remembered that, back in 1985, just before his heart attack, their dad had hired Murdock to kill a man named Salvatore Alaimo.

It was typical of how Dominic did business. Alaimo had no beef with the Musitanos; he was just a janitor at the now-defunct but then-enormous Stelco steel plant. It was Alaimo's brother, Gianni, who was in deep to the Musitanos with gambling debts. Dominic's logic was that a dead man won't pay his debts, so it was pointless to kill Gianni. But there are other ways to get a man to pay.

When the Musitano boys got in touch with Murdock in 1997, he was delighted. Without much else positive in his life, he had developed a great deal of fondness for and dedication to the family, and thought of the boys kind of like nephews. The boys didn't know it at the time, but Murdock had met Dominic in Collins Bay Institution in Kingston and Dominic asked him to take care of his boys if anything ever happened to him. In effect, that made Murdock the Godfather's godfather. The Musitanos gave Murdock a list of four names and indicated they wanted them all killed. They promised him $10,000 cash and a nice big bag of cocaine.

Kenny Murdock

The first name on the list was Johnny Pops. And on May 31, 1997, Murdock shot him dead on Railway Street.

The next name on the list was Carmen Barillaro. Johnny Pops was a secretive, paranoid man who left no clear line of succession. But it was obvious to anyone who knew the situation that, with Johnny Pops dead, the crown would be hoisted by his right-hand man, Barillaro, who ran the Niagara Falls family.

Barillaro was an old friend of Papalia's, and the two moved seamlessly from running heroin to cocaine as fashions changed. He'd gotten in some trouble over the years, too. Caught trafficking in 1979, he was also arrested in 1989 for hiring a woman to kill a debtor — she chickened out and turned informant — and again in 1992 after getting caught with seven kilograms of cocaine and 900 kilograms of weed.

By 1997, though, he was free and clearly the successor to Papalia. His reign lasted less than two months. On July 23, 1997, Ang drove Murdock to Barillaro's house. He parked around the corner so he would not be recognized. Murdock walked up to the house and knocked on the door. When Barillaro answered, he made something up about wanting to know if the Corvette in the driveway was for sale. Suspicious, or perhaps recognizing him, Barillaro tried to shut the door on him. Murdock burst in and killed the older man then fled back to Ang's still-running car.

With Papalia and Barillaro gone, there were no Mafiosi left in Ontario of any merit other than the Musitano brothers. They were now in charge.

And they weren't finished. Although the Musitanos had long hired and dealt with bikers, they didn't like the idea of any major competition in their hometown. Third on Murdock's list was former wrestler and biker Johnny K-9.

Although the Satan's Choice chapter had been slowed down significantly in Hamilton and had kicked K-9 out of the club, K-9 was still active in the city and, sources say, still selling cocaine he bought from Hells Angels. He was small-time, to be sure, but he was competition and he had connections the Musitanos did not want to deal with. Sure they ran the Hamilton Mafia now, but — with suspicions rapidly growing over their involvement with the deaths of Papalia and Barillaro — they didn't have many friends to call on if they had a war with Hells Angels.

On August 20, 1997, with a gun in his pocket, Murdock knocked on K-9's door. The big man answered and invited him in. Murdock shook his head. "John, I've been sent here to kill you," he said. "But I'm not going to do it." Stunned, all K-9 could do was thank him. Murdock told him to be careful and left.

There was a fourth name on the list, but it was never made public. At least three sources have told me that they believed the fourth name was that of Outlaws president Mario Parente.

Whether Murdock decided against killing that fourth target or not, he was apprehended on an earlier extortion warrant. After he was interrogated, the Hamilton cops played him an audiotape of his buddies, the Musitanos. The cops had bugged the Gathering Spot, their pizza restaurant on James Street North, and had recorded them talking about Murdock. They laughed at him, described what a scumbag they thought he was and joked about how much better off they'd be if he somehow met with a tragic accident. Murdock broke and turned informant. In exchange for his testimony, he received a 13-year sentence.

The Musitanos were immediately arrested. Both were charged with the murder of Papalia, and Ang was also charged with the murder of Barillaro. The whole ugly story came out. Murdock said that, despite the promise of $10,000 and a big bag of coke, he

Pat Musitano

only received $2,000. "But I would have done it for free," he testified, because of his love for the family.

The Musitanos — who, in court as well as on tape, made no secret of their disgust with their former employee — surprised the court by entering guilty pleas for conspiracy to murder Barillaro. In exchange, charges related to Papalia's murder were dropped. They were both sentenced to 10 years.

In the space of about a year, the Hamilton — and therefore Ontario — Mafia had effectively ceased to exist. Johnny Pops was dead. The only other man capable of leading, Barillaro, was dead. The Musitanos, flawed as they were, were also behind bars. What was left of the Magaddino Family were under so many legal restrictions and police surveillance that they were essentially handcuffed, and unable to act. But, in truth, there wasn't anybody in Hamilton or elsewhere in Ontario that was up to the task.

At least, there wasn't anyone among the Italians. There were still bikers. And, with biker-hating Papalia out of the way, they were more free than ever to wear their colors and operate their businesses. But there were problems there. The Outlaws were allegedly getting most of their coke from the Italians, and that source had effectively vanished. Satan's Choice, which had the most to gain because they could get an almost unlimited supply of cocaine from Quebec, were taken out of the picture at almost exactly the same time because of arrests linked to the bombing of a Sudbury Police station.

K-9's life was spared just in time for him — and the rest of his former gang — to be thrown behind bars. The chapter's clubhouse on Lottridge Street was taken by the Crown as evidence. Satan's Choice ceased to exist in Hamilton.

The resulting power vacuum affected the streets profoundly. Just months earlier, the province had been literally awash in cheap and easy vice, and now it had dried up almost completely. Keep in mind that most of the drugs that organized criminals were dealing — cocaine, methamphetamine and still a little heroin — were extremely addictive, and that their other services (including gambling, prostitution and loan-sharking) were also in great demand. The people who used these products and services were suddenly desperate for a new source.

Although deprived of their obvious way into the city — K-9's Satan's Choice — Hells Angels were smart enough to take advantage of the situation in a big way. Hells Angels national president Walter Stadnick, through the Sherbrooke Chapter, got in touch with a Niagara region drug dealer named Gerald "Skinny" Ward. An all-time tough guy whose criminal record began when he was 18 years old and listed 21 different convictions by 1999, Ward had been allegedly selling Magaddino-supplied coke received through Hamilton for years.

But he was no biker. He didn't even own a motorcycle. He was just a local guy who sold drugs. Hells Angels reached out to him and he was delighted to hear from them. After a few meetings, Ward quickly became the top coke dealer in Hamilton and Niagara. "Ward was never a biker," Len Isnor, a biker

Gerald "Skinny" Ward.

specialist with the Ontario Provincial Police (OPP), told me. "But Stadnick said, 'You're a Hells Angel now,' and so he became one pretty quickly."

In London, the Coates brothers and their friends were doing a decent business, much to the chagrin of the local Outlaws and the old Annihilators (who had become Loners, then Rock Machine and who were now prospective Bandidos).

In Toronto, Hells Angels supplied the Para-Dice Riders, and what was left of Satan's Choice. And, of course, there were still vestiges of Satan's Choice in Oshawa, Keswick, Simcoe County and Thunder Bay, and the enviably disciplined Kitchener Chapter, remained largely unscathed under the leadership of wily Andre Watteel.

Combined with the independent dealers throughout Northern Ontario, that put a lot of Hells Angels–friendly manpower in the province, even if there was not a single chapter there.

But it wasn't enough. Stadnick wanted Ontario — his own home — for his Hells Angels. So in the summer of 2000, he made a move unprecedented in size and cunning.

With a few exceptions due to bad blood, Stadnick offered Hells Angels membership to every significant motorcycle club in Ontario. And he made them an offer they could barely refuse. He offered Hells Angels membership patch-for-patch to these gangs with no questions asked and no probationary period. Take the deal, and you were a full-patch Hells Angel.

It was remarkable, and not just because it promised instant riches selling cocaine. It represented a chance to be a member of the premier organization in the field. And that is a big lure for many bikers, who crave the fear and respect their bikes and jackets inspire. It can hardly be overstated how much prestige the Hells Angels brand carries in the outlaw biker world. Isnor, who likened it to being invited to play for the Yankees after toiling in obscurity for the Royals or Pirates, put it succinctly: "Nobody makes movies about the Outlaws." To many, it was like winning the lottery.

Stadnick made the offer directly to Satan's Choice, the Para-Dice Riders, the Vagabonds, the Red Devils, Last Chance and the Windsor-based Lobos. Satan's Choice, Last Chance, the Lobos and all but 13 members of the Para-Dice Riders jumped at it. The fiercely independent Red Devils politely declined. So did the Vagabonds, who were still smarting from treatment meted out by Hells Angels to their president, David "Snorkel" Melanson, after he ran afoul of their drug-distribution network.

And Stadnick, through neutral representatives, let it be known that the offer was also open to any and all Outlaws and Bandidos, except the Ontario West Chapter. Stadnick made it very clear that he refused to negotiate with them.

The Bandidos — who had been Rock Machine just a year earlier — were especially responsive. Why should they be prospects for this club in Texas with a silly cartoon Mexican on their backs when they could be full-patch Hells Angels just by agreeing? Both chapters that Stadnick made the offer to — Toronto and Ontario East, based in Kingston and Ottawa — agreed. Even Paul Porter, president of the Ontario East Chapter, who had been one of the founders and primary leaders of the Rock Machine during their vicious war with the Hells Angels in Montreal, changed sides. In his final message before donning his new colors, Porter wrote on a bikers' message board: "Hello to all the RMMC. I wish you all the best with your new colors. 'Bye my brothers." The only holdout of any significance in either chapter was Toronto Chapter president Frank Raso, an old Loner. He'd had enough of changing patches and left the outlaw biker world entirely.

Of course, the offer was made to the chapters, but not to everyone in them. Every chapter had a couple of guys who didn't meet Stadnick's standards and they were told in no uncertain terms that their presence was no longer desired. Denied Hells Angels membership and without their old clubs, those rejects accounted for more than a few disgruntled bikers on the streets of Ontario.

Even a few Outlaws, who had basically ruled Ontario's biker landscape since Satan's Choice founder Bernie Guindon landed in prison in 1977, considered Stadnick's offer. With so many arrests, the club had fallen into disarray with just 70 members in Ontario, and many openly mulled the idea of jumping to the bigger ship. Negotiating with Billy Miller, Raso's replacement in Toronto, some Outlaws — notably Dave "the Hammer" MacDonald of Hamilton and Shaun "Cheeks" Boshaw of London — agreed to patch over. And others, like Mario Parente's old friend and reputed No. 2 Kevin Legere, were openly considering it.

Then Parente stepped in, warning the remaining Outlaws that jumping ship could result in extremely dire consequences. "Most of these guys are what we called 'paper Outlaws.' They were bikers first and foremost and the patch, the Outlaws name and organization, didn't mean all that much to them," Isnor said. "If it wasn't for Parente, who was an Outlaw through and through, they probably would have folded."

For support, Parente called James "Frank" Wheeler, the Outlaws international president in Indianapolis. Wheeler issued his own warning to the remaining Outlaws, and even met with

Hells Angels boss Ralph "Sonny" Barger, who agreed to get Stadnick to stop pursuing Ontario Outlaws for membership in exchange for a promise of peace.

But it was too late. The long run of the Outlaws at the top of a polyglot of biker gangs in Ontario came to an end on December 29, 1999 in Sorel. Outside the shabby Hells Angels clubhouse was a virtual wall of tough guys gathered from puppet clubs — the notorious Rockers from Laval and a local group called the Rowdy Crew. Just beyond them was a scattered throng of police and media types. They knew something was up, but they had no idea what or how big it would be.

A day earlier, Ontario Solicitor General David Tsubouchi — who had caught wind of what was going down — called a press conference at Queen's Park, Ontario's capital building. He announced the formation of a new police task force, the Biker Enforcement Unit (BEU). Then he claimed that outlaw motorcycle gangs were his "top priority" and vowed that it would "not be an easy ride" for them in his province.

Some came by chartered bus and some came by car, but the most conspicuous came by Harley. Even the most experienced and jaded cops were shocked to see Bandidos and Outlaws come to this summit. Then when the Hells Angels rather obviously moved in a well-marked industrial sewing machine, it dawned on them what was happening. And when the bikers started walking out of the clubhouse with brand-new Hells Angels patches — complete with top and bottom rockers — they realized that Ontario was now Hells Angels territory. They counted in the neighborhood of 180 of them. And they noticed that their bottom rocker simply read "Ontario" rather than individual chapters. Maybe it was a half-realization of Stadnick's dream of a single rocker for Canada, or maybe it was because they were dealing with too many chapters in too short a time to order enough rockers.

All of the new Hells Angels were recognized by at least some of the cops. And, of course, everyone knew who Guindon was when he came out of the clubhouse, appearing proud of his new jacket. But not everybody was that impressive. Many of the cops present were surprised that Hells Angels — considered the gold standard among bikers — would accept such lowly gangs as the Lobos and Last Chance into their up-until-then-exclusive club. These were, after all, guys they called "mumblies" because of their drug-addled speech.

But what they didn't understand was that Hells Angels were thinking strategically, not tactically. They were after numbers and cities of importance. Any chapter, they believed, could be improved.

The following day, Hells Angels had chapters in Thunder Bay, Sudbury, Simcoe County, Keswick, Kitchener, Oshawa and Toronto East that had formerly been Satan's Choice. The former Para-Dice Riders clubhouses in Toronto Center and Woodbridge now sported the winged skull. Last Chance gave them a small operation in Toronto West that was still looking for a clubhouse and the Lobos entrenched them in Windsor, an important border crossing. The former Bandidos provided more strength in Toronto (the members there were absorbed by the former Para-Dice Riders in Woodbridge) and Kingston. As a tip of the hat to Porter's weighty status, the Kingston Bandidos were given the Hells Angels' elite "Nomads" title, even though they contravened the original Nomads requirement by having a clubhouse. In this case, the title referred to their powerful status. The Hells Angels who had been operating in London quickly set up a clubhouse and chapter there. And from a strategic, financial and (at least for Stadnick) personal standpoint, Ward and his friends in Niagara Falls were persuaded to buy motorcycles and leather jackets and become the Hells Angels Niagara Chapter. They were to share Hamilton's rich drug market with Watteel's Kitchener Chapter.

That was a total of 13 Hells Angels chapters — admittedly of varying quality — in a province that had had none a day earlier. In fact, Toronto had a greater concentration of Hells Angels than any other city in the world.

Opposing them were largely dispirited Outlaw chapters in London, Sault Ste. Marie, Simcoe County, St. Catharines, Toronto, Windsor, Woodstock and, at least in theory, Montreal. The only club even close to being their allies were the last remaining

Bandidos just outside of London. And they were hardly organized or trustworthy enough to make much of a difference.

It was a tense time. Hells Angels had invaded Ontario and were determined to make it theirs. The Outlaws had an even stronger desire to hold onto the province that had been theirs for a very long time. Many of them prepared for the war that, despite the promise of peace, seemed inevitable.

Chapter 2
The Reincarnation of Satan's Choice

It's 1977. A very different time. All of the post–World War II euphoria has been used up. Years of Vietnam, Watergate, unemployment, recession, inflation and labor unrest have exposed some nerves. It's an angry, violent time — a ridiculously hot summer that sees strikes, recession, riots and serial killers dominating headlines. Crime rates are skyrocketing. Punk rock is emerging. It's ugly. It seethes.

Crime in Canada is burgeoning. The Mafia — usually Italian, sometimes Irish — supplies the goods. They take care of the drugs, the girls, the guns and everything else. But they are facing a big manpower problem. It's becoming increasingly clear that the Mafia members' kids are way more interested in spending their dads' dirty money than they are in making more of it.

While a generation earlier, there was a surfeit of good Catholic boys ready to lay their lives down for the family, by the late '70s that supply had dried up. The sons of those same Catholic boys were now running real estate offices and car dealerships in the suburbs, getting clean money from businesses their dads had paid to start up.

Their mass exodus left the Mafia largely bereft of talent. The foot soldiers that remained were generally old, psychotic, stupid or some combination of all of those things.

But drugs still needed to be sold, strippers still needed agents, prostitutes still needed to be driven around and recalcitrant debtors still needed to be punished. So the Canadian Mafia started to turn to other workers.

It's 1977. It's Canada. White trash abounds. And over the last couple of decades, when white men started considering a life outside the legal norms, they began to grow their hair long, wear leather jackets and start riding motorcycles.

Starting in earnest in the mid-'60s, outlaw motorcycle gangs emerged all over Canada. Although they all had different names, they all basically looked and worked exactly the same way. They had been doing the tough jobs for the Mafia for years, and in many places they had even eclipsed their former masters and had become the dominant crime organizations.

A few years earlier, Quebec alone had, by police estimates, no fewer than 350 motorcycle gangs. But the big boys saw there was lots of money to be made, so they had consolidated down to no more than a couple of dozen.

The rest of Canada had a similar environment — lots of little biker gangs engaging in small-time crime, but none with any kind of real dominance.

Except in Ontario. In the mid-1960s, a charismatic young man from the Oshawa area named Bernie Guindon started a new gang. A championship-quality boxer and a natural leader, Guindon (known as "the Frog" to his friends, associates and enemies) and Satan's Choice quickly began to dominate Southern Ontario's motorcycle gang milieu.

They were actually the second club in Ontario to be called Satan's Choice. But the first version was a very different kind of organization. Don Norris, one of the early members who joined the club after buying a 1952 Triumph from the Saddle Tramps, another Scarborough club, described it in his book, *Riding with Attitude*:

> I hooked up with Satan's Choice and a year later I became president. That would be 1959 or '60. There was only one chapter back then, about 45 members. We hung out at Aida's restaurant at Kingston Rd. and St. Clair Ave. There were no initiation rituals. You just needed a motorcycle and $3 for the patch.

He described the life of the club:

Party, party, party. And some ongoing rivalry with other clubs. The Black Diamond Riders tended to try to wipe out other clubs. I was beaten up a few times. We were treated with respect by people, given a wide berth wherever we went. They saw your patch and they stepped aside.

They disbanded in 1963. Norris, like most former members, drifted in and out of various Toronto-area clubs. He was approached one day in 1965 by an old friend, Guindon, who was by then president of an Oshawa club called the Phantom Riders, to see if he wanted to be part of a newer, bigger club. He had gotten some other area gangs — the Canadian Lancers, the Throttle Twisters and the Wild Ones (not to be confused with the later Hamilton gang of the same name) — to join his club. This new superclub, he said, would be called Satan's Choice. Norris thought it was cool, but decided not to join because of his family.

This second incarnation of Satan's Choice was much rougher. They rode Harleys and wore leather jackets and fought with, chased off or forcibly retired gangs like the Golden Hawks, the Chainmen and the Fourth Reich.

They became notorious nationwide in August 1968, when an undercover reporter from the *Globe and Mail* infiltrated a Satan's Choice party at a resort town called Wasaga Beach. He watched them party and he took pictures. The event that caught the nation's attention and outrage was a game in which a live chicken was set loose in a mob of bikers. They tore the terrified bird to shreds, and a prize was awarded to the participant who emerged with the biggest piece. It caused widespread scorn and outrage, but no criminal charges.

That's pretty well what Satan's Choice was like in the early years. They liked to ride, they liked to fight and they liked to party. They did stupid things. When they fought other gangs, it was with baseball bats and brass knuckles; sure people got hurt, but they didn't die.

They were what bikers always claim to be — a bunch of guys out to have fun, and if they hurt a few people (or animals) or made a mess, that was just too bad. "They were rough guys, for sure," said a retired Ontario Provincial Police officer who had many run-ins with the Choice over the years. "But they weren't gangsters; we'd pick them up for little things — simple assault, vandalism, trespassing, public drunkenness, that sort of thing."

But Sergeant John Harris of the Hamilton police, who investigated bikers for much of their rise to prominence, disagreed. "Guindon had a right-hand man named Arnold Kelly, who was never a member, never wanted to be," he told me. "He made his money in construction and owned a resort north of Orillia." Kelly was not physically imposing. "Believe it or not, he was actually smaller than Stadnick," he said, laughing about his old adversary Walter Stadnick, the biker chieftain who was no fewer than 15 inches shorter than him. "But he arranged everything — drug deals, beatings, shootings — he was probably more dangerous than Guindon himself."

And Satan's Choice, especially Guindon, found themselves drawn to Toronto. Particularly the city's Yorkville district. Back then, it was the polar opposite of the chichi wine bar and gourmet chocolate shop strip it is now. At the time, it was notorious as a hippie ghetto and open-air drug market.

Originally, the bikers were attracted by the freer lifestyle and the girls, but they came to realize that they could make huge profits selling drugs to the itinerant youth culture. They probably didn't realize it, but they made the same discoveries and decisions in Yorkville that the American Hells Angels had in San Francisco's Haight-Ashbury. Drawn to the hippies for esoteric reasons, they evolved into a drug-dealing organization simply because the opportunity was just too good to pass up.

Maybe it was Guindon, maybe it was the lifestyle, the *Globe* article or maybe just the cool name, but Satan's Choice really took off. By 1970, Satan's Choice had 13 chapters, all of them in Ontario except for one in the then-mostly anglophone west end of Montreal.

But with expansion came tension, especially from the Toronto Chapter. By 1970, they were getting bigheaded. Making huge amounts of cash on drug sales and regularly getting away with gang rapes — they called them "splashes" — convinced them they were above any law, including their own club's. They thought they should be running the town, the whole show.

The problem was that two other big-time biker gangs were already established in Hogtown and, although they were prepared to share the city with Satan's Choice, they weren't quite ready to hand it over. When the Toronto Chapter of Satan's Choice began to overstep its boundaries, the Vagabonds and Black Diamond Riders began to rattle their swords. History had proven that neither crew would back down from a fight. An all-out war seemed imminent.

That pissed off the rest of Satan's Choice. "The Toronto Chapter did most of the shit disturbing. Now they start a small war with two of the heaviest clubs going and they're asking us to come in and bail them out," said the road captain of the Brampton Chapter of Satan's Choice at the time, a man who would only consent to be known by the name "Gypsy." "This caused a lot of friction between the other chapters."

That friction wasn't only because the Toronto Chapter came begging for help, but because most of the guys in the other chapters had as much respect for their would-be enemies as they did for their "brothers" in Toronto. "The Vags were a solid club," continued Gypsy. "I knew Edjo, their president; and the BDRs had been around forever."

The potential for war in Toronto divided the club. "The Oshawa, Kingston, Ottawa and Kitchener Chapters and us [Brampton] wanted nothing to do with Toronto's mess," Gypsy said. "Montreal, Hamilton and Brantford were all for it — the other guys [chapters in Richmond Hill, Niagara Falls, St. Catharines and Peterborough] didn't know whether they were coming or going."

Guindon stepped in. It's rare for a national president of any biker gang to intervene and interfere with the goings-on of one chapter, but this was important. Not only was the Toronto Chapter biting off way more than it could chew, it was making decisions that threatened to tear Satan's Choice apart. The undisputed boss called a meeting of all the officers of all the chapters.

"It was a fucking heavy meeting." Gypsy said years later. "Some of the officers were called cowards, others were called fight-crazy idiots." It devolved into a shouting match. Hamilton and Montreal were screaming "Kill! Kill! Kill!" and the other chapters were preaching common sense. Guindon, seconds from losing control of the proceedings, issued an ultimatum. If they decided to go ahead with the war, they would lose him as president. That quieted things down.

Ottawa and Brampton came up with an idea. Why not just dump the Toronto Chapter? Guindon wasn't that stupid. Besides, he really liked Toronto; he enjoyed partying with the hipsters in Yorkville, which was officially Vagabond territory, but where he and his friends could act with impunity. And he knew that even a one-third share of Ontario's biggest drug market was better than none. He suggested another idea. Instead of fighting the Vags and the BDRs, the collected chapters of Satan's Choice would descend upon Toronto. They would remove the "fight-crazy bastards" who were causing all the problems, and make good with their would-be enemies.

On the same night the foot soldiers of the Choice went to Toronto to get rid of the troublemaking members there, Gypsy took Edjo out for dinner and drinks. Peace was established in Toronto. And a precedent was set in Ontario.

Under Guindon's now-totalitarian leadership — he gave himself the title "Supreme Commander" to go along with National President — Satan's Choice flourished. They were so powerful that, in 1973, Hells Angels (at the time the only motorcycle gang in the world bigger than Satan's Choice) sent an emissary from California to discuss a merger (what the bikers call a "patchover") or at least a working agreement between the two clubs. A few of the top members of Satan's Choice — though, notably, not Guindon — met the Hells Angel at the Toronto airport and sent him home. He never even left the terminal. Clearly, Satan's Choice felt they didn't need Hells Angels.

Guindon, as fiercely xenophobic as the Californians who started Hells Angels twenty-some years earlier, had no intention of working with what he considered a "foreign" club. He worked very hard to ensure that Satan's Choice remained "proudly Canadian" — never mind that the bikes their club was centered upon all came from Milwaukee, and their look, language, mannerisms and organization were stolen directly from San Bernardino.

But Satan's Choice certainly didn't mind doing business with Americans or any other nationality. By the early 1970s, members of Satan's Choice were distributing and even manufacturing drugs intended primarily for the U.S. market. Remote Canadian locations made drug manufacturing harder to detect, and Americans paid much more for the same drugs than Canadians would.

The two primary products were "Canadian blue," a cheap imitation Valium, and PCP, a powerful hallucinogen the cops tell us is called "angel dust."

Alain Templain was a member of the Oshawa Chapter of Satan's Choice, and a very rich one. He owned his own floatplane, which he regularly flew up to the luxurious Northern Ontario fishing resort he also owned, catering mainly to well-heeled Americans looking for monster-sized walleyes and pikes.

Guindon had flown up to Templain's lodge on Oba Lake at least once. In Algoma District, about 200 miles north of Sault Ste. Marie, the resort was accessible only by plane and surrounded by miles and miles of rough, rocky forests.

And the cops had a suspicion that Templain was doing more than just guiding vacationers to the best fishing holes and cutting bait. They were right.

In 1976, about a dozen cops from the Ontario Provincial Police (OPP) posing as rich American businessmen stayed at Templain's lodge. In the middle of the night, just before they were scheduled to leave, they raided a shack on a small island in the middle of the lake. Inside, they found Templain and Guindon surrounded by more than $6 million in PCP and PCP-making chemicals and equipment.

Both were sentenced to 17 years.

Without their "Supreme Commander," the individual chapters of Satan's Choice began to grow apart. It happened in a large part because of the nature of the cities they were in. In Toronto, it was all about retailing drugs to kids. In St. Catharines, the focus was on getting product over the border. In Niagara Falls, it was strippers and escorts. Kingston's specialty was supplying the prisons and college kids.

Two cities, in particular, stood out — Montreal and Hamilton. The violent ones. That's because they were both still Mafia towns.

In most of the other places Satan's Choice existed, they were the big dogs, but in Montreal and Hamilton, they still answered to the dons.

You have to realize that the Montreal of 1977 was a very different place than it is today. The separatist Parti Québécois had just been elected and had not yet gotten very far with their subtle form of ethnic cleansing. Montreal was still Canada's biggest, richest and most cosmopolitan city. English was widely spoken, and in the west end of the island, French was rarely heard unless some city workers were fixing a road or maybe a bridge.

The common perception at the time was that all anglophones in Montreal were rich and cultured, but it's not true. There were actually plenty of poor and middle-class English-speakers and some of them became involved in crime. Montreal had two branches of the traditional Mafia — the Sicilian Rizzuto Family and the Irish West End Gang. Both conducted business in English and they worked very closely with the area's bikers. Too smart to rely on just one source of tough-guy labor, both families employed a variety of bikers. The most prominent ones were Satan's Choice in the west end, and the fiercely violent Popeyes in Laval, just north of the city. Satan's Choice generally spoke English; the Popeyes were completely francophone.

There was lots of work to go around. In a city teeming with hipsters and wannabe jet-setters, cocaine was king — and the profits were huge. Heroin was a steady and lucrative business. Prostitution in Montreal succeeded like in no other city. Marijuana was popular, but the profit margins were so low, compared to other drugs, that the trade was dominated by small-timers.

The bikers did some of the cannabis trade. But, primarily, they supported Mafia activities. They sold coke, they imported firearms, they collected debts and they acted as bodyguards for the bosses. It was a very lucrative time to be a biker and recruits were lining up for a chance to get their patch.

Hamilton was — as it always seems to be — another story. The Mafia wasn't there because the city was rich and cosmopolitan. In fact, it was the opposite. But the Mafia was strong there anyway.

It happened naturally. In the early part of the 20th century, a number of small local foundries merged and attracted more business. Hamilton became Steeltown. Although other places in Canada made steel, for most of the century, the lion's share of the country's steel — anywhere from two-thirds to three-quarters at any given time — came from Hamilton.

As the auto industry expanded by leaps and bounds and the world's militaries became increasingly mechanized, the world-wide demand for steel skyrocketed. Hamilton's economy boomed. But while American factories found labor in failed Midwestern farmers and displaced southern blacks, the steel factories in Hamilton had to rely on immigration.

Canada wasn't really comfortable with the thought of people of color quite yet, so its doors were thrown open to Europeans. They came in droves as the steel companies were hiring pretty well any warm male body — as long as he was white.

The steel workers came mostly from Scotland, Ireland and Eastern Europe. But the houses they lived in, the streets they drove on and the markets they bought food in came courtesy of a different group.

Italians — virtually all of them from Racalmuto, a town near the southern shore of Sicily — streamed into Hamilton. Few of them worked in the steel plants, where a workforce with strong English-language skills helped avoid serious accidents, but they found work in other industries.

Racalmuto is a little different from what most of us think of when we think of Italy. Closer to Africa than it is to Rome, Racalmuto gets its name from the Arabic phrase *rahal maut*, which means "dead village." Its history is that of defeat, and the anger that comes with it. Recorded history shows that the area has been invaded and occupied by the Greeks, Carthaginians, Romans, Vandals, Arabs, Normans, Spaniards, Austrians and, most recently, Italians.

While we in North America generally think of Sicily as part of Italy because it says so on a map, the Sicilians don't always agree. Although similar, what people in Sicily spoke before the Italians took over was not really Italian; and many people on the island would have as hard a time understanding a Milanese as they would a Parisian.

They were a deeply religious and superstitious people. They had a great belief in *mal'uocchiu* — the evil eye. Revenge was a significant part of their culture.

In 1860, Giuseppe Garibaldi conquered Sicily and made it part of the new Italian state. Soon thereafter, the Mafia was born.

These days, we think of the Mafia as a group of criminals out to make a quick buck off the common man. But that's not how it began. The Italians ruled Sicily no better than the Austrian princes they deposed. While the Sicilians languished in poverty, the Italians did little more than impose taxes and take young men off to war. There was basically no government in Sicily. No police, no infrastructure, no nothing.

So they made one themselves. The Mafia began as a secret government, a group of local men who could get things done. They were seen as a godsend by the locals who hated the oppressive, distant government who officially ruled them.

But the Mafia — the name actually comes from the Arabic word for bragging — was far from perfect. They were very much what you would expect from a group of rural, uneducated men who had a great deal of power and were accountable to nobody but themselves. They killed their enemies. They settled disputes with bullets and they enriched themselves whenever and however they could. They particularly targeted what they considered foreigners — anyone but Sicilians.

And they came to Hamilton basically intact. There they saw a place that was pretty much what they saw in Sicily, although colder and full of non-Sicilians. The government and the mainstream community, who spoke another language, didn't care for them. Generally, the only contact they had with the state were the cops, most of whom were Irish or Scottish and seemed little different from the Italian military that had kept an eye on them back home. The cops were hard on the Sicilians, with a standing order to break up any group of more than three of them.

When World War II erupted, the Canadian government rounded up many Sicilian men and sent them to internment camps simply for being Italian. It did not build a great deal of trust in the community.

These immigrants established their own territory — north of Barton Street and west of Sherman Avenue — and their own shadow government. The Mafia began in Hamilton minutes after the first boat from Racalmuto landed. They were joined soon thereafter by the Calabrians — people from the toe of the boot Italy is often likened to — who had their own culture and organized crime traditions.

While the Mafia in Hamilton did do some benevolent work, it became involved in criminal activity right away. Protection rackets, kidnapping and loan-sharking were translated directly from the old country. When prohibition hit Canada first and then the U.S., the Hamilton Mafia got rich running booze both ways — first in and then out of the country. When that ended, they moved into drugs. That expanded to other illegal operations, including prostitution.

And it caught the public's attention. Hamilton Mafiosi became notorious and sometimes even beloved celebrities. The first was suave Rocco Perri, who was called "King of the Bootleggers" and "Canada's Al Capone." The exploits of Perri and his outspoken wife, Besha Starkman, were followed by thousands until he was murdered. Perri was followed by decidedly more down-market types like Dominic Musitano, a stone-cold killer who once shot a man for honking his car horn in front of his house. At about the same time, the charismatic John "Johnny Pops" Papalia emerged. When I was growing up in Hamilton, those names were as well known around town as any ballplayers' names would be in another city. The Hamilton Mafia was everywhere in the city and made little effort to hide its existence.

The Mafia had a long history of hiring non-Italians to work for them, often to do the dirty work. Pat Musitano had hired Ken Murdock to murder Johnny Pops and Carmen Barillaro, but smarter Mafiosi knew better than to trust guys like Murdock. The very reason the Mafia works is because of discipline and mutual respect. And that's why Mafia outfits around the world like to hire bikers. Outlaw motorcycle gangs — especially the big ones — have an organizational structure that shares a great deal of similarity to the Mafia's own. Would-be members — usually very young — start out very low on the org chart. They do simple tasks, with limited responsibility and little knowledge of the big picture. Their rewards are small if they exist at all, and the risk of being caught is high.

They do it readily because they can see the payoff. They ride a bike. Their boss has a Chevy. Their bosses' boss has a Cadillac. *His* boss has a Ferrari. They endure the long hours, the low pay, the intense danger of being arrested, assaulted or killed because they believe that some day it will be them cruising around in the luxury car, squiring a couple of beauties and having the whole world at their fingertips.

But there was a problem in Ontario, particularly in Hamilton. Papalia was running most of the province until he was murdered. And of the many things he didn't like (and there were a lot), one of the most prominent was bikers. He found them stupid and without culture, prone to get caught and prone to rat each other out. He didn't like their habit of getting addicted to drugs and he hated the fact that they openly courted police attention with their loud exhaust pipes and their colorful uniforms.

Papalia was smart enough to know that he couldn't rid his province or his city of bikers any more than he could the cops. He reluctantly allowed his own men — and those of his associates — to hire them from time to time, for certain dirty jobs. But he drew the line at Hells Angels. He'd seen what they were capable of in Montreal and he wanted no part of them. As long as he was in charge, Papalia vowed, there would be no Hells Angels' presence in Ontario. At least not officially.

Two and a half years after Papalia's death, that all changed with the Hells Angels mass patch-over in Sorel.

Chapter 3
"God Forgives, Outlaws Don't"

You could hardly make a more perfect breeding ground for biker gangs than Southwestern Ontario, even if you tried. Stretching from Windsor (a declining auto-making town that had pinned much of its economic hopes on a casino and bars and strip joints with laxer laws than those in Detroit, directly across the river) to London (a more economically diverse, but similarly declining city that was also relying on slot machines to attract revenue), Southwestern Ontario is a small, but densely populated region.

The two cities are connected by the MacDonald-Cartier Freeway — called Highway 401 in Ontario and Autoroute 20 in Quebec — that starts in Windsor and ends in Quebec City. London is located where Highway 402 meets the 401. Highway 402 begins at Sarnia, another blighted border city, only this one has traditionally been tied to petrochemicals instead of manufacturing.

The rest of the area is mostly farmland disrupted by a few small cities and towns. With more in common with the Great Plains in a topographical sense than the rest of the Great Lakes Region, Southwestern Ontario is overwhelmingly flat and dry. It's a place where it's hard not to be bored. Motorcycles are a distraction, so are social clubs and drugs, especially stimulants like methamphetamine.

It's a place tailor-made to incubate motorcycle gangs. And it has. Dozens of gangs came out of the area in the 1960s, all basically looking and acting like one another. They were all small-time. And they were, for the most part, absolutely unready when the bigger, more powerful and more aggressive gangs from south of the border came looking for their territory.

While they may not be the best known outlaw biker gang, the Outlaws have a long and storied history.

The well-documented and generally agreed-upon backstory of Hells Angels recounts that the club was one of many formed in Southern California in the years just after the Second World War. The consensus opinion among experts is that it started when a group of disaffected combat soldiers, looking for the kind of adrenaline rushes they experienced in war, banded together, rode customized motorcycles and held rowdy parties. The local youth — alienated by the homogenization of postwar culture — idolized, joined and later replaced those veterans, and eventually ramped up the violence and money-making operations. Due to some sage leadership and an easily marketable name and logo, Hells Angels quickly rose to unparalleled prominence.

But they weren't the first outlaw motorcycle gang. Not even close. That honor almost certainly belongs to the Outlaws. They were formed in 1935 — six years before official American involvement in World War II, in Chicago, during the Great Depression.

While historians and sociologists will tell you that the California bikers were collectively trying to recreate the thrill of battle, the guys who founded the Outlaws were just out for a good time in an era when good times were few and far between.

It all started at the now defunct Matilda's Bar on Route 66, in a small suburb of Chicago called McCook. Even now, McCook, Illinois, is small, working class and overwhelmingly white. It's a pretty boring piece of the Midwest. But back in 1935, it was actually a pretty enviable place to be. While industry was foundering pretty well everywhere else, General Motors had just invested millions and millions in a manufacturing plant for its newly acquired locomotive subsidiary, the Electro-Motive Company, in McCook.

For the next two generations, EMC's LaGrange Plant (it was named after a neighboring city because McCook was then too small to even have a post office) made the most railway engines for the biggest locomotive manufacturer in the world.

It was a haven of relative affluence at a time when any kind of work was scarce. But it was hard, boring work. And the men who worked there drank and partied hard. Some rode motorcycles and hung out at Matilda's. They started as drinking buddies and then emerged as a distinct group who rode, worked and partied together. As they became a cohesive unit, they named themselves the McCook Outlaws Motorcycle Club. It may not have the same satisfying psychological and sociological rationale as the Hells Angels semi-official history, but it's closer to the truth. Members identified themselves with a patch sewn or embroidered onto their shirts. On a black background, it featured a head-on view of a motorcycle in a winged circle.

In a city synonymous with organized crime, which had just a few years earlier seen the likes of Al Capone, the McCook Outlaws made little impression on Chicagoland. They were just a bunch of rowdy hooligans on loud bikes. Despite the name "Outlaws," whatever they did to break the law wasn't serious enough to be written about in the newspapers of the day.

Of course, the war changed things. With much of the McCook Outlaws' membership overseas or working double shifts, the club almost ceased to exist. But it survived and, after the war, the same phenomenal set of circumstances that established motorcycle gangs in places like California, Massachusetts, Quebec and Southwestern Ontario also arose in Chicago.

So when the American Motorcycle Association held an event at Chicago's famed Soldier Field stadium in May 1946, the McCook Outlaws came out in force. It was a watershed moment for the club, which had already gained a number of recruits from outside McCook.

In fact, the club became so popular and widespread that its name was changed from the McCook Outlaws to the Chicago Outlaws after the clubhouse was moved from the suburbs to the south side of the big city. The patch was changed, too; made a little tougher. In place of the winged motorcycle was a crude skull.

Later named "Charlie," the skull is still basically the Outlaws' symbol today. Back then, though, it was hand-painted on the backs of members' jackets. Frequently, the skull was embroidered with white thread on the Chicago Outlaws standard uniform of a black western-style shirt with white piping.

Not long afterwards came an event that changed the outlaw biker world. In 1953, Hollywood released *The Wild One*, starring Marlon Brando. The movie was based on a short story that itself was based on a motorcycle event where the partying got out of hand and the small town of Hollister, California, was terrorized. Each telling of the tale — from media accounts to short story to movie — exaggerated the incident. If you watch it today, the movie is actually pretty hokey, but it was a huge hit back then. Among its biggest fans were the bikers themselves.

In a classic example of real life imitating fiction imitating real life, the look and behavior of the bikers in the movie were quickly adopted by real-life bikers all over the world. In homage to the look of the movie, the Chicago Outlaws changed their logo again, updating and refining Charlie's portrait and putting a pair of crossed pistons behind him. It looked almost exactly like the logo Brando wore on the back of his jacket in *The Wild One*.

The club prospered. At a Fourth of July rally in 1964, the Outlaws expanded by patching over two gangs: The Cult (a small gang from the upstate New York town of Voorheesville) and the Gypsy Outlaws of Milwaukee. The following month at the nearby Springfield Motor Races, the Outlaws accepted another chapter — the Gipsy Outlaws (not previously related to the similarly named Milwaukee club) of Louisville, Kentucky.

They had become the biggest American biker gang east of the Mississippi, with only the California-based Hells Angels any larger. On New Year's Day 1965, the clubs now aligned with the Outlaws incorporated as the American Outlaws Association. Their official logo is a parody of the American Motorcycle Association's own, featuring a rounded triangle with an upstretched middle finger (and sometimes a swastika). But the bikers never wore it on their backs. Instead they still had the same old Charlie with crossed pistons on the backs of their jackets. They dropped "Chicago" from their name, and were commonly referred to as the Outlaws.

In July 1967, the club's brass rode down to West Palm Beach, Florida, and patched over a gang the local media and police called The Iron Cross.

Soon thereafter, the Outlaws adopted the motto "God forgives, Outlaws don't" and members were expected to have the acronym GFOD tattooed somewhere on their bodies.

Unlike the flamboyant Hells Angels on the other side of the country, the Outlaws generally flew under the public's radar. They didn't attract national media attention until December 1967.

There was something suspicious about Christine Deese when she was admitted to St. Mary's Hospital in West Palm Beach after walking into the emergency room. The pretty 18-year-old redhead with freckles had identical puncture marks and exit wounds through both of her palms.

Her story was that she was walking down a country path, had tripped and been impaled by nails that were protruding from a discarded board when she extended her hands to break her fall. Veteran hospital staff didn't believe her story and called police.

Under interrogation, Deese revealed that members of the Outlaws nailed her to a tree because she had violated a club rule. She had withheld $10 from her boyfriend, 25-year-old Norman "Spider" Risinger of Tampa, and Outlaw club rules, she said, commanded that a member's "old lady" was required to surrender all of her money to her man. Since she had hidden the $10 from Risinger, the club decided to crucify her.

News of her torture ignited tempers in South Florida. Risinger and another Outlaw who took part in the incident, Frank "Fat Frank" Link, were quickly arrested. Governor Claude Kirk — an old-school law-and-order Republican — assembled a group of state police to track down and arrest the other perpetrators no matter how far they had fled.

Then he personally led a group of Florida Hotel and Restaurant Commission inspectors to the Outlaws' West Palm Beach hangout — Kitty's Saloon. They shut it down for being unclean, and Kirk's men arrested the owner, 39-year-old Kitty Randall, for maintaining a brothel. She denied the charges, but admitted that the Outlaws frequented her bar and that some of them lived in the spartan cottages behind Kitty's Place that she also owned.

As far as prostitution was concerned, she allowed that it may have happened, but that she wasn't involved. "I introduced some of the girls to some of the guys," she said. "But what they did after that, I don't know."

Under questioning, she told police everything she knew about the crucifixion. She wasn't there, she said, but the Outlaws involved told her all about it at the bar afterward. They told her that Risinger and the others drove Deese to a wooded area near Juno Beach, about 10 miles away from Kitty's Saloon. They then forced her to stand on tiptoes in front of a large melaleuca tree and spread her arms wide. When her hands were in place, the Outlaws drove four-inch nails into each of them, fastening her to the tree and forcing her to hang from them when she could not maintain the tiptoe pose. They sat around her in a semicircle, forbidding her to scream, for about 15 minutes before prying the nails loose and driving her back to Kitty's Saloon.

When asked if this kind of behavior was usual for the Outlaws, Randall said it was and that she was aware that they had beaten Deese on many occasions. But, she asserted, the blows were "never on the face, always on the body."

Soon after, Kirk's posse, having searched Chicago and the surrounding area, found the remaining fugitive Outlaws holed up in the clubhouse of an allied Detroit gang called the Renegades. Sheriff William Heidtman, leader of the detachment, called it "the filthiest place you ever saw."

When Heidtman brought Donald "Mangy" Graves Jr., Joe "Super Squirrel" Sorsby Jr. and John "Crazy John" Wables back to Florida, Kirk met them at the airport. Just before they were led into waiting police cars, Sorsby and Wables began to kiss each other in a way contemporary media called "passionate."

And the Outlaws made enemies well beyond the governor of Florida and his police force.

In the '60s, there was no gang tougher than the Aliens. None.

• • •

Based in Manhattan's then notorious East Village, the Aliens were well known to be violent and to have close ties to the Mafia.

In the summer of 1969, a former member of the Aliens is said to have raped the wife of another member. Although women are not generally held in any sort of high regard by many bikers, they are considered property and the insult was too much for the club to bear. Fearing for his life, the alleged rapist got out of New York and settled in the Midwest. Before long, he joined the Outlaws.

That following December, after some tense negotiations on both sides, the Aliens became the Hells Angels New York City. It did nothing to quell their violent tendencies. It may actually have intensified them.

In the spring of 1974, two members of Satan's Soldiers (a Bronx-based club friendly with Hells Angels) spotted the alleged rapist in Outlaws colors riding his way into New York City. They told the Hells Angels, who sent mammoth sergeant-at-arms Vincent "Big Vinny" Girolamo out to get him. It didn't take long. Girolamo — whose famous quote "When in doubt, knock 'em out" still hangs above the entrance to the East 3rd Street clubhouse — apprehended the man at a friend's house and forced him back to the clubhouse. When the insulted husband showed up, he took the Outlaw outside and beat him until he was sure he was dead.

He wasn't. He recovered and eventually made his way back to Chicago. Enraged, the Outlaws swore revenge.

In April 1974, James Nolan — president of the Outlaws' reinforced South Florida Chapter, which had relocated to Fort Lauderdale — heard from an informant that a pair of Hells Angels from Lowell, Massachusetts, had ridden into their territory. Nolan and four other full-patch members met them at a bar.

The Hells Angels — Edward "Riverboat" Riley and George "Whiskey George" Hartman — told Nolan and his men that they were only passing through their territory to find Albert "Oskie" Simmons, a former Lowell full-patch who had stolen from the club and fled to the area. They didn't want any trouble.

Nolan told them he understood, that he had been in the same situation, and invited them to come back to the clubhouse for some drinks. At first, Riley and Hartman were reluctant, but Nolan told him that he and his club could one day find themselves in similar circumstances and that he would personally guarantee no harm would come to them.

As soon as they arrived at the clubhouse, Riley and Hartman were bound with a pink clothesline and gagged. They were held there until the Outlaws tracked down Simmons and dragged him to the clubhouse. Under Nolan's orders, four Outlaws drove them to a flooded quarry in the countryside. Each had a cinderblock tied to his feet, then was shot in the back of the head by a shotgun at close range. Their bodies were then dumped into the water. Three days later, the bodies floated to the surface.

Nolan and three others were arrested. The president was acquitted, but at a later trial (this one for racketeering) another member testified that he fabricated evidence to help free Nolan of the murders.

After that, it was clear that the Outlaws and Hells Angels were at war. In fact, at a November 1978 summit in Rochester, New York, the presidents of various chapters of Hells Angels officially declared war on the Outlaws.

Although there were many skirmishes — most notably on the Outlaws' turf of Rockford, Illinois, and South Bend, Indiana — it was largely a cold war. The detente that followed it worked out so that Hells Angels controlled New York City, New England and everything west of the Mississippi, while the Outlaws were left in charge of the Midwest and the Southeast and were particularly strong in Chicago and Detroit, as well as Florida.

With the United States effectively carved up, the two outlaw superpowers turned their eyes to Canada.Which brings us back to the hot, angry Canadian summer of 1977.

When Guindon went to prison, he anointed his old buddy Garnet "Mother" McEwen (president of the St. Catharines Chapter) to be national president of Satan's Choice. He would live to regret it.

At its peak under Guindon's reign, Satan's Choice was the second-biggest and second-most powerful biker gang in the world, surpassed only by Hells Angels and outstripping the Outlaws. But with Guindon behind bars, they had slipped significantly.

McEwen called a secret meeting with some of the Satan's Choice chapters he trusted. At it, he convinced Windsor's William "King" O'Reilly and Ottawa's John "Doctor John" Arksey to patch over to the Outlaws. Montreal's Joseph "Sonny"

Lacombe also attended, but made no solid commitment at the time.

If he had known, Guindon would have been enraged. Not only was McEwen compromising the very existence of the club, but he was basically handing it over to foreigners — which the fiercely xenophobic Guindon would have abhorred. McEwen then announced that the club's annual party would be moved three hours down the road from Wasaga Beach on Georgian Bay to Crystal Beach on Lake Erie, less than a ten-minute ride down Highway 3 from the U.S. border. He also announced that it would be a patch-over ceremony. Any chapters or individual members of Satan's Choice who did not want to become Outlaws were advised not to attend. About half the members of the Montreal Chapter — which was still on the fence — showed up. Wisely, McEwen invited a substantial number of American Outlaws and some smaller but ambitious Ontario clubs to serve as reinforcements.

Although the party went off without a hitch, things got ugly soon thereafter. Many of the reluctant members of the chapters that had patched over were chased off. Within days, the once-mighty Satan's Choice was reduced to about 45 members spread between Toronto, Oshawa, Peterborough, Kitchener, Thunder Bay and one very divided clubhouse in Montreal. Making matters worse, the police arrested 40 members and associates of Satan's Choice on 191 charges in August. They were almost totally broken.

Of course, when Guindon found out his empire had been sacked, he was enraged. Effectively powerless behind bars, he issued a $10,000 reward for McEwen's head. It went uncollected.

But that doesn't mean McEwen succeeded with his plan. His bosses from the U.S. caught him skimming $30,000 from club coffers, stripped him of his Outlaws membership and exiled him from Ontario. He later emerged in Calgary, working at a menial job at a hotel.

The local bikers, a gang called the Chosen Few, recognized him, but they didn't know about the bounty on his head and accused him of trying to recruit local bikers for the Outlaws. He assured them he wasn't, using his lowbrow circumstances as a dishwasher to indicate his lack of power, and so they let him be.

But McEwen wasn't done. He was caught stealing again, and one of the Chosen Few beat him nearly to death with his own artificial leg. Tail between his real and prosthetic legs, he limped back to Ontario in 1980 and never did anything of note again.

Although broken by a hostile takeover, defections and arrests, the essentially leaderless Satan's Choice was not quite dead.

On October 18, 1978, a fat man named Bill Matiyek sat at a table in the bar at the Queen's Hotel in Port Hope, Ontario, a quiet and twee little town just east of Toronto. With him at the small, circular table were two other men — a local kid named Richard Sauve and a seasoned Toronto tough guy named Gary Comeau. Matiyek was both drunk and stoned on a combination of marijuana and amphetamines. He had two guns. One was pointed at Sauve's head. The other was stuffed into his left boot.

Comeau was a member of Satan's Choice, Sauve was a prospect. Matiyek was a member of the Golden Hawks, a club many thought had been forcibly disbanded. Further complicating matters was the fact that some representatives from the Outlaws (now the sworn enemies of Satan's Choice) had told Matiyek earlier that day that they were very interested in patching over the remaining Golden Hawks and making him president — if he could get the club back together.

But unbeknownst to Matiyek, the bar was full of armed members of Satan's Choice who had been tipped off by Sauve earlier that day. One of them, a man named Lorne Campbell, had obtained a .38-caliber handgun when he was going through the belongings of Sauve's boarder, Gordon van Harlem, who was away on a big-time bender in nearby Peterborough.

Comeau had originally campaigned to be the one who carried it, but his friends considered him too hotheaded. Campbell, older and more experienced, was chosen instead.

Realizing how serious the situation was, Campbell sent trusted lieutenant Michael Everett over to sort things out. Everett was a big strong man, but he was shocked by what he saw. Matiyek was sloppy drunk and holding a gun on Sauve and Comeau. In his opinion, they were about to die. Instead of talking to Matiyek, he turned around and returned to Campbell, informing him of his view of the situation.

Campbell passed the table and surveyed the situation himself. Matiyek recognized him and the danger he presented and instinctively tried to hide his weapon. As his handgun got caught in his jacket, Campbell (now closer to the bar's exit than he was to Matiyek) drew his gun and fired three shots.

The first passed through Matiyek's thick neck, took a chunk out of his jaw, grazed his left arm and eventually lodged in Sauve's arm. The second penetrated Matiyek's skull and bounced around inside his cranium, killing him. The third also hit him in the head, but he was already dead.

Pandemonium. Everyone who could, stampeded out of the bar. Somebody stopped to relieve Matiyek's body of the cash and drugs stuffed in his pockets.

Police arrived eventually, but not before the bar had been revisited and, according to the guys associated with Satan's Choice, "cleaned up a little." The body was removed by authorities, but not before the crime scene had been grossly contaminated.

The trial was just as comical. Several witnesses changed their testimony three and even four times. One witness's car was shot full of holes while parked in front of his house. The cops were confused. Nobody could explain why Matiyek's gun was never fingerprinted. Much of the Crown's evidence contradicted itself. The forensics were questioned.

But it didn't matter in the end. Six of the eight members of Satan's Choice accused were found guilty of first- or second-degree murder. They received sentences ranging from 25 to 10 years. Campbell was not one of them. Sauve and Comeau each received twenty-five to life.

But the pathetic spiral into oblivion the once-mighty Satan's Choice went through was all just a sideshow to the real attraction. When the Outlaws patched over at least some of Satan's Choice, it was a bold strategic and the first step in what would eventually become a war for organized crime supremacy in Canada fought between two rival American motorcycle gangs.

The Outlaws had gotten there first and they eventually succeeded in Toronto. Almost as soon as McEwen announced that the 1977 edition of the Satan's Choice annual party would be a patch-over ceremony, anti-Outlaws forces in the city mobilized.

The members of the Toronto Satan's Choice who did not want to become Outlaws teamed with other established gangs — most notably the Para-Dice Riders and the Vagabonds — to help keep the Outlaws out of their territories.

It worked for a while. By the summer of 1984, both big American clubs had put a virtual embargo on drugs imported into Ontario. Through intimidation, they prevented the normal suppliers from selling to the Toronto clubs. Most of them — especially the Para-Dice Riders — began to feel a significant financial strain.

One Toronto club, though, was enjoying business as usual. The Iron Hawgs, a large club with more than 30 full-patch members, were selling as much as they had before the big clubs put the hammer down. They had been handpicked a year earlier by the Outlaws to be their beachhead in Toronto. The Outlaws in Detroit supplied the Iron Hawgs with a decent supply of drugs when the rest of the city was practically dry.

They were a wise choice. They were sworn enemies of the Para-Dice Riders because of a 1979 bar fight that got out of hand and ended when an innocent woman was injured when a Para-Dice Rider was beating the Iron Hawgs' president with a loaded shotgun and it discharged. The perception at the time was that the Iron Hawgs were less cohesive and more easily led than many of the other local gangs.

That summer, newly elected Iron Hawgs president Robert "Pumpkin" Marsh put the concept of a patch-over to the Outlaws before his collected club. Unlike McEwen's dictatorial approach, he opened the prospect up to discussion.

As with countless other clubs, the crowd quickly split into two factions. The younger, more ambitious Iron Hawgs were all for it. They had gotten used to the income from drug sales and were looking forward to getting far more once they were Outlaws. Besides, having that well-known and respected patch on their back meant a lot more respect than the comical one they sported now. The Outlaws were the big time, and they wanted to be part of it.

But many of the gang's veteran members were against the merger for exactly the same reasons. Increased sales and increased visibility meant more attention from cops — potentially a different kind of cop, like the RCMP — and other bikers. Those old guys, those who joined the club to ride and party, didn't mind making a few bucks off weed or whatever, but most of them had real jobs and families, they didn't want to become full-time gangsters.

Marsh's guest — Stanley "Beamer" McConnery, a full-patch member of McEwen's old St. Catharines Chapter of the Outlaws — delivered the hard sell. He warned that without a concrete deal with the Outlaws, the Iron Hawgs could see their drug supply dwindle down to the same pathetic level as the Para-Dice Riders had. For those still unconvinced, Marsh reminded them that full-patch members of Hells Angels had been seen partying in Toronto with the Para-Dice Riders for the last year or so. Everybody in Canada knew they had their eye on Ontario. If they were to patch over the much-loathed Para-Dice Riders — and it looked likely — the Iron Hawgs would have to be well armed and well allied.

That was the clincher. The Iron Hawgs became the Outlaws Toronto. It was one of many occasions in which the fear of a biker war in Ontario forced a decision.

It wasn't the Outlaws' first success in Ontario after the Satan's Choice patch-over. In 1982, they negotiated to have one of Ontario's oldest clubs — the Queensmen of Amherstburg, just across the river from Detroit — change their name to the Holocaust, relocate up the 401 to London and serve as a puppet gang.

Meanwhile the Outlaws were facing serious competition on other fronts, namely Quebec. They were not the only ones who came to Montreal in 1977. And while the Outlaws' presence in the city was simply a fortuitous outgrowth of the club's general desire to establish itself in Canada, Hells Angels targeted Montreal specifically.

• • •

While the city fathers would probably prefer to be known for hosting the 1976 Summer Olympics, late '70s Montreal was also well known for being a hotbed of organized crime, racketeering, loan-sharking, smuggling, drug sales and prostitution.

And it was a town full of Mafia. The Cotroni, Violi and Rizzuto families represented the Italians, and the less organized, but still plenty powerful West End Gang represented the Irish. Among them, they controlled most of the crime in town, with an uneasy equilibrium occasionally interrupted by violence.

As in many other places, the gangsters tended to use bikers to do their toughest jobs. It made sense — there were dozens of biker gangs in and around the city looking for easy money, and their presence allowed the gangsters a layer of protection from law enforcement. None of them was especially dominant or all that organized, so if things didn't work out with one club, they could easily switch to another. The almost unlimited supply of competing labor also kept prices down.

But there was a problem. There was a growing resentment among the majority francophones in Montreal towards the anglophone minority who — unfairly, they felt — dominated business in the city. And things were no different among the bikers. While all the gangsters spoke English (when they weren't communicating in Italian), the only English-speaking biker gang of any consequence was Satan's Choice (which became the Outlaws in 1977). That meant most of the time, the powerful English-speaking gangsters were hiring the French-speaking bikers to do their dirty work and paying them a fraction of what they made off them. It was no different, they contended, from the way all business was conducted in Montreal.

But an alternative emerged. In the working-class neighborhood of Saint-Henri, nine of a French-speaking bartender's ten sons began to throw their considerable weight around (the other lived his life as a government employee, and was never accused of any crime). The Dubois brothers — Raymond, Jean-Guy, Normand, Claude, René, Roland, Jean-Paul and the twins Maurice and Adrien — formed a cohesive group of toughs who eventually expanded their individual efforts into organized crime, rivaling the most powerful Mafia families in reach and scope.

It started in the 1950s, when the four oldest brothers — Raymond, Jean-Guy, Normand and Claude — began leaning on local bar owners for protection money and other forms of extortion. They were very good at it, each individually acquiring a few bars by the end of the decade. But they were so good at it that they developed swelled heads. The Quebec Police Commission described them as "ruling like feudal lords." All four were charged with the murder of a waiter who had the nerve to argue with them about their dinner bill, but a lack of evidence and suddenly reluctant witnesses led to their subsequent acquittals.

After that, the Dubois brothers expanded their empire. They had a simple — actually, a crude — business plan, but it was truly effective. A Dubois brother and his cronies would start frequenting a bar. They'd show up every night. At first they'd be friendly. Then they'd start picking fights with other patrons, harassing the staff, vandalizing the establishment and assaulting the owner. It got progressively worse until the owner invariably gave in. Most of the time, they settled for $100 a week. That may not sound like much, but $100 in the early '70s is more like $1,000 today, and each Dubois brother was collecting from literally dozens of bars.

And they did more than that. After the Dubois brothers got their claws into a business, they forced the owner to hire gang members and associates. Of course, they would steal the establishment blind and work for the bar intermittently at best. And they would also operate loan-sharking, gambling, fencing and drug-trafficking businesses from the establishment while they were on the payroll.

Their expansion wasn't always easy. Early in their careers, the Dubois brothers recruited three old friends — Pierre, Jacques and André McSween — to work for them. The francophone Irish-Canadian brothers proved very effective, performing a number of burglaries, truck hijackings and stickups for the Dubois brothers.

But the McSweens were nothing if not ambitious. By the early 1970s, they no longer worked for the Dubois. Instead, they had recruited their own gang and controlled an area bordering their old bosses' territory. They took what they had learned from the Dubois brothers about extortion and loan-sharking and set up those businesses in their own territory. They even had a deal with the official scorekeeper for the Montreal Canadiens under which he would alter game statistics to ensure the McSweens would always collect on bets.

As they got rich, both the McSweens and the Dubois brothers saw that the highest profits came from drug trafficking. And the best drug to traffic, they soon found out, was methamphetamine.

It was cheap and easy to make and highly addictive. Once a user was hooked, he or she would give anything to get more.

By 1973, the competition was too much for the Dubois brothers to tolerate. After a McSween dealer named Real Lepine insulted Adrien Dubois by refusing to sell his drugs, the Dubois brothers declared war on the McSweens. The resulting "West End War" left nine members of the McSween gang — including Jacques McSween — and five Dubois associates dead. With their brother dead, the surviving McSweens surrendered and quickly went back to work for the Dubois brothers.

With the McSweens out of the way and back in the fold, the Dubois brothers began a plan to control all of downtown. Claude, who had worked as bouncer at clubs owned by both the Cotronis and Violis and had learned much from them, was firmly in charge.

His next target was a very profitable trade in marijuana, LSD and particularly meth that operated in Saint-Henri Square. Like Yorkville in Toronto, the area is now quite wealthy and quiet, but in the early and mid '70s, it was a hippie hangout and an open-air drug market.

It was run by a particularly tough biker gang called the Devil's Disciples. Don't be fooled by the name. Of the more than 350 motorcycle gangs identified in Quebec history, a handful — maybe a couple dozen or so — had French names. Even fewer had anglophone membership. The Devil's Disciples were *pur laine* (the Quebec expression for "purely French") through and through. They were, at the time, Montreal's most powerful biker gang.

But because they were operating in what Claude Dubois considered his territory, it just wasn't going to last. The Dubois brothers hired some local tough guys in an effort to get rid of the Devil's Disciples. They succeeded. By January 1976, 15 Devil's Disciples had been murdered and plenty more had been roughed up. In a phone conversation recorded by police, Claude "Johnny Hallyday" Ellefson, leader of the Devil's Disciples, described how he panicked and fled Saint-Henri Square when he found out that Claude Dubois (who he called "the big one") wanted his business. They were gone for good. Ellefson later re-emerged selling drugs from a wheelchair in Quebec City.

What was interesting about that particular battle was that, instead of the usual hired muscle of basically independent tough guys they knew from their neighborhood, the Dubois brothers hired a different biker gang for much of the rough stuff.

They were called the Popeyes. Based in Laval — a large suburb located on a pair of islands just north of Montreal — the Popeyes were a brutal bunch of beer-drinkers who frequently made the short ride into the city on business. They liked working for the francophone Dubois brothers. The Popeyes specialized in muscle for hire, but — inspired by the Dubois brothers — were expanding into other activities, including drug trafficking.

A lot of their success was due to their charismatic and strategically minded president, Yves "Le Boss" Buteau. Tall, strong and blonde, Buteau strove to have a disciplined crew. He forbade the use of stimulant and injected drugs and he encouraged his men to shave, cut their hair occasionally and wear their colors only when necessary. But he was not above using violence when he deemed it necessary. With his statesmanship, though, he rarely needed to. He started a small network of biker gangs, some as far away as Trois-Rivieres, 80 miles down the St. Lawrence. And he had the enviable ability to deal on positive terms with other biker gangs, particularly the Missiles of Saguenay and the ridiculously named Sex Fox of Chibougamau, often inviting them to parties or hiring them for tough or distant jobs.

After they had chased out the Devil's Disciples, the Popeyes began selling Dubois drugs in Saint-Henri Square and the surrounding area. But a large and well-organized police task force had been formed to combat the Dubois brothers, who — after exterminating the McSween gang and the Devil's Disciples — were regarded as the primary threat to the safety and security of the people of Montreal. They were constantly tailed, stopped and searched for minor violations and arrested by police. They all went down pretty quickly.

Almost as soon as they arrived, the Popeyes found themselves in charge of a very large area of downtown Montreal, but — as the Dubois connection dwindled and later disappeared altogether — they had nothing to sell.

That didn't last long. Just like the Outlaws in Ontario, Hells Angels were looking to expand northward. The Outlaws — founded in Chicagoland and later headquartered in Detroit — took the natural step eastward into Southern Ontario. The eastern branch of Hells Angels, however, was based in Manhattan (the former Aliens were the regional bosses), so it was logical for them to look north to Montreal. It was not only much closer than Toronto (a four-hour drive north as opposed to a ten-hour drive west), but at the time, it was also bigger, more cosmopolitan and had a far larger drug market. And, back then, language wasn't a big problem as there was always an English-speaker around to translate.

Hells Angels had been scouting Montreal for a gang to align with for a few years, and one source told me that it was the well-connected Devil's Disciples who were at the top of their list until the Popeyes effectively got rid of them. So, when Hells Angels came to Montreal, they came to Laval.

It was an immediate success for the Popeyes. No less than Hells Angels U.S. national president and celebrity Sonny Barger came to visit. He was so taken with Buteau in fact, that he personally gave him his patch and anointed him as the only Canadian to be allowed to wear the "Hells Angels International" patch.

On December 5, 1977, a wild party in Laval ushered in a whole new era of organized crime in Canada. That night, 35 members of the Popeyes patched over to Hells Angels (the others were chased off). With the founding of the Hells Angels Montreal Chapter, the second of two American supergangs had been established in the country. The era of biker wars had begun.

The situation became even more tense in February of 1978, when the Montreal Satan's Choice made the decision to patch over and become the Outlaws Montreal Chapter. They had seen other former Satan's Choice chapters in Ontario flourish as Outlaws, and realized that what was left of the Choice would be no match against Hells Angels, should they decide they wanted to run the town by themselves.

The patch-over put both American gangs in La Belle Province, both operating in, and vying for, dominance in the city of Montreal.

Chapter 4
Mayhem in Montreal

Maybe they knew it, and maybe they didn't, but on the chilly afternoon of February 15, 1978, Robert Côté and a close friend whose name was never released walked into the wrong bar. At the corner of Saint-Hubert and Castelnau in Montreal's Villeray neighborhood, not far from Jarry Park, sat Brasserie Joey. The locals knew it was a place where the Popeyes — now known as Hells Angels — had hung out for years.

But Côté and his associate weren't from the neighborhood. They were from Saint-Henri, not far away, but very different. And they were Outlaws. They sat near the window, drinking beer and chatting. Nobody else in the bar talked to them, or even looked at them.

Before long, a group of Hells Angels and their supporters walked in and confronted the two men. To their credit, the pair of Outlaws didn't back down. They argued with the locals until they were physically ejected from the building.

Once outside, they stood in the street flinging threats, insults and rude gestures at the people inside. They probably should have left. Minutes after their forcible ejection, a large, light-green car covered in grime and frost drove up. The front passenger-side window opened and someone fired a volley of shots at the

Outlaws. Côté was hit in the head. His friend was lightly grazed. Wisely, he fled the scene. The green car sped away, skidding in the gray snow.

Côté died five days later. The shooter was later identified as Popeye-turned-Hells Angel Yves "Apache" Trudeau, who finally found his calling in life after failing at so many things before. He didn't look like the other Hells Angels in Montreal, and nobody would have guessed he was the club's enforcer and primary weapon. While most of the rest of the chapter were big brutes — including some 350- and even 400-pound behemoths — Trudeau measured just five-foot-six and, by his own admission, tipped the scales at some 135 pounds. And while all the other Hells Angels had long hair and huge beards, as was the biker style at the time, Trudeau was generally clean shaven except for modest sideburns and only traded his Elvis-style pompadour for a sedate parted-at-the-side look well into the '80s.

Côté's death would be just one of the 43 murders the tiny biker later admitted to committing. Ironically, later in life, after he was admitted into the witness protection program, he would go by the name Denis Côté.

Desperate for a show of strength, the Outlaws threw a lavish funeral for Côté. More than 300 Outlaws — many from Ontario and Outlaw strongholds in the U.S. such as South Florida and Detroit — attended, including three convicted felons the Montreal police would later arrest and hand over to immigration.

As is biker tradition, the riders in the procession were helmetless. The cops didn't ticket them. In fact, one told me they appreciate the gesture as it allows them to photograph the bikers' faces and get an approximation of their individual status by what spot in line they have.

Less than a month later, Hells Angels struck again. And the Outlaws clearly hadn't learned to stay on their side of Mont-Royal Park. Gilles Cadorette, president of the Montreal Outlaws, decided to show his friend Donald McLean his newly customized Camaro. It was a heck of a car — assembled in nearby Saint Therese, Quebec, perfected in his driveway in Montreal — and Cadorette wanted to show off it and his newfound wealth to a younger and very impressionable new member.

The problem was that he did it while visiting his girlfriend on rue Bordeaux. The two men hopped into the customized sports coupe, which he'd left parked in the street, allowing it to be tampered with. Cadorette turned the key. That completed a circuit that sent electricity to a blasting cap that ignited a couple of sticks of dynamite duct-taped to the floor of the Camaro right under the driver's seat.

Boom! Cadorette was blown into a number of unrecognizable pieces. McLean was badly hurt.

If the border between the clubs was between the west and east sides of Montreal, Hells Angels violated it on April 25. Although it may be hard to believe now, two Hells Angels — Denis "Le Cure" Kennedy and an unnamed associate — actually knocked on the door of the Outlaws' Montreal clubhouse at 144 rue Saint-Ferdinand and, unbelievably, were let in. Kennedy didn't look like most of the other ex-Popeyes. He was clean shaven, had relatively short hair and was thin. He was also considered talkative and charming. But he wasn't there to make friends. He and his associate pulled out a couple of handguns and started firing. Kennedy's gun jammed, but his friend kept on shooting until he'd spent his entire magazine. Then they ran. None of the Outlaws inside were seriously injured, but they were too shocked to pursue the gunmen. And they got the message.

At about 11 p.m. the day after, a short but tough Outlaws prospect named Anathase "Tom Thumb" Markopoulos was sent out for smokes. The nearest convenience store, Dépanneur Paul, was closed, but the owner was still in the store, cleaning up and getting ready for bed. Markopoulos pounded on the door. She looked up and recognized him. The Outlaws — two buildings over — brought in a lot of business, so she thought she'd open up for the young man. She also knew he'd get in trouble if he came back without whatever they sent him for. So she put down her broom and headed towards the door. Before she got there, she saw a big, pale-green car pull up behind Markopoulos. The passenger window opened, and she could see a handgun sticking out. The man in the car pumped six bullets into Markopoulos, who fell and died before the woman could get the door unlocked.

The Outlaws who'd sent Markopoulos out heard the shots and interpreted it as the beginning of a police raid. Instead of coming to their prospect's defense, the members inside grabbed all the weapons, drugs and cash they could and fled in various directions.

The Outlaws were spooked, and Hells Angels kept the pressure on. The night after Markopoulos was murdered, full-patch Outlaw François Poliseno took his 19-year-old girlfriend Suzanne Harvey out for a drink at Brasserie Industriel on busy rue Notre-Dame. The place was bustling, but that didn't prevent a masked man from barging in and spraying Poliseno and Harvey with bullets from a handgun. Both were very seriously injured.

Other bar patrons described the car to the cops when they arrived. Soon thereafter, they stopped a large, pale-green car just outside the Hells Angels clubhouse. In it, they found Kennedy, a friend he called "Gross Plotte," a mask, a toy gun, binoculars and a bulletproof vest. Later on, the police determined that the bullets fired at Poliseno and Harvey were from the same gun that shot up the Outlaws' clubhouse.

It was a sloppy move, and one they would learn from. In the future, Hells Angels shooters got into the habit of disposing of their weapons at the scene of the crime, reducing the chances of being caught with it or having two crimes associated with each other.

The Outlaws eventually struck back — but ineffectively. On May 12, 1978, a then-minor Hells Angel named René "Canisse" Hébert stepped out of the clubhouse. Someone shot at him from a car. Three bullets missed, one lightly grazed him.

Later that month, Paul Ringuette, a Hells Angels associate, beat Jean Gonthier, an Outlaws supporter, to death in Saint-Vincent-de-Paul prison. Corrections officials told the media that the two argued over a hockey game, although both were Canadiens fans. In addition to assault and bank robbery, Riguette had murder tacked onto his crimes. He served 18 years. And it was later determined he was involved in the notorious Hanna Buxbaum murder plot in St. Catharines, Ontario in 1984.

In the next few months, two Hells Angels associates and one Outlaw died, but it's unlikely they had anything to do with the war. René "Balloune" Francoeur wasn't with Hells Angels, but had been talking to president Yves "Le Boss" Buteau about joining. Before he could, he was beaten to death by an unidentified drug dealer when he tried to pay him with counterfeit U.S. currency. Similarly, Hells Angels member Adrien "Pistasche" Fleury was shot when he tried to steal an unaffiliated biker's Harley. The aggrieved man just happened to have a shotgun handy. Not long after, Outlaw François Ouellette died when his car rolled over after losing a wheel as he drove to his Chateauguay home. Maybe a Hells Angel loosened his rim, but there's no firm evidence to support it.

Up to this point in the war, the Outlaws had taken it on the chin. They were attacked and killed all over Montreal. They had lost a president, their very clubhouse had been violated and shot up. But in October, they pulled off a victory that may have seemed minor at first, but put the Hells Angels' overall effort back for many years.

On October 12, two Americans — one from Miami, the other from Detroit — showed up at Le Tourbillon, a Rosemont bar frequented by Hells Angels. The men were tall and muscular, but their clean-shaven faces, short haircuts, lack of tattoos and outfits (innocuous khaki canvas slacks and nylon windbreakers) indicated they weren't bikers. In fact, the Hells Angels inside the bar were absolutely convinced the two men, who had made only token attempts to hide the fact they were following them all week, were undercover cops.

A hush fell over the bar as the two stepped into the bar nonchalantly, and looked around. They spotted a bunch of bikers in a booth, and approached. On one side of the booth, there were three big toughs who were wearing full Hells Angels colors. They were with three other, less impressive-looking biker types. One of them was actually so small, the Americans weren't sure if he was actually with the others.

The biggest and oldest of the Hells Angels, Louis "Ti-Oui" Lapierre, got up to confront them. He was tired of being followed by these two and wanted to get rid of them before his meeting. Besides, he hadn't done anything wrong and they didn't have anything on him.

He didn't get a single word out before one of the Americans he was confronting pulled a handgun from under his jacket and shot Lapierre in the chest from point-blank range. The other pulled out a sawed-off shotgun and started pumping lead pellets into the men in the booth. He and his partner continued firing and firing until they were sure all the men in the booth were dead. Then, like professionals, they dropped their weapons and ran.

Of the three Hells Angels in attendance, Jean Brochu died immediately. Lapierre and Bruno Coulombe were badly injured, but survived. Their guests — a trio of Wild Ones from Hamilton, who were in Montreal to talk about a working agreement at the very least — fared little better. George "Chico" Mousseau was also dead by the time police showed up. Gary "Gator" Davies lingered a while in hospital, but later died. The only one of the Wild Ones who survived was the little guy, their leader, Walter "Nurget" Stadnick. He had managed to slide under the table, a fact that escaped the assassins' notice.

He rode back down the 401 to Hamilton, alone and frustrated at his inability to make a lasting connection with a big-time club. Hells Angels had been foiled in their attempt to forge a beachhead in Ontario. With the Outlaws and Satan's Choice still large and in charge in that province, they — in particular, Buteau — were looking for smaller, unaffiliated gangs to deal with. One of them was the Wild Ones. The incident set back their plan, but they remembered Stadnick, and reached out to him frequently after the Le Tourbillon massacre.

The war went on. Hells Angels sent their wild beast, Trudeau, after Brian Powers, a well-liked and respected former Outlaws president who was still on good terms with the club. On November 10, Trudeau found out where Powers lived, waited until he knew he was at home, and knocked on the door. Powers answered. Trudeau shot him nine times, mostly in the head, dumped the gun and ran.

Again, the Outlaws tried to make a show of force at the funeral. Of particular interest to Hells Angels (and police observers) was the fact that among the mourners were members of two major Toronto gangs: the Para-Dice Riders and the Vagabonds. The police and media took that as an alliance between those clubs and the Outlaws in an effort to keep Hells Angels out of Ontario.

At the funeral, an informant identified Outlaw Roland "Roxy" Dutemple as the instigator behind the Le Tourbillon shootings. As was now becoming habit, Hells Angels sent Trudeau out after him. On December 8, while walking around in the west end, Trudeau and a friend spotted a man they thought might be Dutemple. They weren't entirely sure, so Trudeau walked up to him to get a better look. The man looked at him angrily. Trudeau asked him (in French): "Are you Roxy?" But before the man could answer, Trudeau shot him in the head.

In the clubhouse the next day, the other members showed him a newspaper article that identified the man he murdered as William Weichold, a non-biker who just happened to look a lot like Dutemple. Trudeau is said to have laughed at his mistake and argued that he should be paid for the hit anyway.

He eventually killed the real Dutemple on March 29, 1979, by planting a bomb in his car. Five days later, Trudeau traveled to the Fabreville neighborhood in Laval, just north of Montreal, and knocked on the door of Robert Labelle, president of a Laval gang called the Huns. There had been a rumor that the Huns were going to patch over to the Outlaws. As soon as Labelle opened the door, Trudeau shot him twice in the face, killing him.

He struck again on May 9. Outlaws rising star Robert McLean — who had survived the car bomb that had killed Cadorette — and his girlfriend Carmen Piché went down into the alley between their Verdun apartment and climbed onto his customized 1963 Harley. The spark of the dynamo that flashed when he kicked the starter activated a bomb that blew the bike and both riders into a million pieces. It had been planted by Trudeau, fellow Hells Angel Jean-Pierre "Matt le Crosseur" Mathieu and president Buteau himself.

The war was not going well for the Outlaws. Other than the Le Tourbillon incident, they had inflicted little pain and suffering on Hells Angels, while they had been gunned down like targets in a shooting gallery.

Chapter 5

Where Jimmy Lewis Died

It was insanely cold as I drove into Hamilton. Still, I parked a few blocks away from the Hamilton Police Service's central station on King William Street, just so I could walk and see how my old hometown was looking. To be perfectly honest, it looked rough.

There were some new restaurants, but it mostly looked run-down and bereft of truly sustainable money-making businesses. I was reminded of a conversation I had with Luther when we were deciding where to meet that day I met Parente in Burlington. Since it was centered geographically between all of us and we were familiar with it, I had suggested meeting somewhere in the Hammer. He audibly scoffed, and asked "Why go into the toilet if you don't have to?" As a native, I was a little offended. But as someone walking through downtown about a week later, I had to admit he had something of a point.

I was there to meet Sergeant John Harris. He's the biggest, most intimidating cop I've ever seen. At six-foot-seven, the former University of Minnesota defensive end towers over lawbreaker and law-abider alike. Other cops talk about seeing him emerge from his car and watching everyone in a vicious confrontation immediately fall silent and still. He relishes being the biggest man in the room, says it makes his job a lot easier, but his quick wit is probably a better weapon. It puts everyone, on either side of the law, at ease.

And he's the most knowledgeable person I have ever met in law enforcement when it comes to biker gangs, especially in Ontario. I called him to tell him I was in town. Rather than talk to me in a coffee shop, conference room or interrogation room like other cops do, Harris prefers to have me interview him while he's working. That means I have to wait for him to arrive in his giant white Suburban. And it also means that we will occasionally stop at crime or emergency scenes.

Once I was inside the huge SUV, he asked me if I had a few minutes before we start. I told him I did. He called down another sergeant who wanted me to sign a copy of my book *Fallen Angel*. Harris signed it, too. Apparently, the sergeant had a friend in Liverpool who, like many non-Canadians, thought Canadian streets were crime-free. And he wanted my help in proving him wrong.

After his friend left and before we started off, Harris told me that Parente had recently called him to check me out, to see if I was okay. He wanted to know if I was honest. Harris told me that he assured him I was. He also warned me not to cross Parente.

Harris knew that I already knew a great deal about the history of outlaw biker gangs in Ontario, so he concentrated on Parente and other goings-on in the Hammer. According to Harris, Parente had joined the local chapter of Satan's Choice in the late 1960s at the age of 18. In an earlier interview, Parente confirmed this. It was a good time to get established in that particular gang. They were big and still getting much bigger. So I asked Harris what Parente was like back then.

He was the exact opposite of hesitant in his answer. "Unlike a lot of guys, as soon as we started noticing him in Satan's Choice, he'd talk to us," Harris said. "Always had something to say, usually tried to be funny." But as personable as he was, Parente also had a darker side, Harris pointed out. "He got in fights, and could sometimes be confrontational." Parente himself told me his first conviction was for assaulting a Hamilton police officer he witnessed beating up a man he'd already handcuffed. Harris confirmed that.

I asked Harris what Parente looked like in those days. He told me that the bikers all dressed alike back then, with leather (or even more often, denim) jackets or vests, jeans and T-shirts. They also favored long hair and beards, and Parente was well stocked in both departments. "He had this huge mop of black hair and a big, long beard," he told me, then thought about it for a second. "He kind of looked like Rasputin."

And that's part of why he got his nickname "The Wop." While most of Satan's Choice at the time could trace their roots back to the British Isles or elsewhere in Northwestern Europe, Parente was very clearly Italian.

But I pointed out to Harris that other prominent members of the Hamilton Satan's Choice — like Anthony Pantonella — were also of Italian ancestry. He laughed. "Pantonella? He was a skinny kid with a big blonde afro. They called him 'Cottonhead.' But Parente looked Italian, he acted Italian." Harris mentioned that he spoke with his hands. I'd seen that myself firsthand.

From my conversations with him, I knew Parente did not mind being called "The Wop." He had even called himself "Mike the Wop" at least once in my presence. So why did he balk at being called Mario?

"He thought it sounded like a girl's name," said Harris.

Parente was, Harris maintained, a likeable enough guy despite being on the other side of the fence. Interestingly, Parente — who referred to most of the other cops we both knew as "bags of shit" — expressed respect, if not admiration, for Harris. Although he did point out that the big man could be more physical than he had to be at times.

Harris said that Parente was always up for a joke, and had a jovial way of expressing things. "One of the things I noticed about him early on was that he was always trying to improve himself, to educate himself," he said. "He always wanted to be more eloquent; and if he learned a new word, you could tell because he would use it over and over again in conversation until he found a new one."

Hamilton was one of the Satan's Choice chapters that patched over to the Outlaws in 1977. Harris immediately noticed a change in Parente. He became more confident. "He was always willing to talk to you, no matter what the situation was like when he was with Satan's Choice. But once he became an Outlaw, he really worked on his personality and he started speaking for the club. He was their spokesman."

He'd offhandedly mention a club event, and Harris would say something like "I'll see you there." And that never failed to get a smile out of Parente. Another time, later in Parente's career, after he had been arrested a few times, Harris ran into him at a bar patio in Hamilton's trendy Hess Village. He was with two other men with Outlaws jackets on. Before he even saw their rockers, Harris identified them as being from out of town, probably from the United States. He sighed and yelled: "Mike, you're getting too old for this; when are you going to give up the life?" Parente, he said, laughed and replied: "It's the only thing I know."

And he was not shy about expressing his association with the club. "He was on his bike all the time," Harris said. "And he wore a lot of jewelry. Not just the Harley stuff all the other guys wore, but always things with the Outlaws logo on them; he was very proud to be part of the club."

One of the pieces of jewelry was inscribed with the initials GLGC, Outlaws parlance for "Good-Looking Guys Club" — which is what they liked to call themselves. Although the transition from Satan's Choice to Outlaws was mostly smooth, there was a minor war between the Hamilton Outlaws and their former brothers in the Kitchener Satan's Choice that left one dead on each side before a truce was established.

There was another problem in Hamilton, a more racially mixed city at the time than any other in Ontario, that involved the Good-Looking Guys Club. Although they weren't actually Satan's Choice members, three men, friends of Parente's — Lloyd Blaquierre, Freddie Weise and Michael Bierce — were very close to the Hamilton members of Satan's Choice, and, according to some, looked like they could eventually become full-patches. But there was a problem — they were black. "The Outlaws said it was whites-only, and they had to abide by that," said Harris. "So those guys were out; you could be Jewish or Mexican, but you just couldn't be black."

So Blaquierre, Weise and Bierce formed their own club. It was officially known as the No-Name Motorcycle Club, but the phrase "Not So Good-Looking Guys Club" was spray-painted on the alley-side wall of the old Cannon Street East storefront they used to rent.

According to Harris, Parente and the newly minted Hamilton Outlaws continued to associate and party with the Not So Good-Looking Guys Club, but "they sure didn't like that name." It wasn't to last, though. The trio later beat a man to death one night over a long-forgotten dispute and dumped his body in Hamilton Harbour. Their subsequent arrests led to the little club's extinction.

• • •

Over those same years, Stadnick climbed the biker ladder in an entirely different way.

Although both were from Hamilton, Parente and Stadnick would consider themselves from different places. You have to consider the social geography of the city. Hamilton is built at the western end of Lake Ontario, and is divided by an escarpment the locals call "the Mountain." Created by the retreating glaciers thousands of years ago, it's not a mountain in the traditional sense, but a nearly vertical cliff that separates two plains. The main part of Hamilton is very flat, then the escarpment lifts about 300 nearly vertical feet and the rest of the city is on another flat

Walter "Nurget" Stadnick

plain. The major north-south streets of the city continue up the cliff, but they have the prefix "Upper" added to their names; Ottawa becomes Upper Ottawa atop the mountain, Gage becomes Upper Gage and so on.

Those who live on the Mountain generally consider those in the rest of the city (which they call "Downtown") to be more ethnic, densely packed and poorer; while those below the Mountain (which they simply call "Hamilton," saving the title "Downtown" for the busiest and oldest part of the city) generally consider their neighbors 300 feet up to be suburban, unsophisticated and boring. Although they share a city, the two groups don't mix all that much, although some Mountain residents work down the hill and — before Downtown fell into decay, and malls on the edges of town took over — many of them did their shopping and enjoyed the nightlife down there.

While Parente lived Downtown — doubly so, as he lived in neighborhoods in or close to the city's Central Business District — Stadnick came from the Mountain. Born to Ukrainian immigrant parents, Stadnick was one of three boys who grew up comfortably in a small, tidy house near a large park.

Always very small — topping out at five-foot-four or five-foot-five depending on who you talk to — and odd-looking, Stadnick was still very popular. That may well have been because he was a drug dealer. Arrested in 1971 (aged 24) with enough hashish to distribute, Stadnick always had money. After high school, he financed a motorcycle gang for himself and his friends, and he named them the Cossacks.

From everything I've been told, they weren't all that impressive. They rode small bikes, mostly British in origin and paid for by Stadnick, and they drilled holes in the tops of their helmets and pulled their hair through them — because Stadnick thought it would look cool. "They weren't a big deal," Harris said. "Nobody paid them any attention." Another police officer told me they were the most polite gang he'd ever encountered.

But over the years, they evolved into a more traditional motorcycle gang. Called the Wild Ones (perhaps in reference to the Marlon Brando movie, but probably not), they switched to Harleys and stopped doing silly things with their hair. And they behaved like the other big-time gangs. Besides drug trafficking, the Wild Ones are alleged to have been in the employ of Hamilton's Italian Mafia. Although they were careful not to step on important, Papalia-connected toes, the Wild Ones are frequently said to have specialized in bombing bakeries and other businesses whose owners fell behind in protection or loan payments.

During most of the 1970s, the Wild Ones were seen as also-rans in the Hamilton biker scene. At the time, the city was dominated not just by Satan's Choice, but also by the Red Devils.

Said to be the oldest 1-percenter (admittedly outlaw) club in Canada, the Red Devils have a more benign reputation than other big-time gangs. There are other, Hells Angels–allied biker clubs around the world called Red Devils, but they are not related to the Hamilton club, which is proudly unaffiliated.

Based on the Beach Strip — a very narrow piece of land that connects Hamilton to neighboring Burlington and protects Hamilton Harbour from Lake Ontario's winds and waves — they are known to keep mainly to themselves. They ride and party and are rarely involved in the sorts of organized crimes law enforcement has come to find commonplace in outlaw biker gangs. They have little time for the politics of the bigger biker gangs, but are generally on positive terms with all of them. "They can party with the Outlaws one night and the Hells Angels the next," said OPP biker specialist Len Isnor. "They get along with everyone."

Before Satan's Choice became the Outlaws, they were fairly tolerant of the Wild Ones, considering them not much of a threat, sometimes partying with them or even employing them occasionally. But, like everything else, those circumstances changed in the fateful summer of 1977.

The same factors that made the Outlaws expand to Ontario made Hells Angels desire the province just as much. And, although Stadnick was responsible for the bulk of the Hells Angels expansion in Canada, it did not start with him. That honor belongs to former Popeyes boss Yves "Le Boss" Buteau, who became Hells Angels Montreal Chapter president and Stadnick's early mentor and champion.

Buteau had made major inroads with some B.C. gangs who later patched over to the Hells Angels of nearby Washington

State before being brought into the Canadian Hells Angels fold many years later by Stadnick. And he had a particular interest in Ontario.

It made sense. Not only was it physically close to Montreal, but its economy (particularly in and around Toronto) was rapidly surpassing Quebec's and it had many major border crossings.

But there was one problem — it was already full of motorcycle gangs, most of which were satisfied with the equilibrium the way it was. The province was also home to a set of powerful Mafia families who weren't too interested in change either.

At that point, the primary gangs in Ontario were the Outlaws and what remained of the still-loyal-to-Guindon Satan's Choice. Of course, there was no way Hells Angels and the Outlaws could have any sort of alliance, and Satan's Choice had already shot down the idea of cooperation with Hells Angels — although they were far more powerful at the time of that decision — making them a hard sell at best.

So Buteau instead targeted the other, smaller gangs with varying levels of success. One such gang was Stadnick's Wild Ones. Although Stadnick and his men were very interested in forming an alliance with Hells Angels, things did not go well for them once the Outlaws found out.

"As soon as the Wild Ones began to associate with the Hells Angels, the Outlaws told them they shouldn't do that," said Harris. "And they probably shouldn't have, as it led to several deaths."

It was the first biker war between the superpowers in Ontario. It was fought between the Outlaws and the Wild Ones, who were, in essence, the Hells Angels' proxy. Over the next few months, the 15-member Wild Ones suffered terribly. Dennis Stewart was killed by a car bomb. Another car bomb took off Danny Powell's right leg. Alvin Patterson's store was shot up while he was in it, and the same thing happened to John "Cataract Jack" Pluim's talent agency.

Two more Wild Ones — Peter Urech and Derek Thistlewaite — died instantaneously when a bomb they were trying to make blew up during construction. But Outlaws hadn't been the intended target of the bomb. Informants later told Harris that it was meant to eliminate or at least intimidate a Hamilton woman who had been gang-raped by members of the Wild Ones, to prevent her from testifying in court.

In fact, the Wild Ones never actually managed to do anything to retaliate against the Outlaws in Hamilton. They talked about it a lot, but never managed to put anything together. And when Stadnick returned from the fateful Le Tourbillon summit meeting with Hells Angels to report that fellow members Gary "Gator" Davies and George "Chico" Mousseau were dead (along with Montreal Hells Angel Jean Brochu), it was over for the Wild Ones. Those who weren't either dead or dismembered quit. Many of them continued to be friends and even business partners with Stadnick in the future, but none went back to the biker lifestyle.

But Stadnick continued to operate in Hamilton. Alone and wary as a Hells Angels associate — and later a prospect of the distant and notoriously violent Montreal South (Sorel) Chapter — in an Outlaws town, he continued to make friends and sell the brand, but he generally laid low in his hometown.

As Harris and I drove around, he showed me all kinds of biker-related landmarks. He showed me a house Parente used to own, but never lived in, instead choosing to rent it out. Then another house he actually lived in with his girlfriend, although he didn't own it or actually pay any rent. Harris pointed out a roofing company owned by a full-patch Hamilton Hells Angel who used to be an Outlaw. Then he laughed when he told me about how another Hells Angel won the contract to pave the new East End police station's parking lot.

Then he showed me the James Steet North restaurant Zucca's, where a wise guy's Yukon Denali was recently shot up and many say what's left of the Italian Mafia still meet.

I asked him if the Mafia still hold much sway in Hamilton, traditionally their base in Ontario, after all the killings and arrests.

"Oh yeah," he said vehemently. "They're still around. Look at the Royal Connaught situation, lots of people got paid, but not a thing's been done." He was referring to Hamilton's last great hotel, which still lies in ruins on the south side of King Street despite tons of public money having been paid out for its restoration.

But he admits they're nowhere near as powerful as they were in the Papalia heyday.

As we kept driving around the city, we stopped to check in on a minivan with a homemade trailer that had been driving the wrong way on a one-way street until it collided head-on with a garbage truck. The minivan was crushed and the homemade trailer was upside-down about half a block away, but Harris' officers seemed to have it all under control, so we left.

Harris then took me to 402 Birch Avenue, right where it meets Burlington Street in the north end amongst the giant, now–mostly empty steel factories and other metal-fabricating businesses. There was nothing there. Literally. I told him I had been there before — having been told it was where the Outlaws clubhouse was — but I thought I had written the address down incorrectly or confused it with Birch Street, a few blocks to the east. "Nope," he told me. "City got rid of it. Used to be a row of houses right there, and the Outlaws clubhouse was one of them." Then he pointed at a triangle of patchy grass and cracked pavement. Then he pointed at the curb. "And that's where Jimmy Lewis died," referring to the killing that landed Parente in prison.

Then we drove around the corner of notorious Sherman Avenue. To me, it looked like the most worthless bit of territory in all of the rust belt; but many Hamiltonians know that it is one of the most fiercely fought-over stretches of land in organized crime history. "There, 409 Sherman Avenue North. That's where the Sherman House used to be," he said. "It was an old-style strip bar where the Outlaws used to hang out; it was owned by Billy Roberts and his wife. They had a 'talent agency.'" There's nothing there now but a parking lot surrounded by high fences topped with razor wire. It was empty except for a couple of rusty old dumpsters.

I mentioned that there used to be a lot of strip joints in Hamilton. "Yeah, there were nine at one point," he said. "Now there's just one." We both know he's talking about the infamous Hamilton Strip, formerly known as Hanrahan's.

"What? Bannister's is gone?" I asked, dumbfounded. The downtown strip joint was an institution. I was first brought there one afternoon when I was 15 by some school chums — they were pretty loose about ID back then — but my memories of the place are not fond.

In fact, I knew it was no longer called Bannister's because its owners had gotten into some serious trouble, but there had always been some kind of strip joint in the building under one name or another.

Harris told me that there hadn't been a strip joint in the building for years and that the only other one nearby was in Burlington. He added that the Outlaws used to hang out there, but don't anymore. "People just don't feel comfortable in those places anymore," he said. "And they can get anything they want these days from the Internet."

Even back in the 1970s and '80s, things did not always go easily for the Outlaws in Ontario, especially in Hamilton. Roland Harper was a high-ranking member of the Red Devils who was outraged by the way the Outlaws treated a young woman he knew. He swore revenge, and decided the best way he could get back at the Outlaws was from inside. So, without telling anyone else about his plan, he quit the Red Devils and joined the Outlaws.

Because he was an experienced biker and a big, strong and bold man, he was accepted right away. And he had another strange ace up his sleeve. Because he was a diabetic, he couldn't drink. That allowed him to stay sober while the other guys drank themselves sloppy. He earned their trust and learned their secrets.

After he became the Hamilton Chapter's sergeant-at-arms, he called Harris and arranged a meeting at the Westcliffe Mall parking lot up on the Mountain where the Outlaws rarely ventured. He told Harris he wanted to work for him as an informant, but that he had to be paid. Harris told me he couldn't help but laugh, then told him he didn't have any money to give him, but he did put him in touch with an OPP officer who could authorize such a situation.

The relationship paid dividends right away. Harris and his men raided the Outlaws clubhouse after Harper told them that the bikers were running an after-hours bar there. At the time, Ontario law forbade bars from serving alcohol after 1 a.m. (last call was 12:30), so after-hours drinking clubs — or "speakeasies" as the locals called them — were not uncommon.

The raid didn't yield any big arrests, but it did get the cops into the clubhouse. They confiscated a number of weapons, including shotguns.

And there were other problems for the Ontario Outlaws. In 1981, Buteau had made friendly overtures to three gangs in B.C. who were called the Satan's Angels. They had developed an enviable network between themselves and their regional puppet gangs, and within a couple of years had become Hells Angels chapters, answering to American chapters in Washington State. But they had little if any communication with the other Canadian Hells Angels chapters in Quebec. To welcome them into the fold, Buteau sent a couple of veteran Montreal Hells Angels to their coming-out party in 1983.

The guys he sent were members of the notorious Montreal North Chapter in Laval. Years earlier, tension between new recruits and the old guard — the former Popeyes — caused the Montreal Hells Angels to split. The old guard stayed in Laval, while the new guys formed a new chapter in a small, industrial town about an hour downriver called Sorel. Although Sorel is geographically north of Laval, it was called Montreal South because it was on the south shore of the St. Lawrence, while Laval was called Montreal North because it was north of the island of Montreal.

Buteau's emissaries were Michel "Jinx" Genest and Jean-Marc Nadeau. Both were very violent (Nadeau was later involved in at least four murders) and addicted to drugs. They left Montreal on July 17, 1983. They took the bus. And somewhere along the line, they picked up a 17-year-old girl.

As they passed through Ontario, they took up the back of the bus. Nobody wanted to sit near them. And when the bus arrived in Wawa, the bikers and their new friend — like everybody else — went into Mr. Muggs, the doughnut and coffee shop that served as Wawa's bus terminal.

While they were inside, a Ford Taurus pulled up with some tough-looking characters inside. They rolled down the windows, pulled out some handguns and filled the bus full of bullets, shattering every window. Hearing the commotion, the passengers ran out of Mr. Muggs just in time to see the men pile into the car and peel out of the parking lot. Three people were mildly hurt when they were hit by shattered glass. At least two witnesses noticed the "Support Your Local Outlaws" bumper sticker on the rear bumper.

When police arrived, they found a handgun and 56 grams of PCP stuffed into an old pack of cigarettes hidden in a garbage can. The bikers were questioned, but nothing stuck to them. They were free to go back to Montreal. The OPP drove the girl back home.

Acting on the eyewitnesses' accounts, the OPP went to the Outlaws' clubhouse in Sault Ste. Marie and arrested Parente, who was visiting from Hamilton, a friend of his from St. Catharines named Roy Caja and a local guy named Ben Greco. When I asked him about the incident, Parente told me in no uncertain terms that he was not in the car in question when the bus was shot up. At least four sources have told me Parente was definitely in the car, but none of them was actually an eyewitness. At any rate, all three Outlaws were arrested for attempted murder and conspiracy to commit murder.

At the preliminary hearing, the Crown prosecutor, Norman Douglas, brought up the specter of "open gang warfare" between the Outlaws and Hells Angels. Parente's lawyer assured him the sentence would be light if he pleaded guilty to possession of a firearm for a purpose dangerous to public peace. He was released on bail. Parente took that under serious consideration.

Upon his release, Parente flew back to Hamilton. That evening, some friends suggested he go out drinking with them. Rather than potentially get into trouble, Parente turned them down and decided to go to Bannister's, the downtown strip joint. It made sense. While other guys were paying for a night out, he could get paid to go to Bannister's.

On that night, he wasn't really a bouncer per se, according to Harris, but more of a

Mario "Mike the Wop" Parente

greeter, like they have at Wal-Mart. Harris dropped by Bannister's regularly. "The owners — Rinaldo Ticchiarelli and Louis
Acciaroli — were big-time coke dealers. They later went to prison
for it," he said, "so I liked to keep an eye on it." He was surprised
and somewhat disappointed to see Parente there. "You're wasting
your talents in a place like this," he told him.

Parente recalled it as a less friendly conversation. Hamilton
had a bylaw that stipulated that any liquor-licensed establishment could be closed (and could potentially lose its license) if it
allowed already intoxicated people inside. Parente understood
that Harris and his men intended to enforce the bylaw vigor-
ously that night, so he and his own men were very choosy about
whom they let pass.

It had been an uneventful night until Brian Lewis showed
up. The Lewis brothers were well known in downtown Hamilton,
the three half-black, half-white (Parente used the phrase "salt-
and-pepper" to describe them) brothers were day laborers and
small-time criminals who had a hobby of scaring and intimidating innocent strangers. Brian, the youngest, was already wasted
when he arrived at Bannister's that night, and Parente (concerned
about Harris' warning) refused to let him in. Brian took offense
and a small scuffle broke out. In seconds, Brian was turfed, and
he bitterly swore revenge before retreating.

After closing, Parente didn't go home. Instead, he went to the
Birch Avenue clubhouse. He was alone. Before long, Brian's two
brothers, Jimmy and Tim, and five of their friends went looking
for him. The police saw the group on a downtown street, but did
not stop them.

When they arrived at the clubhouse, the gang of toughs
called Parente out. He came out and they began to threaten him.
Parente saw that Tim had a handgun and heard someone shout
"Shoot him!" Alone and fearing for his life, as he said later, Parente
brought a loaded double-barreled shotgun out with him. Harris
maintained it was a shotgun he had confiscated in the speakeasy
arrest, but Parente denied that.

The men were screaming at Parente, threatening him. He
saw that Tim had a handgun. When he saw Tim raise the gun
and point it at him, he said, Parente squeezed both triggers of

the shotgun. Jimmy Lewis took the full blast of both shells in the lower back. He fell back against a parked car, exposing a big hole in his torso. He died on the street. The gang scattered. Parente fled.

Two hours later, Harris was paged at home. There had been a shooting at the Outlaws clubhouse. "That could only be one person," Harris recalled thinking.

When he arrived on scene, the investigating officer approached him and said: "They call this guy 'The Wop.' Do you know him?" Harris laughed.

Harris knew Parente had probably gone to a friend's house in St. Catharines, so he alerted the Niagara Regional Police. Their biker officer, Larry Schwedic, put the house under surveillance and, when he saw Parente with another Outlaw named Darrell Sampson, he negotiated a quiet surrender. Parente rode back to Hamilton in an unmarked car and was surprised and dismayed to see that the local cops had made a huge deal of it, putting up a roadblock and escorting the car he was in all the way downtown with flashing lights.

The Crown prosecutor, Tony Skarica, argued for a five-year sentence. But the defense countered that Parente was merely acting in self-defense. Noting that Parente was "not exactly a choirboy," Justice Thomas Callon determined that he "reacted to a serious threat of personal harm to him that included the possibility of death. Parente was sentenced to 30 months for the death of Jimmy Lewis. He was said to have breathed a sigh of relief.

Interestingly, the other Lewises also met violent ends. Tim died in a car crash. And Brian, consumed by thoughts of revenge, years later confronted Parente in a bar. Parente, seriously fearing for his life, turfed the young man again. He told me that he found out that there were two undercover cops in the bar who saw the whole thing, and that he was appalled that they didn't intervene. But Parente didn't kill Brian. Brian killed Brian. He got drunk at a party and held a handgun to his temple. He kept screaming "you wanna know what I'm gonna do to Mike the Wop? This is what I'm gonna do to Mike the Wop!" Then, he slipped or twitched or flinched or something and pulled the trigger. Blew his own brains out.

After the trial in Hamilton, Parente went back to Sault Ste. Marie to answer the illegal possession of a weapon charge resulting from the bus shoot-up in Wawa. He pleaded guilty and received six years. He was shocked, dumbfounded, expecting a couple of months at most. The judge explained that since he was a killer now, he had no choice but to throw the book at him.

Without Parente, the Outlaws' fortunes in Ontario changed, particularly in the Steel City. Stadnick, who had become a full-patch member of the Hells Angels Montreal South (Sorel) Chapter, became much more open about his operations in Hamilton, often wearing his full colors. He operated out of a bar (he didn't officially own it, but everybody knew it was his) called Rebel's Roadhouse at the corner of Upper Ottawa and Fennell on the Mountain.

Roland Harper then told Harris about a plan the Outlaws had to assassinate Stadnick. The Hamilton Outlaws had acquired a pair of LAW (light anti-tank weapon) rocket launchers from connections in the Canadian military, and the plan was to blast Stadnick at the front door as he entered or exited the club. The other LAW was made available just in case the first malfunctioned (they are, after all, single-shot devices). Harris, acting on Harper's tip, found the two bazookas buried in a nearby conservation area. "They didn't have the heart to pull that kind of thing off with Parente out of the picture," Harris said. "Maybe if he was still there, they might have gone through with it, but there was no way without him."

When I asked Parente about the incident years later, he grinned, shrugged and told me, "I don't know anything about any rocket launchers."

Things were about as bad or worse for Stadnick over the same period. He and his friend (and translator) Noël "Frenchy" Mailloux came home to Hamilton from Montreal for Christmas 1982. Realizing he was far outnumbered by Outlaws — the same guys who had killed his friends and colleagues in the Wild Ones simply for meeting with Hells Angels — in his hometown, he decided to lay low. Staying mostly with family and friends, he ventured out rarely and advised Mailloux to do the same.

Instead, Mailloux and his girlfriend, stripper Connie Augustin, went on a two-month-long cocaine binge. It culminated on

February 17, 1983 when he murdered Augustin's friend, 18-year-old fellow stripper Cindy Lee Thompson, and Augustin's son, four-year-old Stewart Hawley. He also shot Augustin several times, failing to kill her, and was finally apprehended in a nearby park babbling incoherently and still attempting to shoot the police with an empty handgun who had surrounded him.

Not only did Stadnick lose a close friend, but it set the Hells Angels campaign for Ontario back years. Outlaw motorcycle gangs rely on at least some measure of public support to survive, and need to find new members, associates and business connections from the local population. Mailloux's actions made Hells Angels look wild and out of control. But Stadnick's ability to keep it together and remove any incriminating evidence from Mailloux's house impressed his brothers in Sorel.

While all of this was going on in Ontario, the war between Hells Angels and the Outlaws was still raging in Quebec, but generally at a low level. And Hells Angels were dominating, with psychopathic Montreal North (Laval) member Yves "Apache" Trudeau killing Outlaws and their associates at a sickening rate of more than one a week.

But the Outlaws managed one big blow on September 8, 1983. A small man with a rat-like face, Gino Goudreau, was eager to become an Outlaw like his older brother. He could hardly have impressed them more.

At a nice little bar and restaurant in suburban Longueuil called Le Petit Bourg, Buteau and his friend Rene Lamoureaux were entertaining a guest from Ontario. Guy "Frenchie" Gilbert was an emissary from the Kitchener Chapter of Satan's Choice — one of the few chapters that did not patch over to the Outlaws and still held a grudge against their former brothers in Hamilton — and they were discussing an alliance between the two clubs.

As the three bikers walked outside for a smoke, Goudreau parked his bike, leaving his girlfriend still sitting on the back seat. Then he pulled a .38 from under his jacket and pulled the trigger until the magazine was empty. Buteau died immediately, Gilbert succumbed a few minutes later. Lamoureaux survived with major injuries.

To many, it looked like it would be a huge blow to Stadnick's status. Buteau was his biggest supporter and universally respected. Without him, it looked like Stadnick (who still hadn't mastered much French) would be sidelined or perhaps disposed of.

Because there was nobody else who approached his status, Buteau's job was divided between two men. Rejean "Zig Zag" Lessard, who earned his nickname from his close resemblance to the guy on the Zig Zag rolling papers package, was named president of the Montreal South (Sorel) Chapter and Michel "Sky" Langlois was named the Hells Angels national president for Canada. Langlois's duties were primarily to communicate with other chapters and to recruit bikers and gangs when possible. Lessard, on the other hand, ran the daily operations of the only genuinely important chapter in the country.

And, as luck would have it, both of them liked and appreciated Stadnick. He was, by that time, bringing significant revenue into the club, had great connections in Ontario and had also earned his "Filthy Few" patch. There are different opinions about how bikers earn that particular patch. Barger's own autobiography claims it's for the club's hardest partiers. Law enforcement says it's reserved for those who have murdered for the club. Either way, Stadnick started wearing it about the time Buteau was killed.

At the time, there was a lot of talk about the Outlaws taking Stadnick out. It made perfect sense: They would have gotten rid of the biggest hope for Hells Angels in Ontario and re-established themselves as top dogs in the province. But while he did once have to fight his way out of a Downtown kidnapping attempt, Stadnick could generally move unharmed in Hamilton. Isnor recalled wondering how unlikely it was that Stadnick could stay alive in a city teeming with people like the Outlaws, the Musitanos, the Luppinos and the Hells Angels–hating Papalias. But he later learned, he told me, that Stadnick was smart enough to either cooperate with or to avoid all of them.

But if the Outlaws had really wanted to assassinate Stadnick, they could hardly have done a better job than was accomplished by an absentminded priest on his way to see the Pope in Montreal. At the same time thousands of the faithful were streaming into Montreal to see the pontiff, the Hells Angels were riding out of town for their own event. On their way to a memorial service in the Eastern Townships town of Drummondville to observe the first anniversary of the murder of Stadnick's mentor and friend, Buteau, the priest missed a stop sign and plowed into the procession of bikers.

The biker in line in front of Stadnick — prospect Daniel Matthieu — took the bulk of the impact and was killed immediately. Stadnick crashed into the priest's car. The forks of his bike were driven into his gas tank and the bike exploded into flames.

Stadnick was airlifted to a Montreal hospital. He was barely recognizable. He'd been burned over most of his body and had lost two and a half fingers and the tip of his nose. "He wasn't good looking before the accident," Harris said. "But he was downright ugly after."

Stadnick's common-law wife, Kathi Anderson, and his lawyer, Stephan Frankel, came to visit him. Anderson was appalled at the care he was getting from the nurses — none of whom spoke English with any degree of fluency — and negotiated with Lessard and Langlois to get him moved to Hamilton.

But there was one big problem: Hamilton was teeming with Outlaws and others who weren't crazy about the idea of a full-patch Hells Angel in their town, and they would not mind seeing Ontario's most prominent one erased completely. The Montreal Hells Angels had a plan; the 13th Tribe — a Halifax, Nova Scotia gang that desperately wanted to become Hells Angels — would stand guard outside his room in the hospital. While that was fine during visiting hours, there wasn't much to keep an Outlaw from sneaking into Hamilton General and holding a pillow over Stadnick's face until he stopped breathing.

So Anderson — out of options — called Harris. She asked him to protect her man. At first, Harris thought it was hilarious. But after some thought and consultation with his chief, Harris agreed. So when the 13th Tribe left at the end of visiting hours, the Hamilton cops took over. It was an uneasy relationship. The 13th Tribe tried to act tough, but they were not prepared for the Hamilton cops who had seen dozens of tougher gangs. And at least one Outlaws associate has assured me that at least one

Hamilton cop let it be known exactly which room the helpless Stadnick was staying in.

But the unlikely, mutually suspicious tag team managed to keep the man safe, and when Stadnick was finally released from Hamilton General, the 13th Tribe became the Hells Angels Halifax Chapter. At the same time, the Sherbrooke-based Gitans (Gypsies) became Hells Angels as well.

And that's how 1984 ended and 1985 began. Hells Angels now dominated Quebec, particularly Montreal, and had a small, fledgling chapter in Halifax to go along with three, small, isolated and suspicious chapters on the Pacific coast. The Outlaws had been virtually exterminated in Montreal, but were the most powerful of the many gangs that controlled the drug trade in Ontario. Their primary rivals were their former brothers in what remained of Satan's Choice.

But nobody was particularly strong in Ontario. Hells Angels — with Stadnick lying at home in bed nursing his horrific wounds — had lost their only hope. The Outlaws — with Parente lifting weights in prison — had lost their heart and soul.

Chapter 6

Open Season on Hamilton Bikers

As 1985 dawned in cold, snowy Montreal it looked like the war had been won. The few Outlaws who hadn't been killed, injured or who hadn't quit never wore their colors in public anymore. Some even refused to come out of their houses.

But that doesn't mean things were going easily for the still-fledgling Canadian Hells Angels. There was an immense amount of tension between the two chapters in Montreal. And the addition of two new chapters — the 13th Tribe, who had become Halifax Chapter, and the Gitans (Gypsies), who had become the Sherbrooke Chapter — gave Hells Angels more manpower and more territory, but also more responsibility.

The two Montreal chapters had developed very different cultures. The Montreal North (Laval) Chapter were the old Popeyes and a few like-minded newcomers. They were old-school bikers who wanted to ride, fight and party. They were responsible for almost all the firepower in the war against the Outlaws, with Yves "Apache" Trudeau claiming 18 of the 23 total victims by himself. Without the discipline that had been enforced by murdered president Yves "Le Boss" Buteau, they fell into disarray. They took their lead from new chapter president Laurent "L'Anglais" Viau, a free-wheeling, cocaine-using man-about-town who used violence when he deemed necessary or simply felt like it. Buteau's group of largely clean-shaven, well-dressed men barely recognizable as bikers had morphed into Viau's sloppy, hairy, hard-partying gang of stereotypical Hells Angels.

They could hardly have been more different from their cross-town brothers, the Montreal South (Sorel) Chapter. Manned by newer members and a few older guys who were put off by the excesses of their brothers in Laval, the Sorel Chapter was more disciplined and business-like. Its president, Rejean "Zig Zag" Lessard, kept up the rules established in the club's better days under Buteau. He forbade the use of stimulant or injected drugs and he was very serious about bikers paying their debts promptly. But, unlike his predecessor, he let the members look and dress however they wanted.

In the winter of 1984/85, Laval's sloppy and costly behavior caused a great deal of friction with the other chapters, particularly Sorel, and Lessard felt he had to do something. Not only were the members of the Laval Chapter consuming a great deal of the drugs they should have been selling, but they were also skimming from payments intended for other chapters. Officially, they owed at least $60,000, but nobody knew how much they had really taken from the organization. And their bad habit of getting arrested for small or unnecessary offenses — often unprovoked acts of violence — put the entire organization in jeopardy.

So Lessard called a meeting with David "Wolf" Carroll — president of the Halifax Chapter — and Georges "Bo-Boy" Beaulieu, president of the Sherbrooke Chapter. The Hells Angels in B.C. still had little contact with the other Canadian chapters and were not involved. Carroll, in particular, had a grudge against Laval. Just days before the meeting with Lessard, Trudeau had gone to Halifax and demanded $98,000 he told them their club owed Laval. They paid him, only to learn that Laval was entitled to just a one-quarter share of that money, and that Trudeau had actually kept it for himself. And Halifax, by far the poorest chapter, still owed Sorel and Sherbrooke (and potentially even Laval) their rightful shares.

At the summit, Lessard railed against Laval, explaining that they had to be eliminated for the good of the organization. Carroll and Beaulieu agreed. The plan, then, was to force two members of Laval into retirement, allow two others the opportunity to join Sorel and kill the rest, including Viau and Trudeau. Years later, Lessard confessed that life was cheap to the Canadian Hells Angels back then, and that few of them would have seen death as an unjust punishment for that size of theft from the club.

After getting permission from his bosses in Manhattan, Lessard put his plan into action. Robert "Ti-Maigre" Richard, the giant, one-eyed sergeant-at-arms of the Sorel Chapter announced that Sherbrooke was holding a party at its clubhouse on Saturday, March 23, 1985. And he said that Laval, Sorel and Halifax were all invited.

Most of the Laval Chapter greeted the news with indifference, but Trudeau knew better. Sensing that something was up, he checked himself into a detox center in Oka, to the west of Montreal. "I saw what was coming," he said later.

Lessard's plan was to kill the Laval members as they walked through the doors of the clubhouse, but it was foiled when he saw that less than half of the chapter had shown up.

Incensed, he called a meeting in which he told the members of Laval that attendance at the party, which would now extend to a second day, was absolutely mandatory. The only excuses for not attending were if a biker was in a jail cell, a hospital bed or on a morgue slab. The next day, all of Laval except for Trudeau and Michel "Jinx" Genest (one of the men the Outlaws shot at in Northern Ontario) attended. Trudeau was in rehab, technically a hospital, and Genest was in Laval, protecting the clubhouse.

Lessard and his men, armed with handguns and shotguns, surrounded the members of Laval and herded them to the center of the room. Then they opened fire. Laval president Viau, Jean-Pierre "Matt le Crosseur" Mathieu, Michel "Willie" Mayrand, Jean-Guy "Brutus" Geoffrion and Guy-Louis "Chop" Adam were killed.

The three surviving Laval members — Gilles "Le Nez" Lachance, Yvon "Le Pere" Bilodeau and Richard "Bert" Mayrand, who had just watched his brother get murdered — were ordered to haul the bodies outside and clean up the crime scene. When they were finished, Bilodeau and the surviving Mayrand were told to leave. Lachance was offered a choice: leave or join Sorel. He picked Sorel.

He and two Sorel members — Jacques "Le Pelle" Pelletier and Robert "Snake" Tremblay — rode to the Laval clubhouse. Genest was still there. They told him what happened in Sherbrooke, and offered him Sorel membership. He took it.

Over the next few days, they looted the Laval clubhouse — grabbing thousands in cash and six motorcycles — and the dead men's homes. The clubhouse was then burned down. The bodies, stuffed in sleeping bags purchased a week earlier by Beaulieu and weighted down with cement blocks and barbell weights, were thrown into the St. Lawrence off the St. Ignatius de Loyola Wharf.

An emissary was sent to tell Trudeau he was out of the Hells Angels. He accepted, and negotiated his safety and the return of his motorcycle in exchange for two murders, including that of Ginette "La Jument" Henri, Mathieu's girlfriend and Laval's accountant.

Genest quickly proved his worth by murdering former Laval prospect Claude "Coco" Roy, and recovering five bags of cocaine from his underwear.

When the Laval Chapter very obviously ceased to exist, the cops knew something was up. The Sûreté du Québec (SQ) correctly surmised from wiretaps that Sherbrooke had something to do with it, and raided their clubhouse. They found little of value.

It wasn't until the first body — that of Geoffrion — floated to the surface and was snagged by a local angler that things began to unravel for the Sorel Chapter. SQ divers went down and found remains of the other murdered Laval members and, as an added bonus, the skeleton of a woman Trudeau had killed in an earlier dispute.

That find had profound effects on the outlaw biker world in Quebec. The first thing that happened was that the Outlaws took advantage of the PR disaster. Not only did they start wearing their colors again, but they distributed leaflets lampooning "Hells Angels Brotherhood" with crude drawings of fish-eating (and vomiting) dead Hells Angels. They bought a farm a few miles north of the Vermont border in an effort to get closer to theAmerican border. Before they could host any parties, though, the SQ seized it because of drug and weapons offenses.

A few Hells Angels weren't exactly on board with the elimination of Laval. Lachance, who was there when his brothers from Laval were murdered and was still profoundly freaked out, turned informant. So did Gerry "Le Chat" Coulombe, a Sorel prospect who was at what the media was now calling "the Lennoxville Massacre" (even though it happened in Sherbrooke, the name came from the fact that the dead men stayed in a cheap Lennoxville motel the night before they were killed) and he was disgusted and unnerved that any organization would do that to its own members. Some smart SQ work also turned Trudeau into a snitch. Sergeant Marcel Lacoste, who was questioning Trudeau about some unrelated charges, showed him an article in a lurid local tabloid that reported that the Hells Angels were intending to kill him. Trudeau believed it, and spilled everything.

From that information, 39 Hells Angels and associates were arrested in connection with the Lennoxville Massacre. After an 18-month trial, 21 of them were found guilty and sentenced to between two and 25 years in prison. Lessard, Luc "Sam" Michaud, Pelletier and Genest were found guilty of five counts of first-degree murder and got 25 years. Richard and Halifax's Michael "Speedy" Christianson was among those acquitted.

The loss of leadership and manpower in Montreal was huge. Laval was gone and numbers at Sorel and Sherbrooke were greatly reduced thanks to the convictions and the loss of members and prospects who quit or turned informant. Making matters worse, days later, the entire Halifax Chapter was arrested for leaning too heavily on a prostitute they represented. When they demanded a bigger cut of her net revenue, she went to police and the entire chapter went to prison for a year.

That's more significant than it sounds, because Hells Angels will pull a chapter's charter if they have fewer than six members free and on the streets at any time. It had happened in Buffalo some years before, and it eventually did sink Halifax in 2003. It looked very much like the empire Buteau had begun to build was falling apart. Laval was gone, Sorel and Sherbrooke were at no better than half strength and Halifax was teetering on the brink of extinction.

With Lessard out of the picture, Langlois took over his job without opposition. As president of Sorel, he instigated a recruiting drive for his chapter and Sherbrooke. And, as national president, he started moving members from other chapters — he even reached out to the long-isolated three chapters in B.C., and they agreed to send some of their men — into Halifax to keep their interests and their chapter alive.

One of the gangs Lessard had been working hard to recruit from was the SS. Named after the universally feared *Schutzstaffel* (protective squadron) of the Nazi party in World War II, the Montreal SS started as a group of young men who believed strongly in white supremacy. As they grew older, they made money dealing drugs and with muscle-for-hire work. Eventually, like many other white gangs around the world, they started riding motorcycles and wearing black leather jackets.

And Hells Angels recognized them as very desirable recruits. Not only were they the toughest guys in a tough neighborhood (Montreal's Hochelaga-Maisonneuve) but they had an enviable drug-selling network.

Things changed after the Lennoxville Massacre. The leadership of the SS — brothers Giovanni and Salvatore Cazzetta and their 400-pound pal Paul "Sasquatch" Porter — were appalled by what Lessard and his men had done. Not only did they vow never to join Hells Angels, but they eventually became the founders and driving force behind Hells Angels' fiercest rivals: the Rock Machine.

But the SS had another prominent member. He was in prison for armed sexual assault at the time of the Lennoxville Massacre, but when he got out, he said he was so impressed by Lessard's strategic move (and claimed to be genuinely surprised that his friends were not), that he immediately quit the SS and joined the Sorel Chapter. He became a full-patch member in a remarkably short time.

He was big and strong, not afraid to fight anyone. And he was smart and charismatic, even charming, and could get along with just about anyone. His name was Maurice "Mom" Boucher.

It was an excellent time for him to join Hells Angels. The old guard — not just the Laval Chapter, but also the leadership of the Sorel Chapter — had been eliminated, and needed replacing. Entry into the Montreal Hells Angels at that time meant quick wealth and rapid advancement.

Almost as soon as he joined, Boucher befriended another young member. Walter Stadnick had recovered sufficiently from his wounds to rejoin the chapter. Although he still had not learned much French by that point, he was already one of the most popular members of the organization. And he was well respected for the income he brought in, his self-discipline, his ability to get along with others and his strategic planning ability. He reminded some, I've been told, of a smaller version of Buteau.

Although he was not present at the Lennoxville Massacre, Michel "Sky" Langlois heard that there was a warrant out for his arrest. Instead of facing it, he fled to Morocco.

To replace him, Boucher became president of the Sorel Chapter, and Stadnick became national president.

Now, I know a cop who maintains that Hells Angels do not have a national president in Canada, and never have. He has even testified to that opinion as an expert witness at a biker trial in Saskatchewan.

I have to disagree. Prosecutors and other cops have shown me graphic evidence that indicates that Stadnick (and others who have held the same post, like Langlois and Buteau) was treated with inordinate respect during his reign. His bike was always at the front of every procession, and in every posed group photo, he is always front row center or just to the left of the club's logo. In other countries, those spots are always reserved for the national president.

And every cop, lawyer, biker and associate I have ever spoken with has acknowledged Stadnick's standing as the top guy when it came to the club's national affairs. And when the club sued a publishing company over the illegal use of the death's head logo, it was Stadnick who represented the club.

So, even if he never printed business cards with the title "national president" under his name, Stadnick performed the duties of one, and was widely acknowledged as such both inside the club and among interested observers. Those duties were primarily concentrated around recruiting new clubs and fostering communication between existing clubs. When he took over the reins, the dispirited Hells Angels were still flailing in Canada. The members in Halifax had gotten out of prison, but were at best a chapter barely fit to operate. Their leader, Carroll, would later move to Montreal, further weakening the only Maritime chapter. Sorel and Sherbrooke were both rapidly reforming after the arrests had robbed them of many of their leaders. They generally answered to Boucher, although Sherbrooke held Stadnick in very high regard. The three chapters in B.C. had much more in common with their friends in Washington and Oregon than they did with anyone in Montreal. And they felt like they were owed something after they'd lent men to fill in for the jailed Halifax Chapter.

But Stadnick had a dream. He told a friend who later turned informant that he had a plan to make sure that the only patch in Canada would be that of the Hells Angels. There would be no need for chapters. Instead, the bottom rocker would only read "Canada."

But there were some things in the way: the other biker gangs throughout the country. Using the many weapons at his disposal — the mystique of the Hells Angels brand, the promise of easy money and his own charm — Stadnick had a great deal of success bringing them over to his point of view. Starting, actually, in Quebec and then in Western Canada, Stadnick managed to bring dozens of clubs into the fold, extending the club's reach from Pacific to Atlantic. But his success was tempered by the fact that he was unable to establish anything in his home province of Ontario.

And there was a problem in Quebec as well. The Cazzetta brothers and Porter didn't join Hells Angels, but that doesn't mean they left organized crime. Instead, they joined with some local bar owners who distributed drugs from their establishments who called themselves the Dark Circle. The members of the Dark Circle were upset that Hells Angels raised and strictly enforced prices, especially for cocaine.

The Cazzettas and Porter recruited a number of street toughs in and around Montreal — including a few Outlaws and guys who had been rejected by Hells Angels — to form a new group called the Rock Machine. In the beginning, they were a gang, but not a motorcycle gang. Of course, the Cazzettas, Porter and a few others rode Harleys, but the vast majority didn't. And, instead of a patch on the back of a leather jacket, members of the organization identified one another with a ring embossed with the head of an eagle. They probably outnumbered Hells Angels, at least on the island of Montreal, and could always rely on the Dark Circle to come up with more foot soldiers.

Their purpose was to supply Montreal with an alternative to Hells Angels as a source of drugs, especially cocaine. The Rock Machine would often charge less than Hells Angels, and that wasn't something Hells Angels could tolerate. In August 1994, they declared war.

In the ensuing years, as the Hells Angels and their puppet gangs killed members of the Rock Machine and their allies with shootings and bombings, more than 160 people, including many innocent people not involved with the drug trade, were murdered. One of them — an 11-year-old boy named Daniel Desrochers, who was killed by shrapnel from a Hells Angels bomb on August 9, 1995 — turned public opinion so far against the bikers in Quebec that it fuelled the government's fight for anti-racketeering laws.

Stadnick's involvement in what the media labeled "The Quebec Biker War" was oblique. At least as far as law enforcement ever found out. It was Boucher's thing — one of his many violent things.

Stadnick had more important things to do. He wanted to make all of Canada, especially Ontario, Hells Angels territory. And he wanted to get rich. Back in his hometown, things took a turn for the strange. With Parente in prison, the Outlaws looked very vulnerable. To take advantage of this, Satan's Choice set up a chapter on St. Matthew's Avenue in North Hamilton, less than a mile away from the Outlaws' Birch Avenue clubhouse.

It didn't last. On August 25, 1985, the bullet-riddled body of Brent Roddick was discovered in front of his house on East 25th Street up on the Mountain. He was the fourth dead biker to surface in Hamilton that month, joining chapter-mate Allan Kinloch, Outlaw James Lewis and Red Devil Michael Carey.

Another Red Devil, Dave Pichet, was also shot, but his assailant underestimated the firepower needed to bring the giant biker down. "He was hit several times," said John Harris. "But since it was just a .22, it didn't do much damage."

The three gangs in Hamilton — not to mention the omnipresent influence of Hells Angels and the danger posed by the Mafia — found themselves in a standoff. Satan's Choice blinked first. The day after Roddick was murdered, Satan's Choice abandoned their clubhouse in Hamilton and, tail between their legs, got out of town. The surviving members went to the Kitchener Chapter.

Chapter 7
The Choice-Angels Alliance

Historically, here are three proven ways for an outlaw motorcycle gang to become established in a new region. They can start from scratch, recruiting members from the general population. They can import members from already-established clubs to start a groundswell in the region to be annexed. Or they can woo existing clubs in the region, getting them to switch allegiance from their own club to the new one.

In Ontario, Hells Angels tried all three, with varying degrees of success. Careful to avoid a war like the one in Quebec, Stadnick and Hells Angels first infiltrated Ontario stealthily and in a small but effective way.

If you look at a map of Ontario, you'll see that it falls into two basic parts. Southern Ontario — defined by Lakes Erie, Ontario and Huron — and Northern Ontario, which begins at Georgian Bay and stretches all the way up to frigid Hudson Bay. And the two pieces could hardly be more different.

Southern Ontario was settled by European immigrants early. Its rich farmland, long growing seasons, water accessibility and proximity to the United States drew migrants in droves. As manufacturing replaced farming as the primary commercial action in the area, the population boomed.

Northern Ontario never took off that way. Virtually uniform in its environment of exposed rock covered in sparse forest interspersed with hundreds of thousands of lakes and rivers, you can't really grow any crops there and it's even difficult to raise livestock. The settlers who came were originally after fur, and then logging as the paper industry took off. Mining was also an important employer, and after World War II increased the value of minerals like uranium, cadmium and tungsten, there was a minor influx of migrants, mainly from Quebec. French is still widely spoken up there, and a quick search of any Northern Ontario phonebook will reveal most communities as having a majority of French last names.

But those industries don't support many people. While Northern Ontario is about eight times the size of Southern Ontario, it has about one-twentieth the number of people. And if you take away its three biggest cities — Sudbury (about 150,000 inhabitants), Thunder Bay (150,000) and Sault Ste. Marie (75,000) — there's about one square mile for every human up there.

With such a small population, cultural events were few and far between at the time. Even TV was intermittent in many communities back then. But Hells Angels had two guaranteed boredom stoppers — drugs and strippers.

The province of Quebec has been a net exporter of strippers for a very long time. Most of them go to Toronto or the cities of Western Canada, but some also go to the U.S. and resorts in places like Mexico and the Dominican Republic.

And, from talent agencies owned by Hells Angels like Scott Steinert of Montreal and Donald "Pup" Stockford of Hamilton, strippers were showing up in Northern Ontario bars. They worked surprisingly cheap because they were being subsidized by the organization. Their job — besides dancing and anything else they could negotiate — was to get to know who ran things in the towns and relay that information back to Montreal. They found out who the tough guys were, who wanted drugs and who could sell them. Hells Angels would then send a representative down to check the guy or guys out. If he met their standards, Hells Angels would start supplying him with drugs. In a very brief period of time, towns that had never seen the like before were full of Hells Angels–supplied strippers, escorts and drugs.

It was a smart plan. And probably the only one that would have worked up there. Some years earlier, Kitchener Satan's Choice full-patch John "Turkey" LeBlanc had also wanted to stake a claim in Northern Ontario. He went back to his hometown — a hard-drinking mining town in the middle of Northern Ontario named Timmins — and tried to form a Satan's Choice chapter there. It didn't work. It wasn't because the community didn't want bikers in their midst; it was because the local drug dealers didn't want to work for someone else. They literally chased him out of town. So Hells Angels learned from his mistake and allowed the guys in Timmins and all the other Northern Ontario towns to think they were in charge. All they supplied were the drugs and the girls at irresistible prices.

One of those northerners was a tall and muscular ne'er-do-well from Thunder Bay named Donald "Bam Bam" Magnussen. Nothing more than a local tough guy at first, he became the leading supplier of cocaine in Thunder Bay and its environs after meeting Stadnick. Impressed by his size and aggressiveness, Stadnick started bringing Magnussen with him on his recruiting trips all over the country. For some time, the two were rarely seen apart.

Although there were no chapters up there (the Outlaws had a chapter in Sault Ste. Marie and Satan's Choice had established themselves in faraway Thunder Bay) and, for a long time, no full-patch members either, Hells Angels quickly rose to dominate organized crime in Northern Ontario. Of course, being at the top of the organized crime heap in Northern Ontario is a little bit like having the best snowplow business in Texas — there's not a lot of money in it. But it did bring in some income for the club, gave it some connections in Ontario and allowed a predominantly safe and Hells Angels–friendly route with a series of pit stops on the way from Montreal to Winnipeg and points west.

While that was happening, Stadnick also decided to import his own gang to Ontario. And he was going for the big prize — Toronto. It might have worked, but he picked the wrong man to be in charge. David "Wolf" Carroll — former president of the Halifax Chapter and a close friend of Stadnick's — introduced him to a young man named Dany "Danny Boy" Kane.

Immediately, Stadnick liked the young man. He was a nice-looking boy with short hair and glasses, but also strong and muscular. He could have passed for just about any occupation. He was friendly, outgoing and chatty. And he came from a trusted source.

He had been with a respected South Shore club called the Condors, and had the backing of their old boss Pat Lambert, a man Stadnick knew well and trusted. A few months earlier, Stadnick had allowed a bigger Hells Angels–affiliated gang on the South Shore, the Evil Ones, to absorb the Condors. Both Lambert and Kane were offered positions in the club — Lambert as full-patch, Kane as prospect — but both declined. Lambert continued to work with the Sorel Chapter as an independent contractor, supplying girls for export and serving as a drug retailer at his bar.

Kane, though, had bigger ambitions and started hanging around with the Sorel Chapter, getting to know Carroll in particular.

From a biker perspective, Carroll's résumé was great. He'd proven himself as a fighter and tough guy, he'd planted bombs and set fires, he'd sold both drugs and handguns and had done time for his organization without complaining or talking to the cops. For Hells Angels, that made him a model employee, one to be groomed for bigger and better things.

But there were a few things about Kane that Stadnick would not have approved of, had he known about them. Kane was flagrantly bisexual, he had some pretty strange tastes, he was paranoid and he had no natural leadership ability.

The plan itself was mostly sound. Stadnick's franchising style of business has often been compared to that of McDonald's, but in this situation, it seemed more like Wal-Mart. He wanted to start a coke-dealing organization that would offer the same product at lower prices than the competition. And then, when they had a decent-sized customer base and had — if all went well — put a few competitors out of business, they could bring prices up to Montreal levels and turn a huge profit into an enormous one. When the new gang grew in size and stature, it could expand, branch off and even perhaps eventually become the Hells Angels Toronto Chapter. And, although it was not expressly in their mandate, anything they could do to intimidate the Outlaws or any other Ontario competitors would be seen as an extra benefit.

But there were problems from the start. Qualified personnel were hard to find. Hells Angels had very few English-speaking options. Stadnick had done some great work in the three Prairie provinces to form working relationships and even patch over full chapters, but the members there were obviously not ready to represent his interests in Ontario. The three B.C. chapters — closer to the Montreal-based leadership than it had been before, mostly thanks to Stadnick — were simply not interested. They were busy with their own operation and were still coasting on keeping Halifax alive. And the Halifax Chapter was still suffering its own chronic manpower shortages, made far worse after their personable leader Carroll left the east coast for Montreal.

So Stadnick staffed this new gang — which Kane named the Demon Keepers as a tribute to his own initials — with Quebeckers, few of whom spoke anything better than rudimentary English. It may seem foolhardy in retrospect, but Stadnick himself, his right-hand man Stockford and their friend Carroll had all succeeded in Quebec with even less ability to communicate in French. Besides, Kane was a francophone (with passable English skills), so it would be his problem to figure out.

The Demon Keepers existed for a little more than two months. After riding out of Sorel on January 29, 1994 with a big launch party, they established their headquarters in a luxury apartment near Toronto's Yonge and Eglinton shopping district. That was the cops' first clue that they were not dealing with a wily group of veterans. The newcomers did their best to hang around bars, looking for people to sell drugs to. But their poor English, clumsy approach and unsophisticated behavior yielded not a single sale. Kane's choice of bars didn't help either. Instead of strip joints or working men's taverns, he took them to discos and nightclubs — even faux dives instead of actual dives.

The OPP and Toronto cops knew how to deal with these guys. Stopping them every chance they could, the cops would frequently take out warrants for their arrest and offer to release them on the condition they leave Ontario for good. Over a very short period, that system eliminated more than half of the Demon Keepers' membership.

And the police also managed to turn one. He didn't have a lot of information, but he knew something big was going to go down with Kane on April Fool's Day. He told them that Kane and his friends would be meeting more Demon Keepers in the parking lot of a Wendy's fast-food restaurant in Belleville, Ontario, just off the 401. They were to look for a yellow Mustang.

Apparently, there was a drug dealer and on-again-off-again manager of a Belleville strip joint called the Go-Go Club named Greg Walsh who owed a friend of the Hells Angels a lot of money. At the time, it was widely believed that the Outlaws were encouraging drug dealers and others in Ontario to renege on payments to Hells Angels and their associates. They offered to protect these people, and offered them drugs at a lower price. It's not known if Walsh contacted the Outlaws or not, but there weren't any with him at the Go-Go that day.

The SQ followed Kane as he picked up some friends in Montreal, and then handed them off to the OPP once they crossed the border. The car — an incredibly nondescript 1992 Chevy Corsica — turned off the 401 at the Front Street exit in Belleville. The Go-Go is located at 320 North Front Street (although the most commonly used entrance is off to the side on Tracy Street), just two blocks south of the 401.

The Corsica turned into the parking lot of the Wendy's at 350 North Front Street, less than 200 yards away from the entrance of the Go-Go. The police were already there, watching the yellow Mustang. When the Chevy pulled up beside it, the police pounced.

There was nothing of incriminating value inside the Mustang, and its passengers were released. But in the Chevy, the cops found a veritable treasure trove of evidence: three Demon Keepers' jackets, two handguns (including a stolen .357 Magnum), gloves with lead stitched into the fingers and an ounce of hash. That wasn't enough hash to make a lot of money selling, so it was forgiven. The real haul was the guns.

Since the other guys in the car — Kane's No. 2 Denis Cournoyer and a talented Montreal meth cook named Michael Scheffer — had basically clean records, the lawyer they met with convinced Kane that it would be best for everyone if he took the blame for everything. The prosecutor couldn't prove any plot against Walsh's life, so the charges were simply possession of the weapons. Cournoyer walked, Scheffer got two months and Kane — who had previously been imprisoned in Quebec for torturing and nearly killing a young man who had stolen some handguns from him — got four months.

Upon hearing this, Stadnick was eager to cut his losses with the Demon Keepers and disbanded them immediately. He then sent a message to Kane telling him there were no hard feelings.

But, as he later told police, Kane — a sensitive and preternaturally suspicious man — came to believe in prison that Stadnick had intentionally set him up to fail: that, for some reason, he wanted to get rid of him. Some commentators in the media have since agreed with that idea. But it's absurd. Stadnick wanted nothing more than to move the Hells Angels into Ontario and the utter failure of the Demon Keepers set that plan back considerably. And the proud Stadnick was personally humiliated by the ineffectiveness of his pet project, a fact that allowed his rival Steinert to mock him and openly talk about forming his own gang in Ontario. In fact, it was at about this point that Magnussen stopped acting as Stadnick's bodyguard and lackey, instead following tall, handsome Steinert around.

But it didn't matter. Kane, who had been so loyal to Hells Angels for years and through much suffering and little reward, changed his mind. He turned. Kane became not only an informant, but a very rich one as the RCMP paid him dearly for his information.

When he was released from prison, he went to go see Stadnick right away. While it's pretty standard practice in biker clubs to see your boss after getting out of prison, I've since been told Kane was also looking for some usable material from the normally immune-from-prosecution Stadnick to give to his new bosses in the RCMP.

He didn't get any. Stadnick was polite, but curt with him; shooing him back to his old sponsor Carroll at every occasion. That convinced Kane that he was right about Stadnick setting him up to fail. But it was later determined that Stadnick was busy putting together his master plan. In fact, in an effort to accomplish it, Stadnick had even given up his title as national president, after eight long and productive years, to giant, short-tempered Robert "Ti-Maigre" Richard, who had been Sorel's much-feared sergeant-at-arms.

Made up of Stadnick's trusted friends and the Hells Angels' best drug-sellers, the Nomads were a new kind of chapter. Welcome at any Hells Angels clubhouse, the Nomads were a sort of super-chapter, a "dream team" whose primary task was the equitable and profitable sale of drugs across the country. The long-range goal — and this perfectly dovetailed with Stadnick's coast-to-coast recruitment drive — was to have a virtual monopoly on all drug sales in the entire country. La Belle Province was becoming just too small a market, and the Hells Angels were fighting a bloody war with the Rock Machine and their allies for control of it.

An added benefit of Nomads membership was that it allowed another layer of protection against prosecution. A Nomad never touched any drugs. He told a Hells Angel to tell a prospect to tell a hangaround to tell an associate to do the actual drug dealing. If any active party was caught, he could only turn in the guy above him. And, as the chain of responsibility got higher, the likelihood of anyone turning informant — at least, according to the plan — was decreased. It's unlikely any street-level dealers even knew who was actually pulling the strings on, or getting the big profits from, their very risky occupations.

It was the antithesis of the traditional motorcycle club model in which individual members were allowed to engage in illegal activities, but the club itself — and, importantly, its management — was not involved and had the ability to deny any knowledge of any illegal activity. That was the key difference between Stadnick's Hells Angels and Parente's Outlaws. Stadnick was involved up to the hilt, but insulated himself from prosecution with layers and layers of lackeys. Parente, on the other hand, could deny any knowledge of any illegal activity undertaken by a fellow member, and certainly would never admit to being involved with anything any other Outlaw did to break the law.

At various times, the Nomads consisted of Stadnick, his right-hand man Donald "Pup" Stockford, former Halifax boss Carroll, Montreal kingpin Maurice "Mom" Boucher, former Trois-Rivieres Chapter president Richard "Rick" Vallée, former SS member Normand "Biff" Hamel, Louis "Me-Lou" Roy, Salvatore Brunetti, René "Balloune" Charlebois, André Chouinard, Denis "Pas Fiable" Houle, Gilles "Trooper" Mathieu, Michel Rose, Richard "Bert" Mayrand, Normand Robitaille, Luc Bordeleau and Pierre Laurin along with prospects Bruno Lefebvre, Guillaume Serra, Paul "Smurf" Brisebois and Jean-Richard "Race" Larivière.

Five of them — Boucher, Robitaille, Houle (despite the fact that his nickname meant "Unreliable"), Chouinard and Rose — stayed in Montreal to administer what was called "The Table," which oversaw the importation, allocation and distribution of drugs (particularly cocaine) to the other chapters. All drug sales involving the Hells Angels or their friends were controlled by The Table, except those undertaken by the Sherbrooke Chapter, which had negotiated a separate deal with the Nomads' brass.

The primary task of the others was to recruit new business and maintain and protect the connections they had already established. Stadnick's job was to oversee all operations outside Quebec.

It began paying dividends immediately. Through a friend of Boucher's, they gained access to a supply of cocaine from the Italian Mafia the likes of which they had never seen before, courtesy of Guy LePage. LePage and Boucher were about the same age and grew up in the same neighbourhood, but didn't meet each other until they were both adults. LePage had been a Montreal cop, but had resigned suddenly after a 10-year career when his best friend on the force was being investigated for fraud. Then he opened a disco. One of his frequent customers was Boucher. The biker plied LePage with gifts and nights out, wooing him to the Hells Angels' side. Before long, LePage had established links with Colombian cartels and the Italian Mafia and the trickle of cocaine coming into Canada through the Hells Angels transformed into a cascade.

Quebec, especially, had higher quantities of premium coke than ever before. And the Nomads were getting rich. Because of this surplus of coke, the Nomads laid down a strict law that forbade anybody in their territory from selling cocaine for less than $50,000 a kilo. The penalty was death. Nobody was immune. The Nomads even killed their own, if they crossed the line. After many warnings about selling for too little in his Trois-Rivieres territory, Roy was a guest of honor at the Nomads' fifth anniversary party. That was the last night he was ever seen alive.

But while the strict adherence to minimum pricing standards improved their bottom line in the short term, it also allowed the Rock Machine to stay profitable. By attracting customers with cheaper coke, the Rock Machine managed not just to stay afloat financially but to erode the Hells Angels' customer base in Quebec and undermine street-level dealers' faith in their dominance of the region.

The Nomads concept paid almost immediate dividends in the rest of the country as well. Stadnick had worked hard to make connections from coast to coast, and the massive profits associated with cocaine trafficking was a very big part of that.

His greatest success was Winnipeg, but it did not come easily or cheaply. For years, Stadnick wooed the two predominant gangs in the city — the Spartans and their hated enemies Los Brovos — while auditioning and grooming them for Hells Angels prospect status. He even started his own small gang there, the cops called them the Redliners, but they were not on the scale of the Demon Keepers. He was in the city so often — making it a third home after Hamilton and Montreal — that he maintained a girlfriend and even had a son, Damon, with her there.

Just after he anointed Los Brovos as the winner of the competition, he tried to strengthen the bond by inviting their former president and best-loved member, David Boyko, to a party hosted by the Halifax Chapter. Once there, a drunken Magnussen (who went with Stadnick, even though he worked primarily with Steinert by this time) punched Boyko and threatened his life over a drug debt Boyko confessed no knowledge of. When Boyko's murdered body was found in nearby Dartmouth the next day, Stadnick had to go back to Winnipeg and report the news.

Not surprisingly, they weren't happy. It set his plan back some months, but Los Brovos eventually became the Hells

Angels Winnipeg Chapter. Not long after, the bodies of Mag-nussen and Steinert — who many believed was responsible for the death of 11-year-old Daniel Desrochers — were fished out of the St. Lawrence River. They had not been hidden. The forensics people determined that they had been tied to chairs and beaten to death with hammers.

And by 1998, according to a police officer I interviewed, Stadnick was supplying "virtually all the drugs in Winnipeg" and plenty more farther west.

At the same time he was recruiting out west, Stadnick was, rather naturally, trying to bring Ontario into the fold. That's when he used the third method of taking over: getting existing clubs to become his allies and eventually his vassals. The hard part was picking which clubs to work with.

• • •

The first choice was an astute one. The Vagabonds — usually called the "Vags" — were large (70 members and prospects), active in the drug trade and located in more or less downtown Toronto. They were also publicity savvy. Every December they hung a festive "Season's Greeting" banner on their Gerrard Street East headquarters (actually they still do) and were always careful to have themselves photographed in full colors at charitable events, many of which they sponsored.

Stadnick and Hells Angels first approached them in 1987. It was a good match. The Vags were happy to have access to the Quebeckers' drugs and were impressed with the fabled Hells Angels patch. Hells Angels were overjoyed to find such a large and well-disciplined club in the heart of Toronto.

But, unlike many other clubs, the Vags did not immediately jump at the chance to become Hells Angels. Many of them were pretty happy just as they were. They made a few bucks here and there selling weed and hash and working as bouncers, but didn't want to get into big-time organized crime, which they knew Hells Angels represented. And they generally thought cocaine was too dangerous — not just the penalties associated with trafficking it and the local competition it could potentially anger, but also the drug itself, devilishly addictive and horribly destructive.

But the majority did not speak for the whole club. Their president — a tall, skinny occasional plumber named Donald "Snorkel" Melanson — absolutely loved the idea. Not only did he want to get rich, but his greatest love was cocaine. Although many have reported he earned his nickname from the impressive size of his nose, it was actually because of its abilities, not its appearance. One of his friends (who was not a member of the Vagabonds) told a local reporter that he had personally seen Melanson use the snorkel to vacuum up a two-foot-long line of coke in one breath. That friend — who can only be identified as "Saul" because he's in the RCMP's witness protection program — discreetly joined Melanson in a deal with Hells Angels that resulted in a small pipeline of cocaine from Montreal to Toronto.

Meeting couriers in strip joints and bars on Yonge Street, well away from Vags territory, and never in colors, Melanson and Saul were fronted bags of coke. While they had agreed to sell it all, Melanson just couldn't help himself. Saul did his best to get his share on the streets, but Melanson not only sucked the bulk of his up the snorkel, he also generously spread much of it among his friends, including many in the club (who never questioned where this bonanza came from). Weeks passed, and Melanson found himself in debt to Hells Angels to the tune of $80,000. The couriers stopped coming. Instead, some big guys — dressed like businessmen, not bikers — met him in a Yonge Street strip joint and demanded an explanation. He begged for leniency, for more time. He'd get the money. They told him they would see what they could do.

Melanson called in favors and got a second mortgage on his house. He managed to get together about $50,000. Saul did his best, too, and was able to scrape up about $20,000 for his old friend. He handed it over, and then — without telling Melanson — drove to the airport and boarded a plane for Florida until things cooled off. "I didn't want to be in the middle of that mess," he later said.

Melanson called his Hells Angels contact and told him he had their money. Great, the contact told him and arranged a meeting at Novotel, a business-oriented hotel at Yonge and Sheppard in the north end of the city.

On the following morning, September 3, a cleaning staffer knocked on the door to his room. No answer. Since there was no "do not disturb" sign hanging from the knob, she let herself in. The first thing she saw was Melanson lying face down on the floor. He had two bullet holes in the back of his head.

Saul heard about it down south and rushed to get back to Toronto. He arrived in time for the funeral. It was a lavish affair at Melanson's parents' church in Markham, north of the city on Steeles Avenue, just west of Yonge Street. After the service, the hearse was followed by a procession of Harleys more than 200 strong. Their riders — who, as was their custom, wore full colors — included Lobos, Penetrators, American Breed, Scorpions and a large number of Outlaws, who were relishing the opportunity to say they had told the Vags what happens when you deal with the Hells Angels. No Hells Angels showed up, but the Montreal Chapter did send flowers.

The next day, Saul approached the police about becoming a paid informant. He told them everything he knew, but it was not enough to achieve a single arrest. It became increasingly obvious that there was a huge rift between the Vagabonds and Hells Angels, and they never really partied or worked together again. While the years have softened hard feelings — and Hells Angels have held out the olive branch at least twice since then — there is still tension between the two clubs. While Vagabonds will attend Hells Angels events as a group, individual Vags still steer well clear of them even though the two clubs are officially at peace.

Don't feel too sorry for the Vagabonds, though. In 1991, Canada Post found itself desperate when its workers walked off the job. They had plenty of replacement workers, but the picket lines were militant and potentially violent. Without any other viable options, the federal government agency hired the Vagabonds en masse to protect their workers past the angry strikers and paid them a remarkable amount of money. Realizing that providing muscle was probably their best way of getting paid, they started hiring themselves out to either side during strikes, either protecting or intimidating replacement workers depending on who had hired them.

With the Vagabonds out of the picture, Stadnick's Hells Angels started looking at other Southern Ontario–based gangs. They went to a familiar face. After Bernie Guindon had been released from prison, he reassumed leadership of what remained of the once-mighty Satan's Choice.

The Choice's Hamilton, St. Catharines, Sault Ste. Marie, Windsor, London, Ottawa and Kingston Chapters had opted to become Outlaws (giving that gang particular strength not just in hot drug-selling areas, but also vital border crossings). Kitchener, Thunder Bay and Guindon's home chapter in Oshawa had stayed loyal. The Toronto Chapter had split, with a breakaway faction becoming the Outlaws Toronto Chapter and the rest maintaining a Satan's Choice clubhouse in the city.

No longer the most powerful biker club in the province, the members of Satan's Choice were still very proud. There were a lot of factors at play. On the pro side of an alliance with Hells Angels were a chance to get back at the much-hated Outlaws, a huge increase in wealth from the sale of cocaine and a bolstering of club power. On the con side of the debate were increased attention from law enforcement and the potential for Satan's Choice to become mere vassals of a more powerful American-based club. Keep in mind that Guindon was fiercely nationalistic — almost to a mania — and had vehemently opposed previous alliance overtures from both the Outlaws and Hells Angels.

Stadnick was insistent and consistent. His visits to Ontario in his black Jaguar sedan with Quebec plates were no longer limited to Hamilton. He could been seen regularly in Oshawa (where he took Guindon and his men to strip joints) and Toronto (where he treated Guindon to gourmet dinners at tony restaurants). He was also a familiar sight in Kitchener, where he befriended local businessman and Satan's Choice chapter president Andre Watteel. And he was even spotted in Thunder Bay, which was much closer to his interests in Winnipeg than it was to any other major city in Ontario.

It didn't take long for the individual members of Satan's Choice to see that a close association with Hells Angels had great benefits. Whatever his personal opinion was, Guindon made a King Solomon–like decision. The members of Satan's Choice would be free to have any business or social dealing with Hells Angels they desired, but the club itself would have no official alliance and a patch-over was not in the offing. In response, Stadnick made it clear that he was also negotiating with other Ontario clubs, in particular the Toronto-based Para-Dice Riders and the Loners of nearby Woodbridge.

The increase in stature resulting from the deal with Stadnick allowed Satan's Choice to do something it hadn't done in a very long time — expand. Two new chapters popped up. One was in Sudbury, a hardscrabble mining city in Northern Ontario that was already getting virtually all of its drugs through Stadnick's friend and fellow Nomad Richard "Rick" Vallée.

The other was in Hamilton. That was widely regarded as a deliberate slap in the face of Parente, who had become the country's most influential Outlaw. "Oh, they hated Parente," a police officer told me. "And they knew it would piss him off to have another club in what he considered to be his town."

Chapter 8
The Rock Machine Targets Ontario

But the Outlaws had troubles of their own. Membership was down. The looming threat of the Hells Angels had put a dent in recruiting and even veteran members seemed to be less interested in staying with the club. After seeing what the Hells Angels were capable of in Quebec and knowing full well that they wanted Ontario, many Outlaws understandably felt nervous about the future of their club.

That tension turned to violence on the night of November 28, 1992. And the intended target appeared to be a familiar and valuable one. At about 2 a.m., Parente's girlfriend — 38-year-old Linda Demaria — had just arrived at Parente's house in Dundas, a nice, quiet suburb just west of Hamilton. She'd spent the night out having dinner and drinks with some friends in nearby Burlington. She was in the passenger seat of the second of two carloads of friends that pulled into Parente's driveway. Just as she was climbing out of the car, she was shot once in the lower back and collapsed. The bullet entered just above her pelvis and exited through her abdomen.

She was rushed to nearby McMaster Medical Centre and quickly put into stable condition. Neither the people in the cars (some of whom were "known to police") nor Parente could provide any eyewitness details. They were described by a police spokes-man as "cooperative to a point."

Despite the extensive use of metal detectors, the shell — believed to be from a 9-mm handgun — was never found, nor was the shooter's location determined. "We can't say: 'was this a drive-by? Was someone hiding in the bushes?" the spokesman said, indicating they had found little useful evidence at all. With nothing in the way of physical evidence and not a useful word from any of the witnesses, the police admitted they had little chance of catching whoever was responsible, but they did indicate that they felt that Demaria was probably not the intended victim. "We still are unable to determine a motive," said the spokesman. "Or even if the shooting was for someone other than the victim; or if it was, in fact, for the victim." Considering the distance involved — since none of the revellers saw the shooter, it's likely to have been quite a long shot — and the inherent inaccuracy of handguns over long distances, the target could well have been anyone in the large group.

But the potshot at Parente's girlfriend, probably taken by a biker or Mafia functionary, was small-time compared to what the police did to Parente four years later. At 5 a.m. on the morning of April 29, 1996, more than 100 police officers from a half-dozen forces launched Operation Charlie, named after the skull on the Outlaws logo. They descended on the Outlaws' St. Catharine's clubhouse, four other locations in the Niagara peninsula and one apartment building on Hamilton Mountain.

After the Hamilton Police shut down the Birch Avenue club-house, Parente had moved his operations about 30 minutes east to St. Catharine's. Because the clubhouse was heavily fortified, the cops attacked it with a front-end loader. They tore down the front wall. They arrested nine Outlaws, but the real prize was Parente. The cops surrounded his farmhouse on Sodom Road, just outside of Niagara Falls, and arrested him when he came out with his hands up. He was charged with two counts of traffick-ing cocaine and one of uttering a death threat. The papers at the time identified him as a former Outlaws national president and current St. Catharine's Chapter president.

That night, the house of an Outlaws member burned to the ground. On the following day, a helicopter was seen to land on the nearby Port Colborne farm of an Outlaw and let off some passengers after dark. The police admitted they found both facts interesting, but had no answers for either.

Being in jail wasn't Parente's only problem. On July 10, 1996, a new inmate was brought into the Hamilton-Wentworth Correctional Centre from just outside Montreal, and within hours of his arrival, he attacked Parente with a makeshift knife fabricated from a toothbrush. The assailant surprised Parente and managed to stab him in the eyes and throat, but failed to do much damage before he was wrestled off him. Parente refused to cooperate with police when they questioned him, and also refused medical treatment.

Just as Operation Charlie was making the papers, the third incarnation of Satan's Choice in Hamilton started to germinate in an East End gym. Bikers like gyms not only because they like to work out, but because they are great places to sell drugs and, in particular, steroids. A small-time Hamilton criminal we can only call Jimmy Rich because he's also in witness protection told his two workout buddies that he had a connection who could make them all very wealthy. Rich's weight-lifting buddies — Gary Noble and Ion Croitoru — quickly accepted.

• • •

Croitoru was a local celebrity. And he was hard to miss. He was huge. Only about six-foot tall, he carried a very solid 300 pounds on his frame. He complemented his intimidating stature with wild eyes, a shaved head and a bushy, black Fu Man-chu mustache. He looked pretty much like what he was: a washed-up professional wrestler.

Years earlier, he'd been in the employ of the World Wrestling Federation (WWF). It can't be overstated how immensely popular the WWF was at the time. Few stars had the magnitude of Hulk Hogan. He was everywhere. People in places like Hamilton wore his likeness, and even his catchphrases, on their clothing.

They watched him in movies and on TV. They loved him. And he fought against Croitoru.

Johnny K-9

Croitoru was what wrestling fans call a "jobber." That's a guy who's paid to show up, look tough, rile up the crowd and then get the daylights beaten out of him by the star. And Croitoru played it up. He'd show up in the ring with tight black shorts and a studded collar around his neck. He'd climb into the ring, acknowledge the boos, and do anything he could to amp them up. Then the star would come in and trounce him. His signature moves were the Stomach Claw and the Flying Headbutt and he became famous as Johnny K-9.

It was a hard way to make a living, even by Hamilton standards. But Johnny K-9 — even though it wasn't his legal name he managed to get a bank account under it, so it has to be considered his real identity — was a major celebrity. At the time, guys like Hogan were thought of as legitimate superstars, so getting thrown out of a ring by him was enough to grant a fairly healthy dose of stardom upon a jobber. Johnny K-9 could barely walk a block in downtown Hamilton without someone offering to buy him a beer.

Professionally, things did not go well for him. After some arrests for cocaine possession and assault in 1991, he was dumped from the WWF. Over the years, he wrestled for increasingly down-market leagues, changing his identity from Middle Eastern bad guy (the Terrible Turk or Taras Bulba) to blue-collar good guy (Bruiser Bedlam). While his exposure and his paycheque dwindled, his credibility on the streets of the Hammer didn't. He was still a star.

After a few months of semi-unemployment, K-9 was ready to make some real money. He, Noble and Rich spent a few months serving drinks at the Toronto Satan's Choice clubhouse before they earned their patch. They bought an old convenience store at 269 Lottridge Street in the North End of Hamilton for a clubhouse. It was about six blocks away from the by-then-destroyed Outlaws clubhouse on Birch Avenue. Satan's Choice paid $40,000 for the building. K-9 was named their president.

It wasn't a wise choice. Isnor, the OPP biker specialist, noticed him right away. He was hard to miss. "After a while, you can tell who's cut out for the life and who isn't. I could tell right away he wouldn't make it," he told me. "Some of the guys would talk to you. If there was a guy who was really into bikes, you could talk bikes, but K-9 would talk about anything, especially himself — he was just stupid that way."

Things were somewhat different in Sudbury. Drugs were already being poured into the city, and the local tough guys were hastily assembled into a barely cohesive group, which became the local Satan's Choice chapter. Their president was a local thug named Michael Dubé. While he had only a few arrests to his credit, police and members of the criminal community alike considered him a dangerous man. Isnor, who said that another biker — a convicted multi-murderer — reminded him of Charles Manson because of the crazed look in his eyes, considered Dubé to be the most dangerous of all the Ontario bikers. And unlike K-9, he did not feel a need to chat with cops.

These new chapters and a close connection with Hells Angels bolstered Satan's Choice considerably. They hadn't come back to anywhere near where they were before Guindon went to prison, but they could make an argument that they were the second-biggest biker club in Ontario after their bitter enemies the Outlaws. They appeared to be the Hells Angels' favorites.

But it didn't come very easily, and it wouldn't be a smooth road for them either. A couple of years before the Hamilton and Sudbury chapters opened, everybody in the outlaw biker world and law enforcement knew that Hells Angels in general and Stadnick in particular were looking to expand into Southern Ontario. Logic dictated that he needed an existing club in the potentially quite lucrative region — boots on the ground, as it were — to break in.

So in the summer of 1993, when Hells Angels threw a massive party in Wasaga Beach (the old Satan's Choice resort town of preference), it was unanimously seen as an audition of sorts. They invited every single biker club in Ontario, except two that were very conspicuous by their absence: the Outlaws and Satan's Choice.

Although Hells Angels and the Outlaws were no longer at war by then, everybody knew that it was a detente and not a real peace. Their not being invited wasn't actually surprising, but a little disheartening for law enforcement. "We knew that if he had invited the Outlaws — especially Parente — then there would be no war in Ontario," one cop told me. "But when they weren't there, it kind of made us a little uneasy."

Satan's Choice was another matter altogether. They seemed the logical partners for Hells Angels. Even though they had been weakened by defections to the Outlaws, they had an enviable network, a strong leadership crew and a deep and abiding hate for the Outlaws. It seemed like a match made in drug-dealing heaven.

But it was not to be. At least not right away. Stadnick was not just playing hard to get. Instead, he had his eye on another gang.

In 1978, Francesco Lenti — who went by "Frank" or "Cisco" — wanted to be a Hells Angel, but they had no presence in Ontario. So, like many in Ontario at the time, he did the next best thing — he joined Satan's Choice.

It didn't work out. Lenti's me-first attitude and obvious sense of entitlement rubbed the Satan's Choice full-patches the wrong way and he never made it past prospect. Insulted and embittered, he left the gang and skulked back to Woodbridge, his hometown, and formed his own gang.

Just north and west of Toronto, Woodbridge has long been a haven for middle-class and wealthy Italians fleeing the rigors of the big city. As such, it has long had a reputation as a hotbed of Mafia activity (and there have been many arrests to back up that claim). In fact, the area's connection with the Mafia is so tied into public consciousness that when a middle-aged Woodbridge couple that had an Italian last name were murdered on vacation in Mexico, the local papers openly speculated about their possible ties to organized crime.

Lenti called his little gang (mostly high school friends and others disenchanted with Satan's Choice) the Loners. They met in a clubhouse he rented across the street from his own house. He even designed their rather elaborate and bizarre patch, featuring a head that is a devil on one side and a werewolf (or so it appears) on the other with blood dripping from its mouth. And the text on the patch is made up of bones.

While most other bikers and law enforcement called them the "Losers," the Loners actually had some success. Most of it came from Lenti, who had two very successful businesses in industries bikers tend to admire — a stripper/escort talent agency and a tow truck firm.

And when Stadnick met with all those Ontario bikers at Wasaga in 1993, he spent most of his time with Lenti and the Loners. My sources say that he was not all that impressed with Lenti himself, but liked the rest of the club and considered them to be in the perfect spot at exactly the right time.

So Stadnick started shipping drugs into Toronto via the Loners. Lenti took care of the books, and when a couple of members confronted him about some discrepancies — mentioning that they knew full well he had stolen money from a previous, now-disbanded gang also called the Loners — he threw a fit and stormed away, never to return. I've since been told the Hells Angels were the ones who planted that doubt.

But he did not disappear. In fact, he started up yet another club — the third he had founded and the latest of at least five he had been in — across the street from the Loners clubhouse in his

Francesco Lenti

own house. Made up of his loyalists and a few kids, they called themselves the Diablos. Since the Loners were right across the street, the frightened Diablos were forced to come to meetings through an alleyway and across Lenti's backyard.

So desperate were the big biker gangs for every square inch of Southern Ontario — especially prime real estate like Wood-bridge — the Diablos were immediately courted. A very short time after they were founded, the Diablos had a working relationship with Satan's Choice, who were as exquisitely angry with Hells Angels for snubbing them as they were with the Outlaws for stealing their best chapters. Despite having already kicked the mercurial Lenti out of their own club years earlier and knowing he had stolen from his own club and been kicked out of yet an-other club he'd founded, Satan's Choice now dangled prospective membership to his newest club, a bunch of nobodies who met in a suburban townhouse basement and were afraid to show their colors on their own street.

The Hells Angels, of course, could not tolerate that kind of insolence, and yet another small biker war was on in Ontario. It began on July 18, 1995 when a member of the Diablos threw a homemade firebomb at a tow truck owned by a Loner. The Loners retaliated by shooting two Diablos, although the injuries were minor.

Everything changed on August 1. Early in the morning, the otherwise quiet Toronto neighborhood of Riverdale shook as a huge boom shattered windows and woke everyone up. The heavily fortified front door of the Satan's Choice clubhouse on Kintyre Avenue had been blown off. Police later determined that it had been shot with a handheld rocket launcher, much like the ones police found in a park just outside Hamilton after the Outlaws' failed assassination plot against Stadnick.

Ever mindful of the biker wars in Montreal that had left piles of dead bodies and saw near-daily explosions, Toronto mayor Barbara Hall was determined to put a stop to it. The often-hysterical Toronto media kicked into overdrive, predicting death and destruction in the streets.

On August 16, two hours after Hall had given a speech about biker violence in the city, a similar explosion rocked Woodbridge.

Someone had blown a hole in the Loners' clubhouse wall. Everyone assumed the Diablos were responsible, but one Loner jokingly told a reporter he suspected a different culprit. "Looks like the cops have stolen our rocket launcher," he said.

Less than a week later, Lenti opened up the driver's side door of his white Ford Explorer. He turned the key, which ignited a bomb fastened to the bottom of the car. It didn't kill him, but it did take a big chunk out of his upper right thigh, incapacitating him for years and giving him a pronounced limp for the rest of his life. The nature of his injuries and his reputation allowed cops and rival bikers alike to start calling him the "half-assed biker."

With Lenti out of the way, the war was over, the Diablos were run off and an uneasy peace was made between Satan's Choice and Hells Angels.

Years later, it came out that Nomad David "Wolf" Carroll had discussed a plan with Rocker Dany "Danny Boy" Kane that would have him and other Rockers kill a few Loners to scare both sides closer to the Hells Angels fold. The plan never materialized for two reasons: Carroll was convinced that too many people knew about the plan and was afraid that someone might rat — and he suspected Kane's friend (and secret lover) Aimé Simard. In any event, the war ended before they could put a conclusive plan together.

But the Toronto media didn't know that the war was over. They urged Hall to take serious action against them, to do more than just talk. Her zoning people got after Satan's Choice for having their clubhouse in a residential area. Determining it was illegal for the building to be non-residential, they prepared a court order against the club. So the club set up a bedroom inside the building and moved a member in. Desperate, Hall offered to buy the clubhouse for almost double what it was worth. The owner, full-patch Larry McIlroy, agreed, but balked at a clause that forbade the club from re-opening in another building in the city. The local media got wind of this, started calling Hall "Biker Barb," and she lost her re-election campaign.

Then the York Region police and OPP raided the Loners' clubhouse. They seized a few weapons, but made not a single arrest.

Things didn't go absolutely smoothly after the Diablos-Loners war. Stadnick was plenty pissed off at Satan's Choice over the whole

Toronto debacle and he was also owed a lot of money by the Thunder Bay Chapter. But he knew better than to keep them enemies.

He started showing up in Ontario more and more often. Despite the constant threat posed by the Outlaws, he appeared frequently at public events. OPP Sergeant Len Isnor recalled being at a motorcycle show at Toronto's Exhibition Grounds when, suddenly, the entire crowd fell silent. He looked to the door to see Stadnick, in his flamboyant, self-designed colors, walk into the show, with a phalanx of bodyguards in tow. Immediately and without any warning, the crowd parted like the Red Sea, affording Stadnick and his men room. Stadnick walked right up to Watteel and the two, surrounded by bodyguards, talked for about 45 minutes. When Stadnick was done, the bodyguards lined up behind him and the crowd automatically separated again to let him through. "I had never seen anything like it," said Isnor. "It was like he was a rock star or something." Years later, at the same show, Isnor was surveying the crowd when he was approached by Parente and another Outlaw. Noting that they were the only two Outlaws in a mass of Hells Angels and Hells Angels supporters, Parente joked: "You'll probably want to stick with us for a little while."

For the time being, the Loners were still Stadnick's favorites. Things were going badly for Satan's Choice. Guindon held a huge party at his large Port Perry property. In a shocking surprise, he announced his retirement from the club. At the time, many suspected he had been tipped off about a massive raid that was coming, but I've since been told that he had already begun to show distinct signs of Alzheimer's-related dementia.

That was actually good news for Stadnick and Hells Angels. Without Guindon and his dogma that the club must remain all-Canadian, the members, even the chapters of Satan's Choice, were now free to become Hells Angels.

• • •

But there were problems just over the horizon. The joint police forces were preparing an immense raid — Operation Dismantle — aimed at arresting every member of Satan's Choice in Ontario and depriving them of their infrastructure and income.

Because they were the newest clubs, Sudbury and Hamilton would have been the hardest to get evidence against had it not been for some bad decisions by the bikers, some good police work by the OPP and a little bit of luck.

Dubé and his guys invited K-9 and his crew — which now included Rich, Noble, Gordie Cunningham and a guy known as Lebanese Joe — up for a get-together. Once the guys from Hamilton had arrived in Sudbury, they started drinking and they all ended up at the Solid Gold, the city's biggest strip joint.

In the spacious parking lot outside the massive, low-slung windowless blue building, the local guys took their jackets off and locked them in the trunks of their cars. K-9 asked what they were doing. One of Dubé's men told him that the club had a strict no-colors policy so they had to take their jackets off before they could go inside. The Hamilton boys laughed derisively. One of them said: "We wear our colors wherever the fuck we want." And the others agreed. K-9 asked rhetorically who was going to stop them.

After a round of "fuck yeahs," the Sudbury members proudly re-donned their jackets and the whole group went into the bar. Minutes later, the police showed up in force and turfed them all from the club. Dubé swore revenge.

Not long thereafter, a bomb exploded at the Sudbury police station. Nobody was hurt, but it left a huge hole in the wall. And it spread fear throughout the community. If the police couldn't keep themselves safe, how could they keep the public safe?

It was just about time for the Victoria Day holiday in 1997. Many Canadians refer to the three-day weekend as "May Two-Four" because it usually falls on or about May 24 and the traditional way of celebrating involves buying and consuming a 24-pack of one's favorite beer. It is the traditional kickoff of summer in Canada, and it brings the first wave of tourists from Southern Ontario to the North.

Isnor was up there, but he was working. On the Friday before the big weekend, he got a call from a local drug dealer who can only be called Ed because he, too, is in the witness protection program. He was behind in his payments to the Vachon Brothers, a pair of tough guys from Sherbrooke who worked for Nomad

Vallée. He promised to tell Isnor everything in exchange for his safety.

Despite the big weekend, Isnor managed to find a motel room for him in Orillia, a cute little town (and home of the OPP's central headquarters) some four hours' drive southeast of Sudbury.

A couple of days later, Isnor received a call at his office. It was from American Express. Their representative asked him if he was in a Peterborough restaurant. He assured them he wasn't, that he was a six-hour drive away in Sudbury. They told him that someone was attempting to pay for a meal using his card number in Peterborough. They also asked him if he had racked up over $2,000 in charges in the last day and a half. He assured them he hadn't, then he told them who he was and that he'd take care of it. So he called some cops he knew in Peterborough and they scooped Ed up and threw him in the "Barrie Bucket" — a notorious and since-closed maximum-security jail in Barrie, a city halfway between Orillia and Toronto.

As soon as Isnor had left Ed at the Orillia motel, the biker convinced the elderly manager that he was in something of a pickle. He told him that he had just ordered a pizza, but that his "brother" (Isnor, who looked nothing like him) had driven off with his wallet. If he could just get his Amex number from the registry, he could pay for his pizza. The manager believed him and gave him the imprint. Armed with this data, career criminal Ed went on a minor spending spree.

A couple of days after Ed had been dragged to Barrie, he called Isnor. The cop swore at him, told him he had a lot of nerve and was just about to hang up on him when he heard Ed say that his cellmate was bragging about blowing up the Sudbury police station. Isnor told Ed he was re-hired.

The cellmate was someone Isnor had recently put behind bars: Gordie Cunningham, a big and aggressive member of K-9's Satan's Choice crew in Hamilton. Raf Faiella, an undercover agent, had made a deal to buy coke from a Hamilton man, a shoe store owner named Mike Parker. The deal was supposed to go down at the Holiday Inn in Barrie, so Isnor and his team put it under heavy surveillance.

The first thing he noticed was that Parker had brought along Cunningham. "I smelled a rip," he told me. Isnor is a veteran cop who knows the terrible things that could happen if he didn't intervene. Faiella, his buddy, could easily be dead. "And, sure enough, it was one." Although he would have rather arrested the men for drug trafficking, he knew it was too dangerous not to intervene on Faiella's behalf. He arrested Cunningham and Parker on possession and threw them into the Barrie Bucket. It was just by pure chance that Cunningham and Ed shared a cell.

Before long, Cunningham made bail and Ed was released after serving a sentence made shorter by his guilty plea and his having made restitution to American Express. The pair had grown quite close in their small cell, and Cunningham had recruited Ed for the Hamilton Chapter. So when he was released, Ed went to Cunningham's house and lived with him.

With Ed wearing a wire, the cops recorded Cunningham making three separate cocaine buys. They had enough evidence to put him away for a very long time. After they put Ed in a safe place (with no access to their credit cards), Isnor, fellow OPP officer Peter Koop and Hamilton biker cop Robert "Biker Bob" MacDonald visited Cunningham at home. Instead of arresting him for the coke buys, they gave him an opportunity to turn on his brothers. He immediately jumped at it and spilled everything he knew.

Apparently, the Hamilton Chapter came up to Sudbury to help their brothers refurbish their clubhouse. When they got bored, they went to Solid Gold. When the cops showed up and kicked them out of Solid Gold, the members of both chapters considered it a major humiliation. Thrown out of the strip joint, the bikers went to the more biker-friendly Coulson Tavern farther downtown.

As the other bikers drank themselves silly, the two presidents walked across Larch Street to an all-night sandwich shop. Dubé told K-9 that he'd do anything to get back at the owner of Solid Gold, the man who ratted him out to the cops simply for wearing his jacket. K-9 told him he knew a guy, Jerry, who could help him out.

Jure "Jerry" Juretta had been in an airborne unit in the Canadian military and knew a lot about explosives. He also happened to be a Hamilton drug dealer and tough guy who worked for K-9's Satan's Choice. Dubé was impressed. He asked K-9 to get his friend to build him a bomb. K-9, always happy to make people happy, smiled and told his colleague that it'd be no problem.

Interestingly, Juretta was an old friend of Parente's. In fact, his sister was married to Marco Roque, a Hamilton Outlaw and even closer friend of Parente's. I asked Isnor about this, especially in light of the fact that I knew that Roque is now a member of the Hamilton Hells Angels. He looked at me with a grin just this side of condescending and said: "I can't believe you still think there's any loyalty among these people."

A few days later, Juretta and K-9 went up to Sudbury with the bomb. They met Dubé and Brian Davis, his right-hand man, at the Tim Hortons at the corner of Highway 69 and Notre Dame Avenue in the Lockerby neighborhood in South Sudbury. Juretta handed the bomb to a delighted Dubé. The plan was to put it into the men's washroom of the Solid Gold. That would teach that asshole to ban colors and call the cops.

A couple of days later, K-9 got a call in Hamilton telling him that the bomb had been a success. There was now a large, smoking hole in the Sudbury police station. "What do you mean the police station?" he shouted. "It was supposed to be the Solid Gold!"

With Cunningham safely taken out of the picture, Isnor put Ed back to work. He accompanied Russell Martin, another Sudbury Satan's Choice member and Dubé's primary gofer, on a few cocaine buys. Isnor and his men approached Martin and showed him the evidence they had against him. They also told him they were much more interested in his boss than they were in him. He nodded. He understood. He knew that Dubé was capable of killing him, and as angry as he was these days, he just might.

Dubé was angry at Martin because he wouldn't do his job. But his job was to help his boss kill his best friend, Brian Davis.

The first time Dubé tried to kill Davis because he was sure he was gunning for his job, he told Martin to tell Davis that he'd found an undefended Hells Angels cottage full of coke. All they had to do was kick in the doors and fill up their pickup trucks. Davis was in.

Martin didn't have the heart to do it. He drove Davis around back roads for three hours pretending to be lost. The second time Dubé tried to kill Davis, Martin slashed his own tires to get out of it. The third time he was rescued by being caught by the cops.

Isnor knew Martin was nothing more than a tool, so he tracked down Davis. He brought him in. He sat him in the interrogation room chair. He used all the tried-and-true cop tactics. Nothing worked. Davis, a tough guy, wouldn't talk. Isnor looked him in the eye. He told him Dubé was going to kill him. In that most fleeting of moments, everything came together and made perfect sense. Davis's face turned stark white. He averted his eyes and said: "You're absolutely right."

In exchange for witness protection, Davis spilled. Even though he was the No. 2 guy in Sudbury, he was deathly afraid of No. 1, Dubé. When they received the bomb from the Hamilton guys, Davis asked his boss how they were going to get it into the Solid Gold. Dubé said fuck that, they were going to stick it in the police station. His reasoning was that the police were the real enemy, not some asshole with a phone in the Solid Gold. He also told Davis that his dream, his greatest goal, was to get a tanker truck full of explosives and drive it through the police station, killing everyone inside — and, presumably, himself. Even though he was no schoolboy, Davis found that image chilling.

It was obvious that none of the local guys from Satan's Choice could plant a bomb at either the Solid Gold or the police station without being caught. But Dubé had a friend who could. Neil Passenen was a local drug dealer, but he cleaned up pretty good and could pass for a contributing member of society. Besides, he was one of the few people he knew who weren't immediately identifiable to even the least experienced Sudbury cop. His mom had been dating a guy whose last name was Young, so he was going by the name Neil Young in those days. And he owed Dubé a favor, so Dubé called it in. He had Neil Young place the bomb in the alleyway between the police station and the credit union next door. He was to be sure to leave it leaning up against the police station's wall.

That was enough for Isnor. He arrested the lot of them. In fact, since Operation Dismantle had begun, the fuzz had managed to arrest 109 of the 125 Satan's Choice members and prospects and seize all of their clubhouses. K-9 went down for his involvement in the Sudbury bombing and for trafficking steroids. Dubé killed himself in jail awaiting trial, hanging himself with a twisted bed sheet. I asked Isnor why he thought that happened. "Johnny K-9 was the only friend he had left in the world, and he knew we had him and he was going away forever," he told me. "Besides the bombing and the trafficking, we probably could have linked him to the [Sudbury coke dealer Michael] Briere murder and then there's Alex Atso, who was Sudbury's No. 1 drug dealer before Satan's Choice took over; I'm sure Dubé killed him, too."

In effect, the police had managed to do what politicians, rocket launchers and Molotov cocktails never could. They had eliminated Satan's Choice from the competition to see who would be the Hells Angels favorites in Ontario. That honor and responsibility now fell squarely on the shoulders of the Loners.

But Isnor, at least, was pretty sure that's how it would have worked out anyway. "Satan's Choice were never the big guys, they were nickel and dime," he told me. "The Loners were always Stadnick's favorites."

But, as always, things were not as easy as they would seem. By the time Satan's Choice was taken out of the picture, things had changed radically for the now financially successful Loners. Two men, Frank Grano and Jimmy Raso, were fighting tooth and nail for leadership of the gang. By the start of 1997, both men had strong factions behind him. And just before Stadnick and Hells Angels were about to give the Loners their blessing as their top puppet gang in Ontario, they split in half.

Grano's half of the Loners showed up at the door of the Para-Dice Riders clubhouse in downtown Toronto, one of the more powerful of the local, non-affiliated gangs. They were welcomed with open arms, opened up a chapter four blocks away from the Loners' clubhouse and called themselves the Para-Dice Riders Woodbridge Chapter. At least two knowledgeable sources told me Stadnick was behind the move, hoping to combine two clubs as a single pro–Hells Angels entity. Raso's Woodbridge Loners stayed where they were and, before long, faded into obscurity. Biker gangs without a steady supply of drugs to sell generally don't make headlines.

The OPP then deduced that the Para-Dice Riders were the entryway the Hells Angels were going to use to get into Ontario and decided to devote most of their energies to them. They were well served to monitor the situation. The Para-Dice Riders were a long-established club, with at least 60 members. The influx of the former Loners had enriched the club in both manpower and finances. And they had a leader. Donny Petersen, though not the president, often spoke eloquently for the club. In the early '90s he had sued the OPP — unsuccessfully, but with a great deal of publicity and public sympathy — over their roadside stop policy for bikers. Not only had it generated a lot of much-needed public sympathy for bikers, but it made him some important friends. He even had the opportunity to address Toronto's prestigious Empire Club, an honor reserved normally for heads of state and titans of industry.

On September 3, 1997, a procession of Quebec Hells Angels roared into Toronto. At one of the roadside stops Petersen had complained about, the police arrested Sylvain Vachon (one of the brothers who ferried Vallée's drugs into Sudbury) on an outstanding warrant. The rest arrived at the Para-Dice Riders' clubhouse on Eastern Avenue, not far from downtown. The prospects for both clubs waited outside while the full-patches talked inside.

They could only speculate as to what went on inside, but that didn't stop the Toronto media from declaring the Para-Dice Riders the Hells Angels' gateway into Ontario and an all-out biker war a certainty.

• • •

But Stadnick wasn't that simple. He had other irons in the fire, other ways to get into Ontario. Remember the Sherbrooke Chapter? The one that had enough juice to opt out of the Nomads' cocaine distribution system? Well, they had a friend from London, Ontario, named John Coates, one of the few English-speaking Hells Angels associates to be successful in Quebec.

He was quite a specimen. At six-foot-seven and at least 300 pounds, he was a huge, intimidating presence. He was well liked by the Sherbrooke Hells Angels and was employed by them frequently.

And he had a brother. Back in London, Jimmy Coates (not quite as big as John, but still a massive man) was a member of the Loners, which still had a fairly active chapter there. The Sherbrooke guys asked John to invite his brother and his friends over. They partied, they got along, they were given drugs to sell.

But they had to do it in secret. The Chatham Loners' most prominent member, chapter president Wayne "Weiner" Kellestine, would never have allowed it. A Loners' purist (even though his old gang, the Annihilators, had patched over to the Loners just a short time before, while Kellestine was in prison), he had no use for Hells Angels. Like Guindon before him, Kellestine didn't like answering to a club based in another country, and he did not like how they treated Raso's Loners. First they backed the enemy, Satan's Choice, then the Loners and when the Loners divided, they went with the Para-Dice Riders, essentially favoring three different clubs in one town over the space of two years.

Kellestine was a man to be feared, even by behemoths like the Coates brothers. He was the biker described by Isnor as looking like Charles Manson. And he reportedly introduced himself to an old friend's brother by saying "Hi, I'm Wayne Kellestine. I sell drugs and kill people."

Although they are often referred to as the London or St. Thomas Loners, the chapter recognized itself as being from Chatham, a small city on the 401 halfway between Windsor and London. The Loners also had a small chapter in Amherstburg, just south of Windsor, and prospective chapters in Oregon and Southern Italy, where many of the Woodbridge guys had relatives.

They were out in Chatham because London was very much an Outlaws town. At this time, Parente was national president and he and his Hamilton Chapter represented the club's power center in Canada. But the London Chapter could probably have made a very strong case for second place. London's not a tough town by any standards, but it is a very rich territory for drug sales. And it was perfectly situated between the Outlaws' world headquarters in Detroit and its Canadian seat of operations in Hamilton, in an area many cops know as "meth alley" because it's Ontario's most active area for methamphetamine manufacture and use.

Because the area is so very desirable to biker gangs, it had been the site of many increasingly violent turf wars. But the Outlaws had kept it theirs and largely peaceful since they had taken over. That changed in April 1998, when two prominent Outlaws from London — chapter president Jeffrey Labrash and full-patch Jody Hart — were shot and killed in the parking lot outside the downtown Beef Baron strip joint.

Working from eyewitness accounts, police quickly issued warrants for the Lewis brothers, Paul and Duane (no relation to the Hamilton Lewises who so bedeviled Parente). The pair claimed they had no biker connections, and their story was that they had been sent to the Beef Baron to repair a malfunctioning video game. They were, they said, minding their own business when they just happened to get into a fight with the two Outlaws. The melee continued outside the bar and ended with both of the Outlaws being shot with the same handgun.

After the shooting, more questions were raised about biker involvement. A few days later, immediately after the funerals for Labrash and Hart, a bomb exploded at T.J. Baxter's, a bar frequented by local Outlaws. And it was full of them that day. Four people, all with some association with the Outlaws, were hurt, one seriously.

While many people in Southwestern Ontario saw it as the beginning of a biker war, police and media biker experts continued to deny any Hells Angels or Loners (who they still incorrectly identified as Annihilators) involvement.

Nine months later, police found the body of locally notorious millionaire businessman Salvatore Vecchio in a marsh just outside London. He was known to have association with bikers of many different clubs, and to have known and perhaps even to have employed the Lewis brothers under the table. Again, police and media downplayed the idea of a biker war.

At their trial, the Lewises claimed that they had gone to the Beef Baron that day for work. When they got there, they said, one of the Outlaws pulled a gun on them for reasons unknown and marched them out into the parking lot. Then, they said, Labrash fired a shot at one of them at point-blank range, but somehow missed (police found no evidence of this). Then Paul Lewis pulled his own gun and fired. He hit Labrash four times in the chest and Hart once in the head, killing them both.

Clearly, the key piece of evidence was Labrash's alleged gun. It was never found, but the defense pointed out that the bar's DJ was an Outlaws supporter, and they asserted that he had taken the gun and other evidence with him when he left the Beef Baron before the police arrived. Police had been unable to locate him — he had fled the country and was hiding out in the U.K. — but it didn't matter. The shadow of doubt was raised, and the Lewises were acquitted of all counts as the killings were attributed to self-defense.

Years later, the Lewises were caught in an RCMP cocaine sting with loads of drugs and cash, including Mexican currency. A subsequent investigation determined that the Lewises had acquired their cocaine from Hells Angels in Sherbrooke. So, while the police and media denied any biker war, the recent killings and the recent influx of drugs into the London area indicated otherwise.

Many Loners — drawn both by security and financial rewards — sought a closer relationship with the Hells Angels, but not all of them did. Kellestine was still adamantly and vociferously against the idea. He made his point at a party late in 1999 when a young Loner was mouthing off about how much better life would be if they were Hells Angels. Kellestine rebutted the argument by beating the man nearly to death with the handle of a handgun.

Kellestine's reluctance to accept the Hells Angels' looming dominance of Canadian biker culture did not go unnoticed. On a cold Friday, October 22 in 1999, Kellestine packed up his SUV to attend a friend's wedding. As he paused at the stop sign where Regional Road 14 meets Regional Road 13, he was surprised to see pickup trucks pull up beside and in front of him, blocking his path. The passenger window rolled down. One of the two Hells Angels associates inside the pickup — David "Dirty" McLeish or Phil "Philbilly" Gastonguay — opened fire at Kellestine's car.

Windows were shattered, but nobody was hurt. Court records didn't make it clear which was the triggerman. When the Hells Angels associate who had the gun ran out of ammo, both vehicles laid rubber and screeched away. The pickup went north to the 401, and Kellestine went south, back home. If there was any chance Kellestine and Hells Angels could have made peace, it was probably killed that day.

To the people of Southwestern Ontario, it looked like Hells Angels had declared war on the Outlaws and the Loners.

Although the assassination attempt on Kellestine failed, it got one desired result: the Hells Angels had come to Ontario. The Coates brothers and their friends were there to stay. "The deal was partly, 'If you do this you become a member,'" said a London cop at the time. "There was some oversight from Sherbrooke, and when they got out and opened up their club here, John Coates was running it."

They didn't have a chapter or a clubhouse yet, but the Hells Angels were already becoming established in London, in Ontario. And they weren't the only ones. In 1999, the Rock Machine surprised everyone in the biker and law enforcement worlds by opening three chapters in Ontario. Despite the fact that their still-bloody war with the Hells Angels was not going in their favor, that most of their leadership was dead or behind bars and despite the language and cultural barriers, the Rock Machine found a way to set up shop in Ontario before Stadnick could.

The Rock Machine — a name that meant only gangland-style shoot-outs and hidden bombs to the people of Ontario — had set up shop in London (a chapter they called Ontario West), Kingston (Ontario East) and Toronto. And as an insult specific to Stadnick, they had changed the bottom rocker of their patch to read "Canada" rather than their individual chapter. The two gangs were officially at peace, but the huge strategic move into Ontario was not greeted without anger by Hells Angels. At the time, though, Rock Machine national president Alain Brunette claimed that his club was "legitimate" and wanted to coexist peacefully with other gangs "for a long time."

It was a very tense year for the people of Ontario. They had watched their neighbors to the east be terrorized by a biker war that was still raging. Shootings and bombings had killed hundreds of Quebeckers — including innocent bystanders, even children — and the bikers seemed absolutely impervious to conviction. They had boldly and callously attempted to undermine the government's authority by murdering prison guards as a lesson to those who stood in their way.

Now it seemed like only a matter of time until it all broke loose in Ontario. The Rock Machine had arrived. The traditional Ontario gang in charge, the Outlaws, who had also fought a bloody war with the Hells Angels in Quebec, certainly weren't going to stand by and let their territory be stolen again. And the Hells Angels themselves — with chapters in B.C., Alberta, Saskatchewan, Manitoba, Quebec and Nova Scotia — were threatening to invade the province both from outside and from within.

Chapter 9

The U.S. Bandidos Make Their Move

Hells Angels knew that the Outlaws wouldn't leave Ontario without a fight, and they, too, prepared for war. They had routed the Outlaws before in Montreal, but this was a very different situation. In Montreal, the Outlaws were far outnumbered and far away from help. They had inadequate leaders and little will to fight.

It was different in Ontario, where the Outlaws (and Satan's Choice before them) had been entrenched for decades. Although Hells Angels now had more chapters and official members in Ontario, the Outlaws could probably recruit as many men, most of them of better quality than the also-rans Hells Angels had recently brought into their tent. They also had the potential for top-notch reinforcements — the Outlaws' international headquarters was in Detroit, and they were said to be enraged by the fact that Hells Angels had managed to establish a chapter just a few miles away in Windsor. And they had Mario Parente, who — both police and bikers have told me — was considered the most feared biker on either side of the divide.

But these weren't the same Hells Angels either. While they didn't have a killing machine on par with Yves "Apache" Trudeau anymore, they did have a corps of veterans battle-hardened after winning a much larger and bloodier war against the Rock

Machine. And they had dozens of chapters throughout the country. They handled hundreds of millions of dollars of drugs and other products and services every year. They had friends all over the country: in the Mafia, in law enforcement, in the military, in the legal business, on First Nations reserves and in many other places the Outlaws didn't. And they had veteran leadership that included the strategic brilliance of Walter Stadnick.

But it wasn't the Outlaws who attacked. Instead, on the early morning of March 28, 2001, it was more than 200 police officers from more than a dozen forces who descended upon every single one of the Hells Angels and puppet club clubhouses in Quebec, as well as hundreds of homes and businesses of members, prospects and associates.

In all, 142 arrests were made, including 80 of Quebec's 106 full-patch Hells Angels. Though most of the charges were for drug-related offenses, plenty more were for murder, the result of the war against the Rock Machine. Seized were 20 buildings, 41 vehicles (including 13 motorcycles, all but one a Harley), 70 guns, a stick of dynamite, 10 kilograms of cocaine, 120 kilograms of hashish, $12.5 million in Canadian currency and a further $2.6 million in U.S. currency.

Particularly hard hit were the Nomads. All of them — except for Maurice "Mom" Boucher, who was already behind bars awaiting a second trial for masterminding the 1997 murders of two prison guards and David "Wolf" Carroll, who miraculously escaped and has not been conclusively seen since — were arrested. Stadnick was taken down by the Jamaican military the day after everyone else. He and his wife were vacationing in Ocho Rios. The police checked flight records and he was spotted by an RCMP officer stationed in Kingston. Some have speculated that he knew what was coming and was fleeing, but he would have, I'm sure, been smart enough to cover his tracks better: spending a month in a Jamaican prison with a communal toilet bucket was hardly part of a cunning escape plan. Either way, the Nomads, his brilliant strategic gambit, effectively ceased to exist. At least for the time being.

Called Operation Printemps (and often referred to by its English translation "Operation Springtime" in the media, although the cops involved generally hate it), it was the culmination of work that armed police with evidence culled from dozens of informants and more than 266,000 different taped and incriminating conversations. Obviously, that magnitude of evidence couldn't have been put together overnight. The initial groundwork for Operation Printemps was put down in 1998, long before the massive patch-over in Ontario. As a result, the only Ontario Hells Angels arrested were Stadnick and his right-hand man Donald "Pup" Stockford, another Nomad. The others were left at large because they weren't Hells Angels when the operation began. In fact, some Hells Angels were charged with crimes committed against Paul "Sasquatch" Porter when he was with the Rock Machine. At that time of the arrests, he found himself rather ironically serving as president of the Kingston- and then later Ottawa-based Ontario Nomads, and one of the country's ranking Hells Angels.

The trials of the dozens of bikers arrested in Operation Printemps began April 19, 2002. With the bombings from the Hells Angels-Rock Machine wars still fresh in the minds of Montrealers, a new, $16.5 million courthouse was constructed. To prevent escape attempts or outside help for the accused, a secure underground passageway was built linking the new courthouse and Bordeaux jail where the accused were being held. Boucher — regarded by many as public enemy No. 1 — was being held separately in his own wing at Tanguay women's prison. The extra expense was considered a small price to pay to keep him from communicating with the other Hells Angels.

While evidence was being heard in the first of the Printemps trials, a verdict came down in Boucher's. He was found guilty of two counts of first-degree murder for ordering the hits on two prison guards on May 6, 2002. Informants Stephane "Godasse" Gagné and Stéphane Sirois claimed that Boucher's plan was to kill enough prison guards, cops, prosecutors and judges in Quebec to intimidate the others into not arresting, prosecuting or finding bikers guilty. It was the kind of terror plan that had worked wonders for cocaine cartels in Colombia and Mexico. Boucher was sentenced to life with no chance at parole for 25 years.

It could hardly be overstated how profound an effect the verdict and sentence in Boucher's case had among law enforcement prosecutors and, in effect, the entire law-abiding population of Quebec. While just two years earlier, a government official admitted that "they [the bikers] kill with impunity," the mighty Boucher had finally gone down — albeit on the province's second attempt to convict him of the same crime. Unless there was a widespread and massive case of amnesia in 2027, he was certain to die behind bars.

Exempt from what were now being known as "the megatrials" were Stadnick and Stockford. They had rather wisely invoked their right to a trial in English. That posed a problem for the Quebec legal system, which had largely been swept clean of English speakers. And they had another weapon at their disposal. They hired Canada's two most famous trial lawyers — Edward Greenspan and Alan D. Gold — to represent them. Fellow Nomad Michel Rose was so impressed that he opted to be tried in English with Stadnick and Stockford. Not a native anglophone, Rose just barely passed an English test that allowed him to be tried in his chosen language.

The Quebec justice department scrambled to find qualified English-speaking staff. For a judge, they settled on Jerry Zigman, an old-school Montrealer who stayed on when the harsh anti-English laws that came down led his contemporaries to flee to other provinces and was rapidly reaching the end of his career. And they lucked out when it came to finding a prosecutor.

Not only was their deputy chief prosecutor, Randall Richmond, completely fluent in both official languages, but he was a top-notch investigator and debater who had done outstanding work for organizations like the UN in places like the former Yugoslavia. He recalled with a laugh that he had studied Greenspan's work extensively while he was in law school. And, as luck would have it, he just happened to be from Hamilton.

Gagné and Stéphane Sirois — the Rockers-turned-informants who were doing so much damage in the trials of the other bikers — could do little aside from establish the fact that Stadnick, Stockford and Rose were Nomads and that Stadnick was the Hells Angels' primary recruiter and negotiator. The real damage came from Dany Kane, even though he had killed himself in August 2000, and Sandra Craig, the wife of a drug dealer killed by the Hells Angels.

Kane had stolen the Nomads' encoded financial records and Craig had translated them. The primary exhibit showed that the Nomads had handled $111,503,361 in an eight-and-a-half-month span, of which $10,158,110 went through an account Craig identified as belonging to Stadnick and Stockford.

Richmond had them dead to rights on the drug-trafficking charges, but could not get murder or conspiracy to commit murder charges to stick. He had tried a novel approach. There was plenty of forensic and verbal evidence around the murders of 13 Rock Machine members and associates, but none of it could be linked directly to Stadnick. But since he had convinced Zigman that Stadnick was in charge of the entire operation, his argument was that Stadnick was just as guilty as the men who actually pulled the triggers and set off the bombs. "Just as a general is liable for any war crimes his men commit," he told me. "We were convinced Stadnick knew about the murders and did nothing to stop them." It didn't stick. They were acquitted of the murder charges.

Even so, Stadnick and Stockford both received 20-year terms, minus time served. Rose plea bargained to a lesser sentence.

While the Outlaws would have liked to take advantage of the disarray Operation Printemps had put Hells Angels into, they had problems of their own. In the late '90s, before Hells Angels had established themselves in their province, the consensus among Ontario police forces was that the Outlaws, as the province's dominant outlaw biker gang, were also a primary threat to public security. By the end of the decade, the police were hitting them hard, arresting them for everything they could in search of a big score.

The peace between the bikers did not hold for long. The Coates brothers in London — bolstered by drug money and the confidence that they represented the future of bikers in the area — decided they'd take things into their own hands. Without the diplomatic Stadnick to stand in their way, the London Hells Angels issued an ultimatum to the local Outlaws: give up your patch or die.

Their point was made at the end of June 2001, when the small Outlaws clubhouse in Woodstock, not far from London, was completely destroyed by an unsolved arson. A week later, the police stopped a car about 100 yards from the Hells Angels clubhouse at 732 York Street, about two blocks from the Beef Baron, the Outlaws-controlled strip joint. The driver was a well-known Outlaw. He was wearing body armor and had a pipe bomb in the car.

The local Hells Angels were taking on other jobs as well. In July, just after the foiled bombing, Hells Angels prospect Douglas "Plug" Johnstone sauntered into a car dealership and demanded a private meeting with the owner, Gerry Smith. Noticing the Hells Angels patch on his denim vest, Smith agreed. Johnstone told Smith that his former partner wanted the $70,000 that Smith owed him. Smith was surprised. The former partner had taken him to court over the $70,000, and a judge had ruled that Smith owed him nothing. To back that up, Smith showed Johnstone photocopies of the ruling.

Johnstone laughed. "I don't care what they say," he told him. "All I know is that you're going to have to pay me the money." Smith refused and asked him to leave. He did.

But he returned later that week with Jimmy Coates. Both men were wearing their patches. Coates and Johnstone played good cop/bad cop with Smith, with the politely pleasant Coates claiming to have his hands tied. He really needed to collect the $70,000. Again Smith refused. The men left without incident.

The third time they arrived, it was much less pleasant. Coates asked for the money. Smith refused a third time. Coates shrugged. "We know where you live," he said calmly. "We know you have a wife. We know you have a daughter." He advised Smith to think about what he said then they both left.

Smith waited until the two big men had left, then he went out and looked to see if they were still out front. Convinced they weren't, he went back into his office and called the police. The police secretly bugged all of Smith's phones, his office and his home. A week passed. Smith was at home with his wife and daughter. Suddenly, they heard a tremendous banging at the front door. It was like the house was going to come down. Smith's wife hid behind a sofa. Smith looked outside; Coates and Johnston — both in colors — were on his front porch with another, also very large and tough-looking, man.

Knowing they would not leave, Smith let them in. The third man introduced himself. He was Thomas Walkinshaw. He said it was his job to collect the $70,000 and that he really "didn't want to see anyone get hurt."

That was enough for the police, they arrested all three men as they exited the home with what they thought was $70,000 in ill-gotten cash.

A few minutes after midnight on what had just become January 7, 2002, four young men gathered outside a house at 434 Egerton Avenue. They were members of a new gang set up by John Coates. Called the Jackals, they were a typical puppet gang. They all wanted to be Hells Angels, but the full-patches didn't think they were ready, so they had to prove themselves in their own gang before they could become prospects. The members of the Jackals earned their spurs by doing whatever Hells Angels told them to. And that night, they were told to pay an armed visit to Thomas Hughes, president of the London Outlaws, at 434 Egerton. The Jackals were there, they said, because of another Outlaw, 26-year-old Marcus Cornelisse. Their beef was with him, they said. All they wanted was for him to come out and talk with them. The Outlaws answered with a gunshot.

A Jackal named Eric Davignon was hit in the gut. What happened next was a nearly comical few seconds of bikers on both sides firing wildly, hitting nothing of importance and running for their lives. It ended with the Jackals retreating to their car, peeling away in a cloud of rubber smoke and the Outlaws firing at the back of their car in full view of their neighbors. One of them, an earwitness, told the local paper: "I was just going to bed when I heard this 'pop, pop!' Then I heard tires squealing, then 'bang, bang, bang!' "

When police showed up, they arrested Hughes and Cornelisse on four counts of attempted murder. After they searched the house, they added charges related to the guns, ammunition and explosives they found.

About 10 hours later, Walkinshaw, Johnstone and Jimmy Coates had their first day in court to answer their charges of extortion and belonging to a criminal organization. Crown prosecutor Elizabeth Maguire argued that the trio didn't need to bring any weapons with them to terrorize Smith and his family because the patches on their backs — and the name and reputation they represented — were more than enough. "The weapon of choice was a Hells Angel," she said in her final summation. "The weapon that was held to Mr. Smith's head, his wife's head, his daughter's head, was the Hells Angels." They all pleaded guilty to lesser charges and were sentenced to three years. The criminal organization charges were dropped as part of the deal.

It was evident that a war was on. Not in all of Ontario yet, but it had certainly started in London. So when the annual custom motorcycle show came around in February 2002, the police and media showed up in droves. Before the show, the local newspaper asked its organizer — former Para-Dice Rider and now full-patch Toronto Hells Angel Larry Pooler — if he was concerned that the floor of his show would become a battlefield. He laughed and said that sort of thing only happened in Quebec because, well, Quebeckers are a naturally combative people. "Their whole society is corrupt and vicious and violent," he said. "It always has been, since the 1600s — that's nothing new." He also pointed out that the police and media pile on bikers because they are an easier target than the people he believed were really behind all of society's problems. "If I was black or wore a turban, my pockets would be lined with gold from civil suits," he said. "But I'm just a poor white-trash biker."

• • •

On the first day of the show, 110 Hells Angels, Jackals and other associated gang members showed up. They were soon joined by dozens of Outlaws. Just after they arrived, a large group of Bandidos, mostly from the U.S., came through the gate and very openly greeted and aligned themselves with the Outlaws.

Combined, the Outlaws-Bandidos alliance numbered at least 120 members.

Amid all these bikers — all with full patches, some with body armor and many with exposed weapons like knives, chains and clubs — were 40 cops. They quickly put themselves between the two factions and politely asked the Outlaws and Bandidos to leave.

They did. Many of the police told local media that they believed their actions narrowly averted a bloodbath. Pooler laughed it off, pointing out that no actual violence took place and any suggestion that it would have was mere speculation. London mayor Ann Marie De Ciccio managed to have Pooler's organization — 2-4 the Show Productions — banned from the London Fairgrounds. He moved the show to nearby Woodstock the following year.

Although much of the leadership of the Quebec Hells Angels was behind bars, that didn't mean they couldn't strike. On March 10, 2002, after a bit of a high-speed chase on the 401, the OPP stopped a Pontiac Sunfire on the Upper Canada Road off-ramp (commonly called the Morrisburg exit by locals). Inside were two men. One was Marc Bouffard, a muscular 27-year-old member of the Rockers who specialized in witness and debtor intimidation. With him was Daniel Lamer, a 37-year-old career criminal who once shared a jail cell with a full-patch Nomad. He was well known from a robbery and 16-hour hostage taking at a Jean Coutu pharmacy in Montreal in 1991. One of his hostages was a police officer whom he shot and wounded in a desperate attempt to escape. He was on parole for a different crime at the time when the OPP stopped him with Bouffard.

When the OPP officer approached the car, Bouffard rolled his window down. The police officer asked for his license and proof of insurance. Bouffard told him that neither he nor Lamer spoke English well enough to continue the conversation. The cop told them to stay put and went back to his cruiser to call a bilingual officer to the scene.

When two more OPP officers arrived, they approached the Sunfire with the original cop. When the bilingual officer — Constable Dan Brisson — began talking to Bouffard, he realized who he was affiliated with, and he asked both men to exit the car. As Bouffard was being seated in the back of the OPP cruiser by two of the officers, Lamer began to get out of the Sunfire to confront Brisson. He was complaining about what he considered unnecessarily harsh treatment by the cops. As Brisson approached him, Lamer pulled out two handguns and threatened him.

When Lamer saw the cops pull out their weapons, he fired at Brisson. The slug hit the cop in the left side of the chest, ricocheted off his bulletproof vest, took a chunk out of his left ear and left a gash in the back of his head. The other officers shot at Lamer. He was also wearing a bulletproof vest, but one of the five bullets fired by the police pierced his head, just above his eyebrows. He later died from the wounds inflicted by that shell.

Besides Lamer's two handguns and bulletproof vest, a subsequent search of the car uncovered two more handguns, a silencer, a pair of balaclavas. Also in the car were pictures of Rock Machine national president Alain Brunette, his customized truck and pictures of every member of the Rock Machine's fledgling Ontario West Chapter, also based in London. Hells Angels and the Rock Machine may have been officially at peace, but it looked very much like Lamer and Bouffard were not coming to Ontario to take in the sights.

In July 2002, John Coates took a call from George "Bo-Boy" Beaulieu, president of the notorious Sherbrooke Chapter that had sponsored London in the first place and still supplied them with drugs. He told Coates to come to a meeting in Toronto with him and some important Ontario guys.

At the meeting, the new power elite of Hells Angels in Canada — North Toronto president Billy Miller and Niagara president Gerald "Skinny" Ward — told Coates and Beaulieu that they couldn't tolerate a Quebec-style war in Ontario. They noted that, in about a year of existence, the London Chapter had made headlines after three of their men (including a full-patch, the president's brother) went to jail for extortion, had lost a very public shoot-out with the Outlaws on city streets, had nearly gotten criminal organization convictions pressed against the club and they had united the Outlaws and Bandidos as a large and viable international force against them.

They told Beaulieu that it was a different time and place, and they wanted to avoid a war like the one he had been part of in Quebec. There was plenty of money for everyone in Ontario and unless they riled the Outlaws and Bandidos into action, they would eventually fade into the background or become Hells Angels as their old guard retired or died off. Miller and Ward didn't exactly say it in so many words, but they were expressing a Stadnick philosophy as opposed to a Boucher one.

Beaulieu said he understood. So did Coates. But they weren't finished with him yet. They told him that they liked him and that he had a bright future ahead of him, but that he was not ready to be a chapter president. They stripped him of his title of London president and relocated him to Ward's Niagara Chapter as a full-patch member.

But the Outlaws and Bandidos didn't know that. Neither did the media, or the politicians or all but a few cops. To all of those people, it looked like the province was a powder keg about to explode, with the events in London acting as the spark.

Chapter 10

Project Retire Clubs the Outlaws

A couple of the cops started laughing. It might seem incongruous now because most of them were on the biggest raid of their lives. But they had been awake since 2:30 in the morning and they were all very keyed up. It was about 6:00 (the sun wasn't up yet) on the morning of September 25, 2002, and about two dozen cops from a few different forces were about to knock down the door to 420 Egerton Avenue, a nondescript two-story home in London. Most of them were on the big veranda, one of them leaning against the white, metal door that led to the upstairs apartment.

There was a huge rottweiler bellowing threateningly in the backyard. And that's what started the laughter. There were two stickers on the door they were about to break down to get into the main floor. One of them said "Never mind the dog, beware the owner," and the other said "Next time, bring a warrant." Punchiness aside, the policemen were laughing because they weren't scared of the dog, and they actually did have a warrant.

A block to the north, another 20 cops were breaking down the door of 434 Egerton Avenue, the much bigger, nicer, field-stone home of London Outlaws president Thomas Hughes. But Hughes wasn't there. He was in jail awaiting trial on four counts of attempted murder for the shoot-out that had taken place right in front of the house.

Hughes' house was the second of three Outlaws-associated buildings that dominated Egerton Avenue at the time. The building next door (and across an alley) from 434 was 440 Egerton Avenue, the clubhouse of the London Outlaws. Other than a solid metal door and grates over the windows, it wasn't really fortified. That was a relief to the cops breaking into it.

A neighbor who didn't want to be identified described what happened next to the local paper: "There was a lot of banging and hollering by the police." And that's pretty much what happened as the huge team of officers broke into the three unoccupied buildings and removed everything they thought constituted evidence.

At the same time, about two hours up the 401 after you turn onto the 403 at Woodstock, the same thing was happening in Hamilton. Well, not exactly the same. The cops in Hamilton weren't after evidence, they were after suspects.

Although it took place more than seven years ago, a woman I spoke with while researching remembered it like it was yesterday. She doesn't want me to use her name either, so let's call her Stella. She remembers being woken up by the noise. She heard cars stopping, their doors slamming and people talking. She looked at the clock. 5:58. It was still an hour and a half before she had to wake up and get the kids ready for school. Stella rolled over and tried hard to get in some more sleep. But she'd hardly settled back into bed when she heard a concussive bang. She leapt from bed, put on her robe and headed to the front door. When she swung it open, she saw that Carrick Avenue was loaded with cop cars. And not just Hamilton cops, but OPP as well.

As soon as she saw what was going on, Stella was relieved. It wasn't an accident or a murder or anything; she knew exactly who they were after. Mario Parente lived at the end of the block. She, like everyone else in the neighborhood knew who Parente was. "He was a biker, you know, a big-time biker," she told me. "He wasn't with the Hells Angels, though; it was some other gang, I forget what they were called."

But while the Outlaws may not have had much resonance in their neighborhood, Parente certainly did. Stella, like pretty well everyone else in the area, knew him by sight. "He was a great guy," she said. "Really nice — I mean, we all knew he was this important biker — but he was never anything other than polite and pleasant as far as I knew."

She was right when she looked out her front door and decided the cops were just collecting Parente. About two dozen cops had showed up just before sunrise to arrest him.

There were similar scenes all over Ontario as more than 500 police officers from 13 forces including the RCMP and OPP descended upon Outlaws and their associates in 13 cities. Most of them came in the "meth alley" between Windsor and London. In all, 56 people were arrested including 35 Outlaws, four former members, 10 associates and three members of the Black Pistons.

The Black Pistons are what law enforcement call a "puppet gang" and many bikers call a "support club." In theory, a puppet gang is a smaller biker gang that does the bidding of the bigger gang — as the Rockers served Hells Angels in Montreal and the Jackals served Hells Angels in London. It's a good system; and the Outlaws strove to copy it, establishing Black Pistons chapters throughout the province. But, in general, the Black Pistons were a far cry from the polished, organized Rockers or even the ambitious and ready-to-go Jackals. Not many of them had motorcycles and most of them were nothing more than small-time hoods. "They were a bunch of pretenders and wannabes," said a cop who knew them. "They never really put anything together."

Besides Parente and Hughes, Project Retire — as the cops called the mass raid — netted a number of big-time players. In faraway Kingston, a city best known for its prisons, they grabbed former London president Andrew Simmons for attempted murder and obstructing justice. Also caught was Marcus Cornelisse, wanted on four counts of attempted murder from the same Egerton Avenue gunfight that had put Hughes behind bars. Thomas Harmsworth, who gained notoriety in 1991 when he refused to tell emergency room doctors or police who had put four bullets in his gut, and his son Jamie Harmsworth, who was grabbed for carrying a restricted weapon in his vehicle, were also swept up. There wasn't a prominent Outlaw free to walk the streets in Ontario.

The hammer fell at a very vulnerable time for the Outlaws. Not only had Hells Angels invaded in huge numbers, but they had taken (or scared off) some of the Outlaws' best talent. Making matters worse, just weeks before Project Retire, on August 12, 2002, William "Wild Bill" Hulko, president of the Outlaws Ottawa Chapter, was found dead in his cell in Quinte Detention Centre by guards. He was awaiting trial on sexual assault charges. Despite the fact that he was just 59 years old, Corrections Canada determined that he died of natural causes after finding no signs of foul play.

Besides the 56 people arrested, the cops involved in Project Retire took in quite a haul. On the first day, the OPP reported that they had confiscated five stolen motorcycles and one stolen pickup truck, a huge selection of firearms including an AK-47 assault rifle and a Mac-10 submachine gun (although they and countless newspaper reporters and copy editors working from their press release misspelled it "Mack-10") and $1.6 million worth of cocaine, methamphetamine, ecstasy and prescription drugs. The following day, they added the Outlaws' clubhouses in Windsor, London, Toronto, St. Catharines and Sault Ste. Marie along with Hughes' residence at 434 Egerton to the booty. Their warrants also yielded 32 motorcycles, three trucks and a trailer, as well as $156,500 worth of cocaine, ecstasy, hashish, heroin, marijuana and Percocet, $29,000 in cash and what they described as "11 long guns (of various caliber, some loaded), one sawed-off rifle, ammunition, blasting caps, gas masks, [a] sword, body armor, knives, nunchukus and gun magazines." Clearly, at least some of the Outlaws were up to no good.

Many of those arrested were charged with the still-untested law that could penalize those associated with what the courts defined as a criminal organization. This, the police pointed out, would make getting warrants and making arrests a far less cumbersome process. "It does make it easier, and we're starting to see the results of that now," said Tony McGowan, Deputy Chief of the London police. "It allows us to more aggressively target and arrest and prosecute them."

Target and arrest perhaps, but not everyone was sold on the idea that anti-criminal organization laws would be beneficial to law enforcement when it came to court. "This is going to attract national attention, and be of national importance because there is hardly any case law on these things," said Syd Usprich, a law professor at the London-based University of Western Ontario. "The stakes are a lot higher under these new offenses than they would have been if you had done exactly the same stuff before the new offenses existed." He also added that constitutional challenges and other legal entanglements were inevitable.

The police involved were uncharacteristically vocal about their success that day. Don Bell, head of the OPP-led joint-forces Biker Enforcement Unit (BEU), was particularly prominent in the press, telling reporters: "We've been able to seize their clubhouses; we've been able to hit them where it hurts." He told them that his crew had been working with Ontario Justice Minister Robert Runciman for three years on Project Retire, the plan to literally put the Outlaws out of business.

Bell also took a moment to dis the Outlaws. "These guys are street punks," he told reporters. "They are involved in an array of criminality."

At that, the reporters began to ask about Hells Angels. Although the Outlaws — and Satan's Choice before them — had dominated the outlaw biker world in London and the surrounding area for decades, the press really wanted to know about Hells Angels. The more informed ones among them knew that Hells Angels dominated organized crime in most of the country, but were just getting established in Ontario. They knew that Hells Angels had fought bloody wars not just with the Rock Machine in Quebec, but also the Outlaws. And they knew that there had been an escalation in biker violence in their own area in the last two years, especially since national president Walter Stadnick had established a toehold for Hells Angels in Ontario. The media wanted to know why the police had targeted just the Outlaws, and not Hells Angels as well.

"The Outlaws were chosen based on priority and opportunity," Bell responded, pointing out that when Project Retire was instigated in June 1999, Hells Angels had not established any official presence in the province yet. "Certainly we were aware of the Hells Angels, but they were not part of Ontario's landscape."

Then he issued them something of an ambiguous warning. "We've got lots of officers," he said. "This [Project Retire] may not be the only thing we're up to." When pressed, he stayed oblique. "Everybody has their day," he said. "Who's to say the Outlaws are our only target?"

McGowan was a little more forceful and specific. "I don't know if the Hells Angels will be celebrating in regards to their rivals, the Outlaws, because they know they're next," he said.

But that wasn't how the bikers saw it. One London-area Hells Angels associate who didn't want his name used said: "The Hells Angels are ecstatic; this couldn't happen to a better bunch." He also pointed out that things might not be so nice for the Outlaws behind bars, as the Hells Angels generally hold sway in Canadian jails and prisons. "The Hells Angels are going to welcome their brothers in arms," he joked. "And the Outlaws won't have the Bandidos to back them up," a reference to the Bandidos show of solidarity earlier that year at Larry Pooler's motorcycle show.

By 2002, Bandidos had already eclipsed the Outlaws as the world's second largest and most powerful outlaw motorcycle gang. Based in Texas, Bandidos dominated the American Southwest and had made significant inroads in Europe. In fact, they had battled Hells Angels there — sometimes winning, sometimes losing and sometimes coming to a standoff. And, because they shared a common enemy, Bandidos and the Outlaws had a strong international working alliance.

But they were never very strong in Canada, and by the time of Project Retire, they were just limping by. It all started after the Rock Machine had been beaten in Quebec. They sought an alliance with Bandidos, but the American Bandidos weren't really interested. Instead they allowed the Scandinavian Bandidos to sponsor a patch-over in Canada and, in January 2001, what remained of the Rock Machine became Bandidos.

But a joint police task force led by the Sûreté du Québec had been targeting the Rock Machine for a while, and struck in June 2002 after they had become Bandidos. More than 60 arrests were made. Since almost all of the evidence came from the Rock Machine days, most of the arrests came in Quebec (in fact, every single one of Quebec's Bandidos was put behind bars). Although a number of arrests were made in Ontario, there were still at least a dozen members at large. None of them had come from the Rock Machine, and none were considered big-time players.

Faced with the Hells Angels' prospects in an Ontario that was now devoid of Outlaws and had no real Bandidos' presence, Bell admitted: "Certainly, things are going to be more open for them [Hells Angels] than in the past."

To counter the idea that the cops were making things easy for the Hells Angels, Bell also pointed out that area police had arrested a number of other bikers that year, including some Hells Angels.

In truth, it was one Hells Angel, but it was one of London's most well-known bikers since the Coates brothers had moved on. Marty Zager had worked as a bouncer at the Beef Baron, but left when it started to become an Outlaws place. He didn't like the Outlaws. But he and his wife became very successful in other businesses.

Zager owned Hardcore Tattoos & Piercing (with locations in London and the nearby resort town of Port Stanley) and, allegedly, a number of rub 'n' tug parlors in the London area. A low-level form of prostitution that begins with a massage, rub 'n' tug parlors are targeted at truck drivers and office workers, both of which London has in abundance.

It was those successful businesses, sources say, that caught the eyes of the Hells Angels. Zager quickly became a member. And he was a very visible one, wearing his colors every chance he got, even at events where he knew Outlaws and/or Bandidos would be present.

Although he was a valuable member, Zager's absence didn't do much to hurt Hells Angels in Ontario. They were solidly at the top of the food chain. The Mafia was all but extinct, most of the other biker gangs had been absorbed or sidelined. The Rock Machine-turned-Bandidos were few in number and not very well organized. If there was any organization that could prevent the Hells Angels hegemony, it had been the Outlaws. And now, thanks to Project Retire, they were all gone.

"Once we had it all wrapped up, a bunch of us were sitting around and the subject came up that without the Bandidos and the Outlaws, there wasn't much to keep the Hells Angels from taking over," a cop who was involved told me. "Everybody just kind of said 'yeah.'"

Chapter 11

Victory for Mario "The Wop" Parente

Elizabeth Maguire was in a familiar place, but in an unfamiliar position. The well-known and highly successful Crown attorney was in a building she felt comfortable in — the London courthouse — but she didn't look comfortable at all. She looked shaken and about to cry. She was being questioned about potential wrongdoing, or at least incompetence, in one of the most important biker trials in Canadian history.

It had started almost seven years earlier, in 2002 when Project Retire arrested all of the Outlaws in Ontario. Most of them made deals right away and were back on the streets, but with so many court-appointed restrictions that they could not operate as a viable organization. But 10 of them, including national president Mario "The Wop" Parente, remained on trial.

At a preliminary inquiry, Justice John Getliffe saw Maguire in a courthouse hallway and asked her to speak with him in his chambers. Once inside, the pair had a conversation that led Maguire to believe that Getliffe had already made up his mind to convict the Outlaws. A few days later, they had another private conversation that Maguire later said further convinced her that Getliffe meant to convict the Outlaws as a criminal organization.

Assuming she already had the case in the bag, Maguire decided against calling in a number of witnesses who had a great deal of evidence against the individuals and the organization. Her logic at the time was that exposing some of these witnesses to cross-examination, especially from Parente's legendarily sharp defense attorney Jack Pinkofsky, could lead to a mistrial or jeopardize Getliffe's ability to give the ruling she was sure they both wanted.

So it came as a tremendous shock when, on June 30, 2004, Getliffe discharged all criminal organization charges against the bikers. In his summation, he mentioned that what convinced him to drop the charge was the fact that Maguire failed to call enough witnesses.

Enraged, Maguire took the rare and fairly drastic step of preferring an indictment. In effect, she went over Getliffe's head to ask the Attorney General to reinstate the charges. A four-person panel (including Deputy Attorney General Murray Segal) considered the case and the evidence already presented. Citing the importance of the case and its likelihood to set an important precedent, they ruled that Getliffe was wrong. The charges were relayed upon the accused.

Years later, Parente told me that he was frequently offered deals under which all other charges would be dropped if he agreed to plead guilty to being a member of a criminal organization. He always refused. That didn't surprise anyone who knew Parente. He was true to his club and its members and made it known that he believed they should sink or swim together. His pride would not have let him be known in history as the man who sold out the Outlaws for a few dropped charges.

It was clearly important to prosecutors all over the country to get someone to admit they were members of a criminal organization. That fixation started during the Hells Angels-Rock Machine war in Quebec. Under a great deal of public pressure, the federal government passed Bill C-95 in 1997. It read, in part, "every one who ... participates in or substantially contributes to the activities of a criminal organization knowing that any or all of the members of the organization engage in or have, within the preceding five years, engaged in the commission of a series of indictable offences ... of which the maximum punishment is imprisonment for five years or more ... is guilty of an indictable offence and liable to imprisonment for a term not exceeding 14 years." So if the Crown could prove that, for example, Hells Angels are a criminal organization, then simply being a member of the club could make someone liable to 14 years behind bars. It would, essentially, outlaw the club.

But it hadn't really seen any real success. The Crown failed to win a single C-95 conviction in the Hells Angels' megatrials primarily because the individual bikers maintained that they were doing business independent of one another, despite the proven existence of the Nomads and their drug distribution organization, which they called The Table.

The next time it was invoked was against the Rock Machine's Peter Paradis, but he turned informant and the charge was dropped. It finally won convictions in 2001 when Philippe Côté, Mario Filion, Eric LeClerc and Simon Lambert were found guilty of operating a drug ring for the Rock Machine. But, by that time, the Rock Machine had ceased to exist, having been patched over by Bandidos.

It finally made some headway in September 2004, when two Hells Angels were found guilty of extorting a huge sum of money from a cocaine-addicted black-market satellite TV equipment dealer in Barrie. Steven "Tiger" Lindsay and Raymond Bonner showed up at the man's house in full colors and demanded $75,000. He refused and called police as soon as they left. They convinced the man to meet with them again in a nearby restaurant. He wore a wire.

According to court records: Lindsay wore boots with the words 'Hells Angels North Toronto' and the death head logo, a belt bearing the words 'Hells Angels' embroidered on it and a death head on its buckle, a T-shirt bearing the death head logo and the words 'Hells Angels Singen [a chapter in Germany],' and a necklace with a pendant of the Hells Angels death head logo and Bonner wore a jacket bearing the Hells Angels death head logo and the words 'Hells Angels East End' and a black T-shirt bearing two death heads and the words 'Hells Angels First Anniversary.' "

The police recorded Lindsay warning the victim that he would send people to his house, and that the money belonged to him and "five other guys that are fucking the same kind of motherfucker as I am."

Judge Michelle Fuerst found them not just guilty of extortion, but also of being members of a criminal organization. "Both Mr. Lindsay and Mr. Bonner went to [the victim's] house wearing jackets bearing the primary symbols of the HAMC [Hells Angels Motorcycle Club], the name 'Hells Angels' and the death head logo," she said in her ruling. "In so doing, they presented themselves not as individuals, but as members of a group with a reputation for violence and intimidation. They deliberately invoked their membership in the HAMC with the intent to inspire fear in their victim. They committed extortion with the intent to do so in association with a criminal organization, the HAMC to which they belonged."

But since Lindsay and Bonner both immediately appealed the ruling — and their appeal wouldn't be heard until 2009 — C-95 was still without precedent.

And Maguire — who had missed a similar opportunity at the 2001 extortion trial of Douglas Johnstone, Tom Walkinshaw and Jimmy Coates — wanted to be the first to bring down an entire biker gang. But while Maguire would get another chance to convince a judge that the Outlaws were indeed a criminal organization, her explanation of why she lost the preliminary inquiry, why she hadn't called on her legion of witnesses revealed something worth investigating. And in June 2005, Pinkofsky filed an abuse of process motion against her.

As a result, Maguire's boss — Senior Assistant Crown Attorney John Hanbidge — ordered her to explain exactly why she behaved the way she did in the preliminary inquiry. Her reaction was immediate and revealing. "Are you nuts?" she shouted. "You're giving my head to Jack on a platter!" It would come back to embarrass her.

At the abuse of power hearing, Justice Lynda Templeton ruled that it didn't matter what Getliffe said to her or whether he had gone back on a deal or not. Clearly she didn't like how he behaved. "For a presiding judge in an ongoing preliminary inquiry to have unnecessarily called the Crown into chambers, and to have proceeded to discuss the case to any extent at all in the absence of opposing counsel was, in my view, entirely inappropriate," she told Maguire. But Pinkofsky hadn't filed against Getliffe, he had filed against Maguire, and so it was incumbent upon her to answer any and all questions about backroom dealings and subsequent cover-ups. And Templeton made sure that Maguire knew that any sort of meeting she had with a judge at which the defense was not present and not even informed of later was not the kind of action that could be tolerated from a Crown attorney. "It is incomprehensible to me that ... Ms. Maguire did not disclose this meeting to defense counsel," she said. "Her obligation to do so was unequivocal; her failure to do so was a breach of duty." And when she heard what Maguire had said to Hanbidge when he asked her to come clean, Templeton said she was shocked that Maguire cared more about "her own status, sense of professionalism and protection from scrutiny" than she was about justice for the accused. She further went on to say that her behavior "sullied" the reputation of the entire Ontario legal system.

Maguire was dumped from the case. Parente, who considered her beneath contempt, was delighted. He still has outstanding suits against her that he can't talk about because they are still active. In her place, the Attorney General's office named Alex Smith — a capable and respected prosecutor but one who was taking over a very flawed and now heavily scrutinized case — to lead the Crown's argument.

Even outside the case things were not going well for the few remaining Outlaws in Ontario. The Black Pistons puppet gang had been reduced to 15 members in two chapters (Simcoe County and London) when their most senior member was arrested on November 10, 2006. Greg Brown — who lived in Ottawa and belonged to the Simcoe County Chapter three hours' drive away — was charged with eight offenses, including possession of a loaded firearm, possession of a weapon obtained by crime and unauthorized possession of a restricted firearm.

On the night of April 15, 2007, Marcus Cornelisse — who had done his time for the Egerton Avenue shoot-out after plea bargaining down to one count of aggravated assault and one of illegal firearms possession — was working at the Solid Gold, a London strip joint not affiliated with similar bars in Sudbury and Burlington that shared the same name. Shortly after 1 p.m., a pair of cops approached Cornelisse and started asking him a few questions. The big biker punched one of the cops in the face. Before they could act, he punched the other cop in the face, knocking him down. He took a moment to kick the prone officer in the head and back and then fled out the front door. The cops gave chase. One caught up to Cornelisse and grabbed him, but the Outlaw punched him again and broke free. He suddenly turned around and ran back into the Solid Gold. The cops followed him in, but lost him in the dark, cluttered bar and he slipped out a hidden exit. He was arrested the next day and, in yet another plea agreement, was sentenced to a year in prison. He was released after seven months.

Cornelisse was hardly the only Outlaw arrested in Project Retire to be back on the streets. Although 56 men were arrested on September 25, 2002, by the autumn of 2008 only three men remained accused. The trial had crawled through the courts as the Crown and the accused were continually wheeling and dealing with charges and potential punishments. It was also slowed down considerably by the Maguire incident. All of the others had made deals, and 16 of them — much to Parente's chagrin — admitted they were members of a criminal organization.

On October 18, 2008, the number of accused fell to two. William Mellow — a full-patch member of the London Chapter and a former national secretary-treasurer of the club — had been arrested in Project Retire and charged with a number of offenses. Police had searched his farm just outside Bolton and found a loaded 10-mm handgun and 50 rounds of ammunition in a bedroom. Handguns of that caliber are rare and extremely powerful. Also in his bedroom, the police uncovered some hash oil, steroids and a syringe. In his garage, they discovered an unloaded 12-gauge shotgun wrapped in a black plastic garbage bag. The shotgun's barrel had been sawed off. And in his Cadillac, they found $11,065 in cash.

After more than six years of severe bail restrictions, Mellow was ready to deal. He had his load of charges reduced to one simple count of possession of a handgun without a license. He was sentenced to a year's probation.

While that punishment seems remarkably lenient in light of what the cops had against Mellow, it also came down with a court order that he may not be in possession of a firearm or be in association or communication with any members of the Outlaws, Hells Angels, Bandidos or Black Pistons. Any violation would earn him a long prison stay.

And it was typical of the deals the other Outlaws arrested in Project Retire had made. In exchange for very light sentences, the guilty were subject to court orders prohiting them from keeping company with each other or any other bikers. Clearly, it was far more important to the Attorney General's office to break up the Outlaws as an organization than it was to put individual members out of commission. Take Cornelisse for example. He shot another biker in the abdomen with what appeared to be intent to kill and beat up two cops before escaping — and he spent just a few months behind bars and was forbidden to be a biker anymore.

Two Outlaws held out. One, to nobody's surprise, was Parente, and the other was also from Hamilton. His name was Luis Ferreira. A much younger man (33 to Parente's 60), nobody I spoke with considered Ferreira to be a big-time biker. "He was a local bad guy, a buddy of Parente's," recalled Hamilton biker cop Sergeant John Harris, who knew them both well. "He became an Outlaw, but was never a major guy. Nobody ever really knew what he did to deserve membership, but he was always a loyal guy."

The primary evidence against Parente came from a Sault Ste. Marie Outlaw who had turned informant. Parente told me that he did not know the man very well, that the man in question was made a member when Parente was in prison, so he had no opportunity to check him out, so he had little to do with him on purpose. But OPP investigator Len Isnor told me that the pair were in frequent contact and that he'd seen "at least three [cocaine] buys" occur between the two.

And on March 12, 2009 — just a few days less than six and a half years after the arrests — it was his turn to talk. But to everyone's surprise, he wasn't in court that morning. Instead, Alex Smith, the Crown prosecutor told the Justice Lynda Templeton that he was withdrawing all charges due to a lack of evidence. The informant, he said, had changed his mind; without him, the Crown had "no reasonable prospect of conviction."

Thinking quickly, Jack Pinkofsky, Parente's lawyer, asked Templeton to make it part of the public record that the informant declined to testify of his own free will, not because of any threat from Parente, Ferreira or anyone else. Templeton asked Smith if he had any objection to that. He said he didn't. Parente and Ferreira were free to go. Pinkofsky later said he had "a hunch" the trial would end that way.

I asked Parente why he thought the informant declined to testify. He told me that it was because the informant didn't actually have anything on him, he just wanted to get paid. When I asked Isnor the same question, he answered with a different opinion. "After six and a half years, he was tired, not as sure he could provide accurate evidence," he said. "I've got to hand it to Pinkofsky for dragging the trial on that long."

"Sometimes true justice takes that kind of course," Pinkofsky said. "Sometimes it takes a long time for justice to be done."

After he left the courtroom a free man, Parente stopped to talk with reporters. "I'm just glad everything is over after all this time," he said. "It's been a long, long road; and I never had any doubts that the matters were going to turn out the way they did."

It had indeed been a long, long road for him. Arrested in 2002, he was held in jail until Justice Getliffe dropped the criminal organization charges against all the accused. He was then released on $250,000 bail. Then when Maguire won her preferred indictment, he was thrown back in jail. When that was overturned and she was dismissed from the case, Parente was offered bail once again, only this time for $400,000. He was forced to find work immediately, had a strict sundown curfew and was required to check in with London police — even though he lived and worked on the other side of Hamilton, at least three hours' drive away — three times a week.

And it wasn't just him. Parente's girlfriend, Nadia Kosta, and a common friend, Silvana DiMartino, lost their security clearance at Toronto's Pearson International Airport where they both worked as passenger-information representatives. Without it, they were as good as fired. The reason, their superiors gave, was that they had put up surety for Parente. Kosta was shocked. She had put up surety for Parente once before in 1996, and had acquired her security clearance in 2001. Kosta was adamant in the media that she had made no secret about her relationship with Parente, and she felt that changing the rules on her now was petty and unnecessarily punitive.

An inquiry noted that Kosta had been in court with Parente and had been rude and combative with court officers. They also claimed DiMartino and her boyfriend were both good friends of Parente's and knew about his criminal record. They even brought up the fact that a deck of playing cards with a "Support Your Local Outlaws" logo on them was found in DiMartino's purse. Kosta said they were hers. The women later regained their right to work at the airport, but had been suspended without pay and were dragged through hours of inquiries and other proceedings.

In all, Parente spent about 30 months behind bars, had turned over hundreds of thousands of dollars of his own and his friends' money and had his life held hostage for 42 long months. Always jovial, he had taken to calling himself and Ferreira "the last men standing" and — in protest of his treatment by the legal system — refused to shave for the last six months of the trial. By the time he was freed, his beard flowed long, white — almost Santa Claus–like — down his chest. "I was prepared to sit in there forever if I had to," he said. "As far as we're concerned, we fought this to the bitter end; I was prepared to go on as long as I had to to prove otherwise."

He was free and he was, he said, proven right. He had managed to get off when so many other prominent bikers — Stadnick, Boucher, the Cazzettas, the Vachons and countless others — had gone down.

But unlike Stadnick and Boucher, he didn't have a club to go back to when he was finally free. When the entire organization was arrested in 2002, he told them to stay firm, to stick together and that they would all get out of it as a unit. Other than Ferreira, a small-timer, none of them did. In fact, more than a dozen of them pleaded guilty to being members of a criminal organization, a move that endangered the very existence of the club.

Particularly galling to Parente, members of law enforcement have told me, was the betrayal of the man they identified as his No. 2, Woodstock Chapter president Kevin Legere. He pleaded guilty in February 2005.

And, when Parente needed cash for bail, none of his so-called brothers came to his aid. "The club has never donated a nickel," he said. "So that's how much of a criminal organization this club in Canada is." He had to sell virtually everything that he owned that hadn't already been confiscated by police. When last I heard from him, he was still trying to get thousands of dollars' worth of property back from the government. They claim that it's theirs because he was a member of a criminal organization, even though he personally beat that charge. But they maintain that because others in the same organization pleaded guilty, his stuff is now theirs.

So he publicly quit the Outlaws. He gave a three-hour interview to reporter Peter Edwards explaining why. "I'm disgusted with everybody," Parente told him. "I wash my hands of them all." He later explained that by "everybody," he meant the legal system, law enforcement and his former fellow Outlaws.

He made it clear that he was shocked and still bitterly disappointed by the fact that the other Outlaws did not support his defense, which, he maintained, would have helped them all. "They were out partying and didn't donate a dime to help out," he said. "I [didn't] get a nickel of support from anybody to fight something that implicates everybody."

He acknowledged that some of the Canadian Outlaws were criminals, but that since they acted individually within the organization, it didn't make the Outlaws a criminal organization. "If someone was dealing coke, he wouldn't tell me about it, it wasn't my business," he told me at one of our meetings. Then he gave me an example of how the Outlaws worked. "One time a guy comes up to me and tells me he is selling a trailer full of chickens — didn't tell me where or how he got it, and I didn't ask. All I said to him was, 'What the hell am I going to do with a trailer full of chickens?'"

Had the Outlaws gone ahead with it, Parente's plan may well have worked. In fact, Hells Angels had used that very defense against similar anti-racketeering laws in the United States and won.

But it didn't happen, and Parente summed up his opinion of the Outlaws in his typical wry style: "With brothers like that, who needs enemies?"

Soon thereafter, Parente — through his friend Luther — approached me about writing his life story.

Many people have said that the charges being withdrawn against Parente were a huge victory for the bikers in Ontario. Isnor disagrees. "My job was not to put Mario Parente behind bars," he told me. "It was to put the Outlaws out of business in Ontario."

And he certainly did manage that.

Chapter 12
Trouble on the Horizon

With all the Outlaws behind bars, it looked like Hells Angels controlled organized crime in all of Canada. After all, the Walter Stadnick–led expansion had established chapters from Nanaimo on Vancouver Island to Halifax, more than 3,500 miles away. And he and his gang had finally invaded Ontario where the last holdouts had held sway. His patch-over of hundreds of bikers on December 29, 2000 was just the beginning. With all of the Outlaws behind bars because of Project Retire and the Mafia in complete disarray, Hells Angels were virtually unopposed in Ontario, unless of course you include law enforcement.

But there were some remaining pockets of resistance: the holdouts, rejects and odds and ends Hells Angels couldn't account for. Most of them, after Project Retire, were located in the South-western part of Ontario.

One very important one was in Windsor. Just a mile south of Detroit, Windsor is almost as tied to the auto industry as the Motor City. These days, of course, that's bad news, but in the 1960s and 1970s, it meant jobs for everyone. It attracted all kinds of people, including a Calabrian family called the Muscederes.

Every day, on their way to and from elementary school, Giovanni Muscedere and his little brother Joe were bullied.

Their family had recently emigrated from Italy to Windsor and the boys still didn't speak English all that well. Some of the area's other boys thought the Muscederes' attempts at communicating in their new language was comical, so they teased them. After a while, the teasing became verbal abuse, and that evolved into physical assaults.

After being beaten up a couple of times, Giovanni Muscedere vowed to his little brother that he would never lose a fight again, no matter how big or how many his enemies were. He learned to box, he worked out. He grew big, strong and fearless. He stopped calling himself Giovanni, and switched to John. John Muscedere turned the tables on his bullies and then became something of a bully himself.

Years later, Muscedere lived in Chatham — about an hour's drive east on the 401 from Windsor, halfway to London — and had a steady job as a forklift operator at the Rockwell International (later renamed ArvinMeritor) brake plant in Tilbury, about half-way between Chatham and London. He was a jolly guy who made friends easily and liked to party. He also taught kids how to box, earning him the nickname "Boxer" among his friends.

Giovanni Muscedere

He was also a biker. Muscedere originally ran with a low-level gang called the Annihilators. Based in a lonely little shack in a hamlet called Electric about 20 minutes northwest of Chatham and not far from Sarnia, the Annihilators were big-time partiers and small-time crooks. Muscedere himself had gotten into some trouble with break-and-enter charges and the odd assault.

But his rap sheet paled in comparison to his old friend and Annihilators president — Wayne "Weiner" Kellestine. Although he was first arrested many years earlier, Kellestine began to enter law enforcement's collective consciousness in a serious way in 1982. At the trial of another man, a witness testified that it was common knowledge that Kellestine had murdered a man named John DeFilippo and wounded his father-in-law Vito Fortunato in a Woodbridge home invasion back in 1978. Police investigated, but couldn't muster enough evidence to bring charges against Kellestine.

A couple of years later, Kellestine was charged with assault after he punched a bouncer who was trying to eject one of his friends from a London bar. He paid a $700 fine. Months later, police found $325,000 worth of cocaine and LSD and a semiautomatic handgun on Kellestine's farm in Iona Station, a village not far from London. But again, they couldn't build enough of a case to lay any serious charges.

Wayne "Weiner" Kellestine

Kellestine kept out of serious trouble until December 1991. On a cold morning, a black SUV screeched to a halt in front of the emergency admitting entrance to the Elgin General Hospital in St. Thomas. A rear door opened and a body wrapped in a blanket was thrown out of the vehicle. EMTs rushed the man inside and hours of surgery saved his life as surgeons took four bullets out of his gut.

The man was 34-year-old Thomas Harmsworth. He was a full-patch Outlaw who came from Iona Station, the same 300-resident hamlet just west of St. Thomas that had produced one of the 20th century's greatest minds — economist John Kenneth Galbraith — and, more dubiously, Wayne Kellestine.

Once he was conscious, police questioned Harmsworth. But he refused to speak. If he knew who shot him, he wasn't saying. The cops proceeded to investigate without his cooperation, but quickly abandoned the case in January 1992.

The official reason was a lack of evidence — which was completely plausible since Harmsworth wouldn't talk — but others in the area had a very different opinion. A couple of sources I spoke with said that the cops knew Kellestine was behind the shooting, but they made a sweetheart deal with him.

Just two days before they officially dropped the Harmsworth case, police announced they had found the body of David McNeil in a shallow makeshift grave on a lonely country road just outside another nearby village named Dutton. His corpse had three holes in the back of its skull, the result of three .38-caliber bullets fired at extremely short range.

McNeil had been wanted for the September 19, 1991 murder of an Ingersoll police officer named Scott Rossiter. While nobody has come out — even off the record — to tell me that Kellestine killed McNeil, the consensus among the cognoscenti in Southwestern Ontario is that Kellestine at least knew of McNeil's death and led the cops to his body in exchange for a quick end to the Harmsworth investigation.

Two months after the McNeil incident, local police forces and the Ontario Provincial Police (OPP) mounted Project Bandito (this was long before the Texas-based Bandidos had any presence in the country, so the name is just a coincidence), in which more than 100 officers raided the clubhouses of the Outlaws and Annihilators, along with the residences of many of their members, prospects and associates.

Kellestine was caught red-handed. When police broke into his house, he was passed out on his living room couch, surrounded by drugs, cash and weapons. And there was an unregistered, semiautomatic handgun within his arm's reach.

Faced with mountains of evidence — including videotape of him selling cocaine, ecstasy and a handgun to an undercover cop — Kellestine pleaded guilty. He was given six years.

It is a custom in the Canadian correctional system to release prisoners after two-thirds of their sentence unless there are some extenuating circumstances. The parole board twice denied Kellestine's bids to leave prison before his six years were up, citing his continued association with "known and active criminals" and for failing mandatory drug tests while in custody.

Things shifted in the Ontario outlaw biker environment while Kellestine was in prison. Changes in Toronto reverberated through the rest of the province, and the southwestern corner was no different.

After the Loners won the great Toronto biker war of 1995 against the Diablos, they split into two distinct pieces. One was absorbed by the Hells Angels–aligned Para-Dice Riders, while the other stayed nominally independent.

Kellestine — eager to be on the side against Hells Angels but reluctant to align directly with the Outlaws — accepted the Loners' offer of a patch-over. The Annihilators ceased to exist. Although police and the media generally refer to this new chapter as the St. Thomas or London Loners — perhaps because most of the members lived in or around the city — they always identified themselves as being the Chatham Chapter. Soon thereafter, the Loners established another, smaller chapter based in Amherstburg — a small town just south of Windsor.

Things got complicated after that. The London Outlaws fought a small and largely indecisive war with Coates' Hells Angels. Two Hells Angels operatives had tried and failed to assassinate Kellestine, probably in an effort to bring them into the war as well.

The Rock Machine — supported by the Texas-based Bandidos — set up three chapters in Canada. Then on December 29, 1999, Stadnick pulled off his massive Ontario patch-over, in which all kinds of bikers — the Para-Dice Riders, the Vagabonds, Satan's Choice, Iron Hawgs and others, even a few Outlaws — became Hells Angels. Many observers in the media and law enforcement were aghast. "They were truly scraping the bottom of the barrel," one cop I know told me. "They were trading patch-for-patch the legendary Hells Angels patch for some of the lowest of the low."

But still, the remaining Loners who had not joined the Para-Dice Riders were among the few gangs in Ontario not offered Hells Angels patches. The Woodbridge Loners continued to survive as a nominally independent but, in practice, pro–Hells Angels club. The next time they made news was in January 2001, when the club attempted to keep its mascot — an 800-pound, neutered, declawed lion named Woody — on a farm north of the city in the face of widespread protests.

The Chatham Loners, however, were another story. Because of Kellestine, Hells Angels wanted no part of them. Instead, they, along with the Rock Machine chapters in Toronto and Kingston, became a prospective Bandidos chapter.

Like many motorcycle clubs, Bandidos were formed by a man who admired Hells Angels, but couldn't join them. Bandidos formed in 1966 in the Southeastern Texas town of San Leon when a longshoreman and former U.S. Marine named Donald Eugene Chambers met a fellow dockworker who had been with Hells Angels in upstate New York. Despite the number of ports there and the proximity to Mexico, there was virtually no Hells Angels' or Outlaws' presence on the Gulf Shore of Texas.

The gang took off very quickly. Bandidos took over the region, and expanded rapidly, attracting Vietnam veterans the same way Hells Angels and the Outlaws had veterans of World War II and the Korean War a generation or two earlier. It has frequently been reported in the media that Chambers, a Vietnam combat veteran, took the name and look from the Frito Bandito, a cartoon mascot the Frito-Lay company used to sell its corn chips, but that logo actually debuted in 1968, well after the club's formation.

By the time Stadnick conquered Ontario, Bandidos had eclipsed the Outlaws as the second most powerful biker gang in the world, behind only Hells Angels themselves. They had a few advantages. While Hells Angels have a strict whites-only rule (the Outlaws' views on this vary from chapter to chapter and country to country, but they are still overwhelmingly white), Bandidos readily welcomed some non-whites, and are very heavily Hispanic or even predominantly Muslim in some areas. And while Hells Angels do have many foreign chapters, Bandidos have been far more aggressive when it comes to recruiting overseas.

And it was actually from Sweden that the first Bandidos' presence came to Canada. In the late 1990s, when the Rock Machine was losing what had become a very one-sided war against the Hells Angels in Quebec, a high-ranking member of the Rock Machine named Fred Faucher asked the Swedish Bandidos for help.

He was impressed by what the Scandinavian Bandidos had accomplished in what the media called "The Great Nordic Biker War." In a battle waged from 1994 to 1997, Bandidos (along with a few Outlaws and smaller clubs) managed to fight Hells Angels and their allies to a stalemate. Although there were far fewer casualties — 12 deaths (including one innocent civilian) and 96 wounded — than in the Quebec Rock Machine-Hells Angels war, the conflict in Scandinavia made more headlines worldwide. That was probably because the war crossed international borders — Sweden, Denmark and even Finland were involved — and because the bikers (many of whom had ties with their countries' militaries and/or white supremacist groups) used machine guns and rocket-propelled grenades to settle their differences. It got so bad, in fact, that the Danish government actually passed a law forbidding biker gangs from buying or renting property as clubhouses. The law was later overturned as unconstitutional, but it lasted long enough to make a big difference. The Bandidos and Hells Angels even signed a truce in Denmark, live on national television.

The European Bandidos — especially in France, a place where Bandidos are quite strong — welcomed the Quebeckers with open arms. But things were different with their bosses down in Texas who had the final say on everything. At first the Texans weren't crazy about the idea of the Rock Machine. They knew little about Quebec, the war with the Hells Angels or the gang itself. But when some arrests and casualties led to Faucher becoming acting president of the Rock Machine by default, he invited Bandidos from around the world to a huge party in Quebec City, and things quickly changed. The Rock Machine may have ceased to exist, but it wasn't because of the Hells Angels. Instead of surrendering, Faucher and his men wanted to get stronger.

It happened, appropriately enough, in Woodbridge, a town best known for its Mafia connections. In recent years, it had been home to at least three separate incarnations of the Loners, the Diablos, Satan's Choice, the Para-Dice Riders, the Rock Machine, Hells Angels and, now, Bandidos. The Rock Machine negotiated with Bandidos, and the patch-over was official.

And on Saturday, January 6, 2001, a banquet hall in Kingston was the site of a huge party. At it, what remained of the Rock Machine in Ontario and Quebec patched over to Bandidos as a prospective chapter. While it was the Scandinavian Bandidos who sponsored the Canadians and were considered responsible for them, the Americans were ultimately in charge.

Soon the Canadian Bandidos went looking for other gangs to recruit. A group of American Bandidos — led by Oklahoman Edward Winterhalder, who had been assigned the task of patching over the Rock Machine and getting them up to speed in Bandidos' rules and philosophy — visited the Woodbridge Loners in February. Although he was very impressed by Pietro Barilla, their leader, Winterhalder didn't have much hope of patching them over. The Loners they met indicated they didn't hate Hells Angels — usually a prerequisite for Bandidos membership — and had, in fact, just kicked out a promising and prominent member for being "too anti–Hells Angels."

While the Woodbridge Loners didn't patch over to Bandidos, the others — including Kellestine's Chatham Chapter — did. It happened while Kellestine was in prison and Muscedere was acting in his place. Muscedere was made president (el presidente in Bandidos' parlance) of Ontario and vice-president of Canada, second in rank behind national president Alain Brunette (who had replaced the recently convicted Faucher).

Soon thereafter, in 2002, the combined forces of the Royal Canadian Mounted Police (RCMP), OPP and Sûreté du Québec (SQ) launched Project Amigo, which was originally aimed at eliminating the Rock Machine from Canada. Since the club's name had changed, but its membership by and large had not, it was now aimed at Bandidos. And they cops did a pretty good job, using evidence gathered during the Hells Angels-Rock Machine war, they arrested almost every single Bandido in the country. By Winterhalder's own admission:

> There were 65 [Canadian] Bandidos in prison or out on bond awaiting trial. There were another half-dozen who had gone underground to avoid arrest. Left on the street and not in trouble with the law were fewer than 15 Bandidos in Ontario — and none in Quebec!

Bandidos actually issued a media release that admitted that the club was dead in Quebec, but survived in Ontario and was planning to expand into Western Canada. Since the evidence was gathered against the original Rock Machine, the more recent patch-overs — including Muscedere's and Kellestine's former Loners — were not part of the raid.

Years later, in 2003, they found themselves as the only Bandidos chapter in Canada. After the arrests from Project Amigo left the Canadian club with barely more than a dozen members, all in three distant Ontario chapters, they were consolidated into one chapter based in Toronto. Muscedere was their president and, with Brunette behind bars for a long time, found himself as national president as well.

The few remaining Canadian Bandidos didn't have a club-house, but instead met in a run-down bar in Toronto's notorious Parkdale neighborhood. Few of them lived in Toronto, though, and many of them had long commutes to their meetings.

Faced with the prospect of having just one small, loose-knit chapter in the whole country, Bandidos went on a major recruiting drive. They established probationary chapters in Winnipeg and Edmonton — two cities that had been particularly receptive to Stadnick's Hells Angels sales pitch — with bikers who had become disillusioned with or passed over by the big guys.

The Edmonton experiment ended on January 30, 2004. Two men from the Rebels, the club charged with leading the Bandidos expansion into Edmonton, went for a night out on the town. Joey Morin and Robert Charles Simpson were just getting out of Morin's car when they were approached by some other men. Morin was somewhat famous in the city after he pulled three men from a blazing truck as a teenager in 1989. But because he avoided media coverage and award ceremonies — including the Governor General's Award for Bravery and the St. John's Ambulance Award of Merit — he was known throughout the city as the "Shy Hero."

But there was little heroic about what he was doing that night. He and Simpson were headed into Saint Pete's Mens Club, a large and popular strip joint in the northwest section of the city. Although owner Peter Bodenberger claimed his club had no affiliations with any particular gang, people in the area knew

it as a Rebels' hangout. Neither Morin nor Simpson were wearing colors when they arrived. Just as they slammed the doors of
Morin's car, the men who had approached pulled their guns and
started firing.

The police never said how many shots were fired (or even how
many shooters there were), but there was enough hot lead in the
air to nearly sever Morin's arm. The police did admit that both
men had been shot in "nearly every part of their bodies."

Simpson died at the scene. Morin was rushed to Royal
Alexandra Hospital where he lingered a few hours and died in the
arms of his mother, Sharon Trottier.

Although some Ontario Bandidos attended the funerals, what
was left of the Rebels — who had gained a great deal of notoriety
in 1991 when a member named Daniel R. "Coyote" Wolf wrote
a PhD thesis about life in the club that was later published as a
book — renounced their Bandidos membership, and threw their
lot in with Hells Angels.

• • •

It was during this period — just after Project Amigo and the de-
mise of the club's hopes in Edmonton — that Kellestine got out
of prison. He went in a Loners chapter president and came out a
Bandido. The bosses in Texas made it clear that they did not want
Kellestine in charge, so Muscedere did not step down for him to
return as president when he was released in August 2004. Instead
he offered him the position of sargento de armas (sergeant-at-arms).
Kellestine accepted, but was well known to be angry at the fact that
he was now taking orders from his old flunky.

The Bandidos gained some traction in Winnipeg, a city with
a long tradition of rival biker gangs and strong-willed factions.
Their recruiting took off when a small, anti–Hells Angels gang
signed on. They had been called Los Montoneros. Police recognized them as a Bandidos puppet gang when some were arrested
and on their crest was the acronym SYLB — "Support Your Local
Bandidos." They also had a yellow-on-red patch, the reverse of
the Bandidos red on yellow. It's commonplace for puppet gangs
to wear the reverse of their parent club's colors, such as the Black

Pistons' black-on-white patch which indicates their relationship with the Outlaws, who wear white on black.

The media often reports that the name Los Montoneros means "the Wolf Pack" (and the Montoneros may well have believed that themselves), but it actually has a more complex meaning. In Spanish, the suffix "-ero" means someone who does something, like a profession, much like the English "-er." And "monton," depending on where you are in Latin America, can mean to pile or stack or it can simply mean a lot of something. The name Montoneros originally came into use in the 1960s when the left-wing Argentine guerrilla group Movimentos Peronista Montoneros fought against that country's right-wing dictatorship. Basically, it means "the workers" or "the masses."

Before long, Los Montoneros started wearing a new patch, the familiar "fat Mexican" of Bandidos. And under the logo was a rocker that read "probationary."

Their leader, Michael "Taz" Sandham, was a big tough guy who had been an auxiliary police officer in Ste. Anne, Manitoba, and a full constable in East St. Paul, Manitoba. Both of those communities are small and relatively afflu-ent suburbs of Winnipeg. He worked very, very hard to keep his law enforce-ment past a secret from his fellow bikers.

Sandham had spent a lot of time communicating with the Toronto Chapter, eventually coming to a

Michael "Taz" Sandham

party on Kellestine's farm. His aim, he told the guys back home, was to get Winnipeg elevated from a probationary chapter to a full chapter (or at least to get a timetable on when they could expect that to happen). But he went home disappointed. Muscedere had little to say on the matter, and Kellestine kept telling him that they just didn't know enough about him or his guys to move forward.

There are lots of different opinions and even a few fabrications about what happened next. But what we do know is that, by early 2006, the Canadian Bandidos were a gang very much divided.

In December 2005, the Bandidos leadership in Texas officially revoked the membership of the only remaining official Canadian chapter. Most sources said that the Americans felt that the Canadians were not pulling their weight financially, and others indicated that the Americans were unnerved by how sloppily the Canadians went about their business, believing they were flagrantly courting prosecution.

While those concerns may have been valid, the Bandidos' Texas leadership's major complaint was that the Canadians wouldn't communicate with them, a matter made worse by the fact that none of the American Bandidos with any authority to check up on them could cross the border because of felony convictions and/or outstanding warrants. Bill "Bandido Bill" Sartelle, the Houston-based national secretary boss, wrote an e-mail to every Bandido chapter in the world indicating the Texans' official position:

> To whom it may concern: For the past year or more, we, BMC USA, have attempted to make communications with Canada. We have directed face to face visits from whoever is in charge up there. Up till now there has been no visit from the proper person. It has been decided that due to a lack of participation, Canada's Charter is being pulled. Effective immediately: Return all Bandido patches and property to the following address [Sartelle's home in Friendwood, Texas]. In approximately 30 days we will make notification to all that we no longer have a Chapter in Canada and that any person wearing our Patch, in Canada, is not sanctioned. Bill 1%er

The Toronto/Canada president, Muscedere, responded by sending increasingly pleading e-mails back to Texas in an attempt to get them to reconsider. He wrote to Sartelle:

> ... there is no reason too take something the canadian brothers value more than there own lives when a brother is down

you reach out your hand too help him up not kick them I feel like a knife has been driven in my heart would you beleave it my own brother has done what my enemys could never do without my death ...

That rubbed the Texans the wrong way; they clearly wanted a less philosophical and more practical discussion. "You can't come here, we can't come there, but you do not want to answer any questions," Sartelle wrote. "There are issues that need to be resolved. I have made attempts to get these answers, but have not gotten fuck all."

Sandham had a different, and very telling response. He wrote to Sartelle: "I am just hearing about this problem with Toronto. I hope this does not reflect on us [the probationary chapter in Winnipeg] ... Also, Bandido Wayne 'W' would like someone their to call him. He is in London, Ontario [Kellestine's home phone number]."

When Muscedere's e-mail exchanges with the Texans failed to move anything forward, another Toronto Bandido named George "Crash" Kriarakis tried his hand at convincing the Americans to reverse their decision and let them stay in the club. He wrote on international guestbooks and forums that "Ontario is standing tall," indicating they were refusing the Texans' orders to give up their patches.

When Sartelle repeated his demands, Kriarakis confronted him directly. "Give us a fair and reasonable chance," he implored, then changed tack and insulted Sartelle, calling him "a peace of work."

Sartelle, clearly a more careful speller but still not a consummate grammarian, wrote back: "Yes, I am a piece of work, and proud of who I am." His demand stood.

When attempts to negotiate with the Texans failed,

George "Crash" Kriarakis

Muscedere wrote begging messages on the guestbooks of Bandidos' sites around the world, appealing to them to stand up for the Toronto Chapter, which Muscedere claimed was being treated unfairly. Nobody — not even their Scandinavian sponsors — came to their aid, or if they did they were quiet about it and not very successful.

Finally, Muscedere sent the following e-mail to every Bandidos chapter in the world:

> We ask that our Brothers make there voice heard from all over the world and stand tall with us in support of us as we have all our brothers. We would like a worldwide vote from all our brothers from around the world before we return our Bandidos property.

The highest-ranking member of Bandidos, el presidente Jeff Pike from the Houston Chapter, had the final word on the matter when he sent an e-mail to Muscedere that told him: "Bandidos don't vote, they do what the fuck they're told."

Although they kept their Bandidos patches, the Toronto Chapter (many of whom, like Muscedere, actually lived in Southwestern Ontario and commuted to the club meetings) renamed themselves the No Surrender Crew, a name borrowed from a particularly violent faction of the Irish Republican Army. The Toronto version of "No Surrender" referred to the fact that these Bandidos wouldn't give up their patches without a fight.

Kellestine was a different story — as he always seemed to be. With some excessive drug use and bad business ideas, he had gone into severe debt, and one of his biggest creditors was the club itself. He had also forged a bitter divide between himself and the rest of the club by complaining bitterly of their lack of desire to make money and because they always called him late for meetings, not taking into account how far away he lived. And he had made some new friends outside the club. The crystal meth trade was flourishing and growing in Southwestern Ontario, and Kellestine had acquired several close associates in the business of manufacturing and retailing the drug. They assured him it was easy money, exactly what he needed to get out of his money troubles. Still, Muscedere and the bulk of the Toronto Chapter did not want to get involved with Kellestine's new friends or their business. It was, they decided, just too dangerous.

But some others did want to get involved. Kellestine had reached out to Winnipeg's prospective Bandidos, who lived in a place where meth had been very popular for a much longer time. The members of the probationary chapter there had grown very impatient with Muscedere, whose incompetence and poor relationship with the Texans they felt was the real reason they had been prevented from getting recognized as an independent full-patch Bandidos chapter.

At the start of April 2006, it all came to a head. The Americans had ordered Muscedere and his men to relinquish their patches more than five months earlier. But the No Surrender Crew were determined to stay on as Bandidos anyway, and wanted to do it without Kellestine and his meth. Kellestine wanted to make money selling meth and, if possible, remain a Bandido. Winnipeg wanted to be Bandidos making money selling meth and saw Muscedere and his crew standing in the way.

The Americans had given Kellestine the task of collecting his chapter's patches and returning them to Texas in March 2006. The job was too big for him, and he knew it. So he stalled. But when four representatives of the Winnipeg prospective chapter arrived unannounced at his Iona Station farm to ask him why he hadn't stripped his brothers of their patches (strongly intimating that they'd pull his own patch unless he acted quickly), he knew he had to do something.

The Winnipeggers were tough guys, sent on purpose to intimidate Kellestine. The tacit message was that if he didn't take care of it, they would do it themselves and they would take care of him, too.

Besides being a former cop and martial arts instructor, Sandham had been in the Canadian military, had undergone special-weapons training and had been known to associate with members of the Winnipeg Outlaws. He was easily the most important member of the prospective chapter and president-in-waiting should Winnipeg ever become a full-patch chapter. But the members of his gang were pressing him to do something about Toronto, and he, too, was in danger of losing his status among them unless he acted.

Sandham was actually with Kellestine at a March 2006 meeting with the American Bandidos at the Peace Arch Park on the British Columbia-Washington state border when the original orders to pull Toronto's patches came down. The park is unique in that there's a picnic table there that allows people on opposite sides of the border to meet face to face without entering the other country. This is important to bikers of many clubs because many of them are banned from crossing the border due to felony convictions or outstanding warrants.

The orders to "unpatch" the No Surrender Crew came from Peter "Mongo" Price, a 350-pound monster with long hair he liked to dye a brilliant shade of orange. Price was the Washington State Bandidos sergeant-at-arms, and was known to carry two guns, two knives and a chain with him at all times. He is said to have told Kellestine that if he succeeded in removing Toronto's patches he would be in charge of the Toronto chapter and be Canadian national president, while Sandham would become president of the newly official Winnipeg Chapter, and second-in-command of the Canadian Bandidos. He also indicated that if Kellestine failed, he would be in the same boat as the rest of the Toronto chapter and the duty (and rewards) would then fall to Sandham.

Police recorded Kellestine talking to Keswick-based full-patch Cameron Acorn just after the meeting. He told him that "The people in the States are super, super, super fuckin' choked." In biker parlance that means upset or disturbed. When Acorn acknowledged that he knew that, and that Kellestine had been out west to talk with them about the situation, Kellestine told him: "And don't say a word, just ... uh ... just leave it at that."

Later in the same phone conversation, he told Acorn that there was trouble on the horizon: "For some strange reason they [the Americans] seem to ... oh, fuck ... anyways there's gonna be some major changes, man ... I'm telling you that right now you protect yourself ... it's not my doing, I want no part of this, but I'm gonna try to salvage as many guys as possible."

When Sandham arrived at Kellestine's farm, he brought along full-patch Dwight Mushey — a former kick-boxer turned boxer who had a rather disheartening 7–32–1 record as a pro. He had already been arrested for selling meth at least once back in

Manitoba. Also with them was prospect Marcello Aravena — a professional tae kwon do instructor and strip-club bouncer. There was another man in the group, another big guy, Mushey's workout partner who was a full-patch and is now in the federal witness protection program and may only be referred to as M.H. He was a police informant before April 2006, but did not have any significant information about the upcoming meeting to share with police.

The four men showed up, they said, at the urging of an American Bandido who was identified as Keinard "Hawaiian Ken" Post. Post wanted to know why it had taken Kellestine so long to pull Toronto's patches.

Instead of just giving up and allowing the Winnipeggers to pull his patch, Kellestine explained his situation and recruited them to help him and two local friends — career break-and-enter man Frank Mather, who was originally from New Brunswick but now lived with Kellestine, and 21-year-old Brett "Bull" Gardiner of no fixed address — to strip Muscedere and his men of theirs.

Chapter 13
Bloodbath at 32196 Aberdeen Line

Kellestine's visitors must have noticed that the first floor of his house at 32196 Aberdeen Line was decorated entirely in red and black, with swastikas, Iron Crosses and other Nazi memorabilia all over the place. He was obsessed with two things — guns and the Nazi party.

And he wasn't the only one. Kellestine's self-confessed "right-hand man" was a local character and truly massive full-patch Bandido named David "Concrete Dave" Weiche. He earned his nickname from his work at his father's immense contracting firm. And his father — Martin K. Weiche — wasn't just well known because he was wealthy and successful. The elder Weiche, like Kellestine, decorated the family house with Nazi memorabilia, including oil paintings of Adolph Hitler and an autographed copy of *Mein Kampf*, Hitler's autobiography.

Virulently racist and thoroughly atavistic though they may have been, at least the elder Weiche came by his views somewhat honestly. He had been in the Hitler Youth and had fought for the Nazis in World War II. After emigrating to Canada and becoming very successful, he ran in the 1968 federal election in the riding of London East as a National Socialist. The word "Nazi," it's important to note here, is actually a short form of the German phrase "Nationalsozialistische Deutsche Arbeiterpartei," which means "National Socialist German Workers' Party" and was the official name of Hitler's organization.

Under that red-and-black banner, Weiche received 89 votes. He was later connected to some violent clashes, a couple of local cross burnings and was alleged to have put up the money for Operation Red Dog — a failed coup attempt in Dominica, which was aimed at establishing a white supremacist government on the small Caribbean island after expelling all of its black residents.

Although the younger Weiche had been at the Peace Arch meeting with Kellestine, Sandham and Price, he had left South-western Ontario for Winnipeg about three months before Sandham and his crew showed up at the farm. There has been no evidence to indicate he had any involvement with or even any knowledge of what happened next.

Many locals who had no connections to outlaw motorcycle gangs knew about Kellestine's attitudes. He had a habit of doing things like interrupting London's annual Pride Day Parade by dancing around with the Confederate war flag (the familiar stars and bars) — but only, he told friends, because he could be indicted if he used a Nazi flag; he considered the Confederate flag to be a decent second choice.

His racist and anti-Semitic views were well known, but they were not considered bad enough to get him thrown out of or even disciplined by the club. Some sources have told me that, while his beliefs may have been flamboyantly displayed, they were hardly rare in his milieu.

But they caused some friction in Toronto. Because, while Kellestine was a constantly stoned, frequently violent arrest-waiting-to-happen, the club had a few promising prospects like Jamie "Goldberg" Flanz. His friends called him "Rogue," but the Bandidos, particularly Kellestine, usually called him "Goldberg."

Originally from Montreal, the strapping former hockey player was a well-liked and intelligent young man, but he had a habit of breaking laws. He was the son of a well-known and well-heeled Montreal lawyer and something of a computer expert. In 2003, Flanz had been hired by a big American company, but was fired because he had set up a website that was in direct competition with the one they paid him to establish. His wife left him, and nobody in the computer business was interested in hiring him. So, he took a job as bouncer at a bar in Bradford, Ontario, (about

Jamie "Goldberg" Flanz

an hour north of Toronto) and lived in nearby Keswick.

Although Keswick had been a Hells Angels' stronghold since the mass patch-over, the muscular Flanz shaved his head, grew a goatee and started running with the Bandidos. Police were well aware of it, too. When they found the beaten and burned body of Keswick-native Shawn Douse in Pickering on December 8, 2005, they arrested four Bandidos (two of whom were already in jail on other charges) and searched Flanz's apartment. Douse was known to have been an active cocaine dealer, and was seen at a meeting at Flanz's apartment earlier that week. They found no evidence of his involvement and Flanz was never charged.

As charming as Flanz could be, Kellestine hated him. Everybody knew that it was because he was Jewish. And so, at the start of April 2006, when Kellestine accused Flanz of being an informant, Muscedere and his crew attributed it all to Kellestine's rabid anti-Semitism and his growing paranoia. So when he invited them to his farmhouse in Iona Station to discuss the matter, they agreed. Their plan was not to entertain Kellestine's wild accusations, but to kick him out of the club.

So on Friday, April 7, 2006, the Toronto Bandidos, other than Kellestine himself and two others who were out of town, drove down the 401 from Toronto to Iona Station to meet Kellestine and the Winnipeg prospective chapter. Both sides were determined to take the patches of the other.

Paul "Big Paulie" Sinopoli

One of them, 400-pound Paul "Big Paulie" Sinopoli, tried repeatedly to beg off due to a bleeding ulcer that he claimed made him weak and nauseous.

Since the Douse murder, many of the Bandidos had had their phones tapped. Sinopoli — who lived in the basement of the Jackson's Point home of his parents Onofuco and Antonetta — was the best source of information. The police listened as Sinopoli called Flanz to tell him he couldn't go. Flanz said he should go out on the town instead — suggesting he go see a Tragically Hip cover band that was playing at a bar the Bandidos frequented. But Sinopoli claimed he was so sick that he couldn't move.

Later, Kellestine called him and basically ordered him to go. Tape recordings of an April 7, 2006 conversation between the two included Kellestine singing an improvised version of Roy Orbison's 1959 hit "It's Now or Never" to the reluctant biker.

Kellestine sang: "It's now or never, hold me close, kiss me, you homely little bastard, be mine tonight."

Sinopoli was silent.

Kellestine stopped singing. "Howdy doody, whaddaya doin', Big Paulie?" he asked.

"I could be better," the obese and ailing Sinopoli replied.

"You've been sick," Kellestine acknowledged. "You're a sick man. Never mind you're sick — I still love you."

"I know, I know," Sinopoli replied.

Kellestine then pointed out that — sick or not — Sinopoli had a responsibility to stay in touch. No matter how sick he was, even if he couldn't visit the farm, he could have at least called.

"What's up, buds?" Kellestine asked. "You don't love me no more?"

Sinopoli went back to his only excuse. "I've just been sick, bro."

Kellestine then basically ordered him to come to the meeting at the farm, noting that it was of utmost importance.

Then he added a detail that seemed to surprise Sinopoli. He mentioned that he may run into some visitors who had stopped by the farm. But he also indicated that they could be gone before he arrived. "There's some people passing through town right now," Kellestine told him. "They're not gonna be around for much longer."

Sinopoli then called his old friend Kriarakis. Kriarakis told him that he was attending the meeting but it didn't seem to be about anything important, so Sinopoli could probably miss it without getting into too much trouble.

About five hours later, Francesco "Bammer" Salerno called Sinopoli from his house in Oakville to make sure he was going to make the trip. He told him his standing in the club was in great jeopardy. "Bro, uh, Boxer's freaking out, bro. You're on your last legs, you're almost out the door. So if I was you, I'd get yourself to church tonight," he advised.

Then he suggested that it was in Sinopoli's best interest to bring a large sum of cash to the meeting. "You better bring it. Don't come there empty-handed, brother, and don't bother phonin' him and telling him you're sick."

After Sinopoli again pointed out how ill he was, Salerno made his final argument. "I'm telling you what to do. If you don't want to listen to me, that's your problem. Don't come crying to me after."

Salerno then called another full-patch member, Oakville-

Francesco "Bammer" Salerno

based Pierre "Carlito" Aragon, to underline the importance of the meeting: "Yeah, brother, I don't know what the agenda is out there, but ... uh ... it's not to have dinner at fuckin' J.C.'s house [the house of Sandham's second-in-command in Winnipeg,

Jamie "J.C." Korne], that's for sure, ya know what I mean? I suggest you call this fuckin' Taz fuckin' piece of shit and order him as a Canada Rocker [full patch] to get his fuckin' ass to where you are. What is this, a fuckin' joke?"

He went on in this profanity-laden rant to point out that Korne was eight months behind in dues, "so whatever he's fuckin' got there fuckin' that's worth something, like his motorcycle, fuckin' has to be fuckin' grabbed." He made it sound very much like Toronto had a lot of questions that Winnipeg had to answer or lose *their* patches.

Sinopoli reluctantly made the drive. Almost all of the chapter went — Muscedere, Salerno, Sinopoli, Kriarakis, George "Pony" Jessome, Luis Manny "Chopper" Raposo, Michael "Little Mikey" Trotta and Flanz.

Interestingly, the bikers weren't alone on their trip down the 401. Two OPP agents, who had been investigating Muscedere for months, were on their tail. In an unmarked vehicle, they followed the bikers all the way to Kellestine's farm. When they got there a little after 10 p.m., the cops were disappointed. They decided that all these Bandidos visiting Kellestine was unlikely to be anything more than a party and they didn't have a search warrant anyway, so they figured there was no use in sitting on some lonely country road watching a bunch of idiots get drunk. They turned around and went back to Toronto.

After they got out of their cars, Muscedere took Flanz aside. Flanz knew Kellestine was an anti-Semite and that he didn't like him, but he didn't know that he had accused him of being a rat. Muscedere wanted to prepare him, but not spook him too much. "You're going to have some kind of a bad reception over there," he told him, "so you might have to stay outside."

Before Muscedere and his cohorts arrived, M.H. testified, he, Kellestine, Sandham and the others made preparations. They sent away Kellestine's wife and daughter, as well as Mather's pregnant girlfriend. Aravena and Gardiner — unknown to the latest set of guests — were instructed to say they were from the nearby Oneida First Nations reserve. Gardiner was then ordered to search the property for old shotgun shells or anything else potentially incriminating.

And they had pizza, tons of pizza. Earlier that day, Kellestine and his friends had gone to the nearby Oneida First Nations reserve. Somebody had told them there was an unguarded trailer full of smuggled cigarettes in a field. They'd gone and opened up the trailer, but instead of smokes, they found about 200 frozen pizzas. Although the cash value of their prize was far lower than what they had expected, from all reports Kellestine was anything but disappointed. He and his men took the pizzas home and from that point forward there was a constant supply of hot pizza at the Kellestine farm.

They put on rubber gloves underneath their normal riding gloves. Then they went up to the roof of the back porch. Kellestine, M.H. testified, peeled up some shingles, revealing an impressive cache of weapons. They spent hours collecting, cleaning and loading the weapons. Someone asked what they were doing. M.H. said that Kellestine answered, "Just in case, let's prepare for the worst."

Aravena later testified he heard Kellestine telling Sandham that they might be able to "salvage Crash, Pony and Big Paulie."

Things got a little tenser as the time for the party approached. Kellestine looked at the others and told them: "If we kill one, we kill them all." Sandham put on a bulletproof vest.

Mather, Aravena and Gardiner were instructed to stay in the house. Mather had a gun. Aravena — whom Kellestine and Sandham had allegedly discussed executing earlier — was armed with a baseball bat. His job was to watch for the approaching Torontonians and tell the guys in the barn through a two-way radio Kellestine had set up earlier. Gardiner was told to monitor Kellestine's police monitor.

Kellestine waited in the barn with a Lakefield-Mossberg .22 rifle. Mushey was with him. Sandham was hidden in the loft with a more deadly World War II–vintage Lee-Enfield .303 bolt-action rifle. M.H. was out back, armed with a Remington Wingmaster pump-action shotgun.

The Toronto contingent were lead into the barn and told to surrender their wallets and cell phones. They reluctantly put them in a pile on top of Kellestine's old white freezer near the entrance. A space had been made in the middle of the otherwise cluttered barn. Things like mattresses, furniture, an old plastic kiddie pool and other detritus had been piled up to make room. The walls were made of pressboard and were adorned with busty young women dressed as construction workers or posing on Harleys along with Kellestine's usual Nazi propaganda. An old aluminum stepladder led to a loft. The guests from Toronto were instructed to stay together in the middle of the cleared-out area.

Shortly after the Toronto Bandidos arrived, M.H. reported that he heard gunfire, which he said "sounded like popcorn." Mather and Aravena rushed into the barn. Aravena later testified he left his post and ran to the barn because he "had a good friend in there."

When they arrived, Kellestine ordered Aravena to get beer for him and water for his men. He then told him to tell everyone on the roof that everyone's okay. Aravena wondered what he was talking about because there wasn't anybody on the roof. He later attributed it to Kellestine's predictably eccentric behavior.

Luis Manny "Chopper" Raposo

According to M.H., they saw all eight of the guests lying face down in the barn, except for Raposo. He had fallen, and was seated on the floor with his arm hanging from a couch he was propped against. M.H. reported that he could see wounds in Raposo's neck and chest.

Sandham later tearfully testified that Raposo had seen him, armed, in the loft and fired at him with a sawed-off shotgun he had hidden under his jacket. Surprised by what he considered an unprovoked assault, Sandham said he "flinched," which accidentally led to him firing back.

No matter how it happened, Raposo was dead. When the dust settled, Muscedere asked Kellestine to get his fallen brother some medical help. Kellestine refused, telling his old friend: "He's already dead." It was later determined Raposo died of wounds inflicted by two different guns.

Kriarakis had taken a shell in the abdomen. Sinopoli had been shot in his right thigh. Kriarakis, losing blood, started praying in Greek, and Sinopoli began crying and complaining about how his wound would complicate his diabetes.

Salerno, much older and tougher than the other victims and with holes in his own legs, shouted at them to keep their mouths shut. "We're bikers," he reminded them. "We're not the fucking Boy Scouts — so stop your whining."

Kellestine shouted up to Sandham, demanding to know who shot first. "Was it fucking Chopper, or was it you?" he demanded.

"Chopper shot first," Sandham shouted back, pointing out that his bulletproof vest had saved his life.

Then things got a bit weirder. Kellestine starting singing "Das Deutschlandlied," the national anthem of Germany. Or, at least, he sang the first line of the first stanza, "Deutschland, Deutschland über alles" (Germany, Germany above all else), over and over again.

German politics are tricky at the best of times, but since the first stanza of the song is strongly associated with the Nazis, it is rarely sung in Germany anymore. Kellestine also danced a celebratory jig, reminiscent of the one British propaganda showed Hitler doing again and again during the war.

While concerned with their own wounds, the bikers quickly recognized that Raposo was indeed dead. Muscedere led them in the Lord's Prayer — Kellestine dropped to one knee and joined them. When they finished, Kellestine ordered Trotta and Flanz to wrap Raposo's corpse up in an old area rug and take it out of the barn. They were instructed to put it in the cargo area of Muscedere's silver 2001 VW Golf.

Sandham testified that he then surrendered his gun to Kellestine — whom he described at that point as "a man to be feared" — and went to the aid and comfort of Kriarakis in the belief that "they were all going home." Except Raposo, of course.

Kellestine told those who were left that he was pulling their patches "by order of the States." He kept his rifle trained at

Muscedere, and told Mushey that he'd "shoot Boxer if he moves from that fucking spot."

Then he approached Flanz. He hit him with the butt of his gun and accused him to his face of being a police informant. Then he laughed and said "I'm saving you for last, you fucking Jew." Muscedere tried to reassure Kellestine that Flanz wasn't an informant. He wasn't listening.

All of the cell phones on top of the freezer had rung at least once during the ordeal. But one of them rang repeatedly. Muscedere admitted that it was almost certainly his wife, Nina. Kellestine told him he could answer it, but warned him: "Don't say anything fucking stupid."

Muscedere answered. He told his wife that he was at "church" and that he'd be home in an hour or two. He also told her he loved her. Then he hung up and started crying. He looked up at his old friend Kellestine and said through his tears: "Do me. Do me first. I want to go out like a man."

Kellestine laughed and said he was going to let him go. Then he ordered Muscedere out of the barn. Aravena followed him. Outside, Aravena later testified, Kellestine led the way, Muscedere was in the middle and he brought up the rear. They walked from the barn to Muscedere's VW Golf, which already had Raposo's corpse in the cargo area. Kellestine warned his old friend not to get too close.

"What are you talking about?" snapped Muscedere. "I'm right behind you, and I'm not doing nothing."

When they got to the car, Kellestine ordered him to get inside. Muscedere refused. "I'm gonna get two bullets in the back of my head," he said, challenging Kellestine. But, after a brief stare-down, he relented. As he sat down, Kellestine shot him in the face through the open door.

Aravena testified that he initially thought that Kellestine had missed because Muscedere "had a big smile on his face." Then he saw the hole in the man's head.

Kellestine then leaned into the car, put his gun under Muscedere's shirt and shot him again.

Then, Aravena later testified, Kellestine pointed his gun at the Winnipeg prospect's chest and threatened him. "I ain't doing

25 years for you," he snarled. "If you say anything, I'll kill you and your family."

"I ain't saying shit," Aravena replied as calmly as he could. "I'm not a rat."

Inside the barn, M.H. reported that he heard more "pops" of gunfire.

When they returned, Sandham took the visibly shaken Aravena aside and told him that Muscedere was the only one they were going to kill, that the others were going home.

Gardiner came running from the house to the barn where he met Mushey at the door. "Did you fucking hear that?" he asked, clearly disturbed. "I should go check on Wayne."

Mushey ordered him back into the house. Kellestine and Mather made sure he went.

Kellestine and Mather came back into the barn. Nobody spoke until Kellestine ordered Mushey to help him take Kriarakis outside. They did. M.H. heard more pops. Aravena was recruited to stow Kriarakis' body in the tow truck. He later testified that he thought they would take him to a hospital because "it was still warm" (despite having helped dispose of Raposo's body and having seen Muscedere murdered before his eyes). Kellestine said that they would drop the body off in Toronto where they could "make it look like a drive-by."

Back in the barn, Sandham later testified that he considered shooting Kellestine to put a stop to the murders, but had already given up his gun. Then Kellestine asked for someone to help escort Jessome outside. M.H. said he volunteered. With their guns trained on Jessome, they walked out to his tow truck. Kellestine ordered him to get into the rear passenger seat. As Jessome was complying, M.H. said that he saw Kellestine shoot Jessome in the head, then lift his shirt, put the gun under it and shoot him again in the chest. He then ordered M.H. to push the body into the truck and shut the door.

Kellestine then sized up the logistics of his operation. He told M.H. to move the bluish-green Chevy tow truck to the farm's entrance, and then park Flanz's gray 2003 Infiniti QX4 SUV behind it. M.H. then got in the other side of the tow truck, with a man he had just seen get murdered in the back seat, and followed orders.

Kellestine waited for him, and walked back from the site of Jessome's murder to the barn, complaining bitterly all the way. "He was bitching about doing 'wet work,'" M.H. testified. He also told the court he took the phrase to mean murder.

Michael "Little Mikey" Trotta

Back in the barn, Kellestine ordered Trotta and Flanz — both of whom were still prospects and not full-patch Bandidos — to clean up the barn with bleach and water. Sinopoli, the reluctant one, was led out of the barn — still crying and complaining — by Kellestine and Mushey. They shot him in the head and stuffed his giant corpse in the back of Flanz's Infiniti. Yet again M.H. reported hearing "pops" from outside the barn.

When they returned, it was Salerno's turn and he knew it. He got up and faced M.H. Salerno offered his hand. M.H. did not shake it. Neither did Aravena, who later testified he wouldn't shake Salerno's bloody hand because he was "wearing new clothes" and didn't want to get them dirty. Salerno then turned to Mushey and shook his hand before leaving the barn with him and Kellestine.

M.H. testified he heard still more pops.

In an effort to break the tension, Flanz asked Sandham about how his kids were doing.

Mushey and Kellestine took Trotta out of the barn. Once again, M.H. heard, but did not see, him get shot.

Then Kellestine took Flanz outside. According to M.H, everyone who was still alive — himself, Sandham, Mushey, Mather, Aravena and even Gardiner — followed. M.H. watched as Flanz was forced into the back seat of his car. By this time, Sandham had acquired a handgun. But then M.H. said he turned around, and then he heard a gunshot and saw a flash. He turned back around. This time, Mushey had the gun in his hand. M.H. turned around again. He heard another shot and saw another flash.

Sandham later gave his own perspective on the death of Flanz. He said that Kellestine and Mushey ordered him to kill the last remaining victim. Sandham said he refused, and that Kellestine told him he could "get in the car and join them." At that point, Sandham said, Kellestine turned away, Mushey grabbed the gun and killed Flanz. Sandham said that Mushey told him he "owed him one."

All eight targeted men had gone to their deaths without a fight.

By this time, dawn was approaching. Kellestine told the other men to collect the keys for the four cars the Toronto Bandidos had come in, and one extra so that they could return after dumping the bodies far away. Since Muscedere's body was still behind the wheel of his VW Golf, nobody wanted to drive it. Instead, it was decided that it would be attached to Jessome's tow truck.

Although they had intended to drive far away to dump the bodies, one of the vehicles was almost out of fuel, so Kellestine made the call to ditch. They were traveling northeast on Highway 3 (which many locals call the Talbot Line) and pulled over into a lightly wooded spot less than 10 miles from Iona Station, next to a farmer's field down an unlit dirt road just outside the tiny hamlet of Shedden, Ontario — the self-proclaimed "Rhubarb Capital of Canada."

When they returned, the men collected the slain bikers' possessions. They assembled all of their IDs, cell phones, keys and anything else that could potentially be incriminating, which Kellestine put in a bag that he later burned. Kellestine took all the change taken from the dead men's pockets and put it in his daughter's "Potty Mouth Jar" — an old glass jar she was expected to put money into each time her parents caught her swearing.

Sandham, Mushey, Aravena and M.H. went back to Winnipeg. Gardiner decided to stay at Kellestine's farm, joining Mather, who had already been there for a few days.

The following morning, at about 8 a.m. a neighbor saw Flanz's Inifiniti in a lot owned by Mary and Russell Steele.

She called her friends and told them about the car on their property. The Steeles drove out to where the friend had spotted the car and discovered the slate-gray Pontiac Grand Prix Trotta had rented for the trip. At first they thought some revelers had been partying on their lot and had passed out or been too drunk to drive back home. But when they saw the tow truck with the Golf, it unnerved them. They went back to the house and called 911.

Curious, they went back to the site before the police showed up. Russell — or "Rusty" as his wife calls him — went up to Flanz's SUV, but he couldn't see inside the car because the windows had frosted over.

Just after they went back home, an OPP officer arrived. The officer approached the Infiniti SUV and noticed that the driver's side window was open. He looked inside and saw Salerno's body in the back seat. Undaunted, he went around to the back of the car. He put his hand on the handle of the latch. It was unlocked. He opened it. The next thing he saw was Sinopoli's gigantic belly. His body was folded up in the Infiniti's cargo area. By that time, another OPP officer had arrived on the scene. Circling the Infiniti, he noticed Trotta's body on the other side of the back seat.

They called for help. Two more OPP officers arrived. They found the VW hooked up to the Superior Towing truck. Inside, they found the corpses of Muscedere, Kriarakis and Raposo.

They called paramedics. While on scene, one of the paramedics looked in the back seat of the tow truck. He discovered the body of Jessome. The cops kept searching, and discovered Flanz's corpse in the back seat of the Grand Prix.

By noon, dozens of police were keeping hundreds of media and curious locals away from the crime scene.

At about 8 p.m. that evening, two old friends of Kellestine's — Eric Niessen and his common-law wife Kerry Morris showed up at the farm with a couple of cases of beer. They had driven unannounced from their home in Monkton, about two hours to the north. Niessen was an official Bandidos supporter — a position for which he was required to pay $25 a month, although he later said he'd only paid it once. Before that, he was an Outlaws supporter. A piece of lined, legal-sized paper later recovered from

Salerno's house and used as evidence against him noted that he was a "hangaround."

But he was no biker. Niessen attended Bandidos parties and knew all the guys — he even knew Kellestine had plans to reform the Toronto chapter and relocate it to London with himself in charge — but he wasn't the type to actually be in a gang. And although he was never charged with any drug-related offenses, according to police, Niessen's name came up in several different meth-related investigations.

When they arrived, he saw that the house was surrounded by police cars and what he — hey, he'd been around — recognized as unmarked police cars. He told Kellestine, who he later said didn't seem surprised.

Also inside the house were Mather and Gardiner. As he began to make himself comfortable, Niessen saw more police arrive. After watching television, Niessen realized that the cops were there because of the bodies found in Shedden. Although Niessen never publicly said he suspected his old friend of the crime, he realized it wasn't a huge intellectual leap for the cops to think that the baddest biker in the area may have had something to do with eight bodies found less than 10 miles away. Especially since the TV news had reported that all eight of the dead were bikers themselves.

Kellestine fielded phone calls about the murders all day. Niessen recognized Raposo's car and Jessome's truck from Toronto-based Superior Towing on the news. Just before midnight, Niessen called Muscedere's brother to tell him that he believed the bodies found in the field were Muscedere's and Raposo's. He did not mention any others.

Niessen began to harbor suspicions when he noticed the other people in the house destroying things that could potentially be used as evidence. Later, at Kellestine's request, Niessen went out to an old freezer Kellestine used to collect rainwater and brought a number of buckets of water to Gardiner who was cleaning up the barn.

Police later reported they saw Niessen searching the farm, especially in areas where they later determined the murders had occurred. They did not, however, find any hard evidence that he had destroyed or hidden anything that could be used as evidence.

Later that day, the police moved in. After an uneventful stand-off, they apprehended everyone inside the house — Kellestine, Mushey, Gardiner, Niessen and Morris. They were all arrested and charged with eight counts of first-degree murder. Inside the barn, the police found blood spatters and bits of human flesh and hair among the beer bottles and Nazi flags. Gardiner had done a lousy job cleaning up.

Interestingly, at her trial later on, Morris testified that she thought the Hells Angels were attacking when the police moved in.

The media leapt on the story. Sinopoli's giant so-white-it's-blue belly was on the front page of every newspaper and led every night-time newscast. They called it the biggest mass murder in Ontario history. They called it the Shedden Massacre (even though the killings happened in Iona Station and the bodies were dumped just outside Shedden).

About a month later, on May 6, all murder charges were dropped against Niessen and Morris. Interviews with the accused had convinced police they were not present at the farm at the time of the killings. Instead, they were charged with being accessories after the fact.

• • •

Back in Winnipeg, Sandham continued as though nothing had happened, raising money and recruiting prospects for Bandidos. But a new rival emerged. One of the few surviving Ontario Bandidos, Aragon, who didn't make the trip to Kellestine's farm because he was out on bail and cautious of being watched by police, was attempting to reorganize the Toronto chapter with himself as president. He saw Sandham as an obstacle to this and began a campaign against him. He told the Americans that Sandham was a former cop. Sandham, lying, explained to the Texans that his only experience with the police was a mandatory special-weapons course he participated in while he was with the military. And he retaliated against his accuser, claiming that Aragon — like many Toronto members — was breaking a Bandidos' bylaw by not owning (or even knowing how to ride) a Harley.

The American reaction showed anger at the pair of them, frustration that the Canadians still couldn't get their act together and confusion as to why two Bandidos "brothers" would be so openly hostile to each other. Houston's Carlton "Pervert" Bare was given the duty of communicating with them. He told Sandham that cops and ex-cops could never be Bandidos and that if he found out Aragon's allegations were true, he'd pull Sandham's patch. And he told Aragon that without Harleys, he and his men couldn't consider themselves Bandidos either.

Sandham promised to visit Texas and iron everything out; he also promised to tell them more about Aragon. For an extra bit of ammunition, he signed on to Mushey's e-mail account and, pretending to be him, wrote the Texans a long and strident letter in support of Sandham and his leadership skills, noting that he believed that Sandham had never been a cop.

Just as that crisis was looming, on June 16, police in Winnipeg arrested Sandham, Mushey and Aravena and took M.H. into protective custody.

The American Bandidos denied involvement, and no charges related to the Shedden Massacre were ever laid against them. There was never any evidence that the Americans ordered or even authorized Kellestine or Sandham to use force when taking Toronto's patches away.

On December 8, Niessen and Morris came to trial. All charges were dropped against Morris, who had spent six weeks in jail before making bail. Niessen received a two-year sentence for obstruction of justice.

The accused Bandidos first showed up in court on January 8, 2007. And Kellestine was immediately a problem. When he was led into the courtroom for his preliminary hearing, he gave the collected reporters the finger and swore at the courtroom artist. When asked about his client's behavior, Kellestine's lawyer chalked it up to stress. "He's got a lot of pressure on him," Clayton Powell said. "I don't know, it seems okay to me."

Sandham wept openly and would sometimes cover his ears when certain grisly details of evidence were discussed.

Some of the lawyers complained about being searched on their way into the courtroom.

After suffering a brutal beating in the jailhouse shower later that month, Kellestine was moved into protective custody.

On March 27, 2008, an unknown assailant set the Kellestine farmhouse on fire. It was destroyed, but the big, ominously black barn where the initial confrontation took place still stands intact.

• • •

The trial opened in September 2009, 41 months after the incident. As in most biker trials, there were some ridiculous incidents. The accused complained there was not enough meat on their ham sandwiches. They were later caught flushing ham down toilets, which allowed the court to dismiss their claims.

Kellestine told a story of how he demonstrated to the other Bandidos how stupid Gardiner was by sending him out of the house to pick pickles off his pickle tree. He also said that Mushey pushed a note up against his cell partition that read, "You're a dead man." When asked where it was, Kellestine said Mushey had eaten it.

Gardiner motioned to a local reporter that he wanted to talk with her. When he did, he handed her a note, it read:

> My name is Brett Gardiner and I was wondering what had happen to the comic strip. I am currently residing at Elign Middlesex detention center, so you have to understand that it gets boring and redundant in this place so please understand that the best part of my day is opening up the today section of your paper and reading your comic strips mostly the De-flocked strip. I love reading that stupid sheep and I keep all the one's that I get my hands on, but know I have orderd your paper for one of those reasons. So please consider returning the comic's as they where.
>
> Sincerily
> Brett Gardiner

Sandham too was in protective custody, and his clear plastic partition was later covered in paper to prevent the other bikers from intimidating him. He testified that he only joined Bandidos in an effort to become a highly paid police informant.

He also likened Bandidos membership in Canada to a "revolving door," and said that members were stripped of their patches all the time in a nonviolent way. While that concept perfectly rationalized his argument that he arrived at the unpatching ceremony without any idea that violence would be involved, it did not explain why he was armed with a powerful rifle and wearing a bulletproof vest.

M.H. — who was an actual police informant — described the Canadian Bandidos succinctly: "They were at the very bottom rung of biker gangs. Some were in their forties but still lived with their parents. They were not making any money, many of them had been rejected by Hells Angels and half of them didn't even own a motorbike."

And various details of Kellestine's character — beyond his Nazi fixation and fondness for firearms — came out. Sandham mentioned that he heard Kellestine muttering to himself about murdering two of the Toronto members and "cutting them into little pieces." When the court asked why he didn't take that as a warning sign, Sandham replied that he thought Kellestine was joking, When the court was aghast, he explained by saying, "He has a very, very dark sense of humor." To emphasize this, Sandham told a story of how when he and Kellestine were walking in some nearby woods, they came across some deer droppings. Kellestine popped them in his mouth and started chewing. When he saw Sandham's horrified reaction, he started laughing uproariously.

And Sandham wept often, citing a fear for his life and how he worried about what would become of his daughter. He had earlier testified that he "technically" had four children, but only mentioned concern for one.

Mushey and Gardiner fired their lawyers. They didn't explain why. Local media speculated that it was a move intended to make it appear as though they were not helping put the other bikers behind bars. Realizing they were both facing serious prison time, both Mushey and Gardiner would have been well served to appear as little like rats as possible.

Closing arguments were heard October 19. Sandham's lawyers accused Kellestine of being a psychopathic mastermind who found an opportunity to guarantee his standing while getting a chance to kill people. Kellestine's lawyers accused Sandham of being a Machiavellian genius attempting to use violence to get ahead in the biker world while trying to frame Kellestine for the whole thing.

The jury went into deliberations on the morning of October 29. The following morning they had a unanimous verdict. Kellestine, Sandham and Mushey were all found guilty of eight counts of first-degree murder. Mather and Aravena were each found guilty of seven counts of first-degree murder and one count of manslaughter. And Gardiner, bringing up the rear as usual, was found guilty of six counts of first-degree murder and two counts of manslaughter. Of course, under Canadian law, even one count of first-degree murder guarantees life imprisonment with no chance at parole for 25 years. And that's the maximum penalty for crime in Canada anyway, so the individual tallies of murder and manslaughter convictions were largely academic.

As the verdicts were read out, most of the accused remained stoic. Aravena buried his head in his hands, Gardiner looked like he was crying a bit (but it was hard to tell) and Mushey bowed to the judge. Kellestine, ever the showman, looked over at the media, grinned and gave a "whaddaya-gonna-do?" shrug.

Just as Superior Court Justice Thomas Heeney was thanking the six-man, six-woman jury for their patience and hard work, reality set in for Aravena. He exploded. "They're fuckin' goofs!" he screamed at the jury while giving them the finger with both hands. "You know some of us are innocent! You're pieces of shit!" His lawyer, Tony Bryant (who made headlines years earlier as Paul Bernardo's defense attorney), tried to restrain him. Aravena kept waving his arms and shouting. "Fuckin' Tony! Fuckin' Tony!" Then he started shouting unintelligibly, and a group of OPP officers stormed in to restrain him.

Although it may sound childish and comical, the word "goof" is considered perhaps the worst insult among Ontario's likely-to-go-to-prison set. At least two murders in Kingston alone since the '80s were reported to be the result of someone calling someone else the G-word.

Angry cries of appeals were heard immediately. But, of course, such high-profile verdicts are virtually impossible to overturn.

Sandham, Mushey, Aravena and Gardiner (who was from Southwestern Ontario, but had moved to Winnipeg in an attempt to become a Bandido there) were sent to prison in Manitoba. Mather was sent back to his native New Brunswick. Only Kellestine went to Kingston.

Chapter 14

Mongols, Mexicans and B.C. Bud

In January 2008, while Kellestine and his accomplices were awaiting trial, a court in Georgina (about an hour north of Toronto in good traffic) heard the case of the Shawn Douse murder. Accused were four Bandidos members — would-be president Aragon, full-patch Acorn, and prospects Randolph Brown and Robert "Bobby" Quinn. Also implicated were Sinopoli and Flanz, but, of course, they were both dead.

Most of the evidence came from a woman who testified they recruited her to help them "get back at" a friend. The woman, who knew Douse and also knew he was a cocaine dealer, was urged on December 7, 2005 to call him and invite him to Flanz's house on Hattie Court in Keswick so she could make a purchase. She was also aware that the Bandidos and Douse had some beef and Acorn explained that he was annoyed with Douse for selling cocaine to his family and friends, especially his girlfriend's sister, whom he said he was worried about because she was on the verge of breaking her probation.

The bikers were hiding behind the door when she let Douse into the house. Immediately, they began to beat on him. Brown stuffed a gag into his mouth, the others — although notably not Flanz — began to punch and kick him. After a brief struggle, it was obvious that Douse was dead. Brown then ordered the horror-stricken witness to clean up the blood, which had splattered on the walls and had drenched the entrance hall carpet so completely that it was running down the basement stairs.

The Bandidos then wrapped Douse's body in sheets and a sleeping bag, put it in a car and drove away. A man walking his two dogs found it the next day — burned beyond recognition — in a deserted field in Pickering, just east of Toronto.

All of them were charged with second-degree murder. Since asphyxiation was a major contributor to Douse's death (along with the beating and acute cocaine poisoning), Brown of nearby Jackson's Point was the only one who couldn't plea bargain. Acorn and Quinn — both of Keswick — pleaded guilty to manslaughter, while Oakville-based Aragon bargained down to aggravated assault. They all went to prison for a minimum of seven years.

$\bullet \bullet \bullet$

You might think that with the Shedden Massacre crew behind bars for twenty-five to life and four more Bandidos from the Douse murder also in prison, it might have been the last gasp of Bandidos in Ontario, but you'd be wrong. And the Shedden Massacre wasn't the last time Bandidos made headlines.

On the night of December 1, 2006, David "White Dread" Buchanan went out with friends to celebrate his 33rd birthday. Buchanan wasn't just any guy. In fact, he was sergeant-at-arms for the Hells Angels West Toronto Chapter. That rank is usually reserved for the toughest and most aggressive member of the chapter. The job, in a nutshell, is to act as the chapter's disciplinarian and primary offensive weapon. The muscular, tattooed Buchanan was up to the task.

And Buchanan wasn't any biker, either. His nickname — usually shortened to "Dread" — came from the fact that, though white, he was born in Jamaica. Like many other Jamaicans, his family immigrated to Canada and settled in the crime-ridden Rexdale neighborhood in the northwest corner of Toronto, bordering Woodbridge.

As a youth, Buchanan ran with a mostly black street gang called the Mount Olive Crew. It was based in a high-rise apartment complex located at 1 Mount Olive Drive at the corner of Kipling Avenue. They were notorious in the neighborhood for drug sales and retaliatory (and even random) violence. And just as small-scale biker gangs strive to become Hells Angels or Bandidos, the Mount Olive Crew became the Mount Olive Crips sometime around 1995.

While Buchanan never led the gang, he was a very respected and valued member. He provided not just muscle, but income as well. He had a reputation as the area's primary gunrunner. "He was certainly a source [of weapons] for the street gangs in the Rexdale area," said Toronto Detective-Sergeant Kevin Torrie. "He was certainly very well known in the Etobicoke [western Toronto] area, that's for sure. He certainly had no problem flexing when he was younger."

His exploits and assets did not escape the notice of the local Hells Angels, who many in local law enforcement say supply the black gangs with drugs and weapons. They recruited Buchanan from the Mount Olive Crips, and made him a member quickly. His skills and connections guaranteed him a solid position, and he became sergeant-at-arms before long.

The bar he went to on his birthday wasn't just any strip joint either. Club Pro Adult Entertainment is located on Doughton Road, near the corner of Jane Street and Highway 7 in Concord, just north of Rexdale and east of Woodbridge.

It has a reputation as a rougher club than most in the region. When I was talking to a Toronto prosecutor about strip joints in the area because of a case that involved a 13-year-old stripper from Bosnia-Herzegovina, her child-soldier-turned-drug-dealer boyfriend from El Salvador and legendary Hells Angel Maurice "Mom" Boucher, she summed up the club's reputation pretty succinctly. "You have to put [downtown club] The Brass Rail at the top, and Club Pro at the bottom of the list," she said. "Club Pro has earned its name, if you know what I mean."

It was something of a Bandidos hangout. In fact, perhaps the most prominent of all of Canada's remaining Bandidos worked there. It was none other than Francesco "Cisco" Lenti, the former Loner, Diablo and Satan's Choice member, who had been a fixture — albeit something of an eccentric one — in the Toronto biker scene for decades. He was 57 and walked with a pronounced limp from when his right leg was almost severed by a car bomb, but he still commanded some respect in his milieu.

His job at Club Pro was to be a "cooler." Not a bouncer per se, a cooler's responsibility is to calm situations and disputes down in an attempt to prevent violence. Lenti would approach troublemakers and use his talents as a negotiator to cool things down. He was also charged with the task of preventing customers from bringing drugs and weapons into the building. Club Pro owner Domenic "Mimmo" Marciano described the position by saying: "He was kind of the buffer, the cooler, to eliminate the other element that we didn't want."

Lenti knew from experience it was a dangerous business to be a biker from another gang in Hells Angels' territory. Back in June 2006, some West Toronto Hells Angels met with him in a restaurant and offered him membership, no questions asked. Lenti politely refused.

Insulted, the Hells Angels (according to a police informant) decided not just to kill Lenti, but to display his body — in full Bandidos colors — on a public highway as a warning to others. That sort of thing is common practice in Mexico and Colombia where bodies (or more often, just the heads) of informants, rival gang members and police are often displayed as a terrorist tactic. It was, the Hells Angels said, intended to discourage anyone from joining Bandidos.

But one of the three men given the task of assassinating Lenti, Stephen Gault, happened to be a police informant. The police arrested the other two — full-patch Nomad Remond "Ray" Akleh and Hells Angels' Oshawa chapter president Mark Cephes Stephenson — and warned Lenti of the plot. After that, Lenti began to carry a loaded 9-mm handgun with him everywhere he went.

And on the night of December 1, 2006, it was tucked into the waistband of his pants.

Lenti had his hands full that night. Buchanan hadn't come to celebrate his birthday alone. In fact, he brought with him some considerable muscle — fellow members Dana "Boomer" Carnegie and Scott Desroche, along with prospect Carlo Verrilli.

Lenti had been at work for a little more than two hours when at 12:53 on what was by that time the morning of December 2, he went from the club's office to the bar to get himself a coffee and a water. He recognized the four Hells Angels, even though they were not wearing their colors. He sat at the far end of the bar.

Whether by plan or by chance, the Hells Angels noticed Lenti and surrounded him in his chair. They began to argue. The Hells Angels forced him to acknowledge his identity and affiliation with Bandidos and accused him of attempting to establish a Bandidos chapter in their territory.

Realizing he was in a poorly lit part of the room that was out of the view of the club's security cameras, Lenti got up from his seat and went into the brighter, more exposed lobby. The Hells Angels followed, and the argument resumed. A small crowd gathered to watch. Witnesses swore that Lenti appeared to be doing his best to calm the men down. Surveillance video backed them up. Buchanan was seen to be carrying an empty beer bottle by the neck.

One of the club's bouncers decided to help Lenti out, and asked the men to leave. He was told to shut up, then pushed and eventually punched in the face by one of the bikers. Then Buchanan turned back to Lenti and punched him in the eye, knocking him down. When he got up, Lenti decided that Verrilli and Desroche were closing in on him. At that point he claimed he saw Buchanan flash a gun. So Lenti pulled out his own handgun. "I seen that guy pull it [a gun] out," Lenti said later. "I went boom, boom, boom, boom. I just went for it. I shot him to death." (No witnesses reported seeing any of the Hells Angels with a gun and none showed up on tape.)

As soon as he saw Lenti pull out his gun, Desroche jumped into a janitor's closet. He would continue to hide in it throughout the incident.

Lenti kept shooting. He hit all three of the visible Hells Angels. Buchanan and Verrilli fell to the floor. Carnegie managed to flee out the front entrance. After a few seconds, Buchanan stirred. He rolled onto his back, and realized he couldn't get up by himself. He offered his right hand to Lenti, in effect asking him to help him up. Instead, Lenti shot him just under his left eye. It killed him instantly. Lenti ran toward the door. Just before he left the building, he shot Verrilli — who was lying on the floor in a full-fetal position — one more time. Lenti took the gun with him, but left seven 9-mm shell casings on the floor. No other guns were recovered from the Hells Angels or the club.

Somebody called 911. Desroche left the closet and fled the scene, but returned minutes later to attempt CPR on Buchanan. When the ambulances arrived, Verrilli was taken to Sunnybrook Hospital, while the less seriously wounded Carnegie managed to drive himself to the much-closer Humber River Regional Hospital.

Lenti surrendered to police the next day, and later pled guilty to manslaughter in the death of Buchanan and to aggravated assault for the shootings of Verrilli and Carnegie. He was sentenced to six years in prison. About a year after the incident, Verrilli sued Club Pro for $1.1 million for the "psychological and physical injuries" he claimed to have suffered at the bar.

The Bandidos name flared to prominence one more time. On the unseasonably cool morning of August 30, 2007, a man named Jason "Salami" Pellicore was on his way to his daily workout at the Complete Fitness club in Richmond Hill, just north of Toronto. It was 9:25 a.m. and Pellicore was traveling from his car to the club when he was confronted by a man wearing a full-face motorcycle helmet. The man then pulled out a handgun and shot Pellicore four times in the head and abdomen.

A woman who was passing by saw the shooting and ran into the health club screaming for help. Tony Farrah, a friend of Pellicore's, jumped off a treadmill and ran into the parking lot. He was joined by his nephew and a health club employee named Frank who initiated CPR as the two Farrahs did their best to minimize Pellicore's blood loss and make him comfortable. Soon paramedics arrived and took him to York Central Hospital where he was pronounced dead after a short revival effort.

Witnesses said the assailant escaped on a small motorcycle or scooter. Definitely not a Harley. A man and bike matching the descriptions was captured on surveillance cameras, circling around the club before the shooting, perhaps waiting for Pellicore to arrive.

Pellicore had been in some trouble before he was murdered. York Police Detective-Sergeant John Sheldon told media at the time he believed the murder "was a targeted hit." He said that Pellicore was well known to local police and that they had visited his home many times in the past. Some sources said he made his money as a Mafia debt collector, but wasn't always in their good books because he didn't always return with all of his bosses' money.

Pellicore was actually out on bail awaiting trial along with a Pefferlaw man named Jose Silva for uttering death threats, extortion, weapons charges and mortgage fraud. And he had some problems with local bikers; in fact, the Hells Angels.

Earlier in his career, Pellicore was a prospect for the West Toronto Hells Angels, but he had quit because of the menial and degrading chores full-patch members forced him to do. A few weeks before the shooting, Pellicore had suffered a beating from some Hells Angels. He then went to police and told them he felt his life was in danger. He had become convinced that a Hells Angel had stolen his girlfriend. The same Hells Angel had since been kicked out of the club for excessive use of crack cocaine, but after the assault, Pellicore was sure the club had it in for him.

Perhaps he meant it, or perhaps he just wanted to irritate the man who stole his girlfriend, but Pellicore started telling people he was going to establish a new Bandidos chapter in another small community north or Toronto, his hometown of King City.

American Bandido Edward Winterhalder, who has become something of a go-to guy for media concerning the gang (especially in Canada), said he believed that Pellicore had some involvement with the club, but opined that the hit was not related to a Hells Angels-Bandidos war in Ontario. "This will probably be something that is not club-related in the end," he said. "I think it will have something to do with his private life. Normally, when something like this happens, it's traditionally over either women or over drugs — he, to my knowledge, had no interest in drugs at all."

Someone claiming to be Pellicore's cousin posted a memorial on the guestbook of Bandidos' official website (which is now based in Denmark), and many people have written their condolences for him on another biker-oriented site — Levack, Ontario-based White Trash Networks, which can be found at bikernews.org — most of them mentioning his affiliation with Bandidos.

His killer was never caught.

• • •

By the fall of 2007, the Shedden Eight were dead, Pellicore was dead, Weiche was in hiding (his father says he's in Winnipeg, but other sources have told me Alberta), Aragon was laying low, Lenti, Kellestine and his friends were all behind bars. There really wasn't much left of Bandidos in Canada. And on October 1, their extinct status became semi-official. A post showed up on Bandidos' official website guestbook that read: "As of October 2, 2007, the Bandidos MC 1% Canada is officially shut down. There isn't no more Bandidos MC membership in Canada." It has since been removed.

It was signed by "Cisco 13. 1%er Canada." Cisco, of course, is Lenti's nickname. As Bandidos' top-ranking survivor, he would be the person in charge of closing up shop. The extenuating circumstance that he was in prison was trumped by the fact that there was nobody left to delegate the task to.

The 13 probably signifies the letter M, which is the 13th letter of the alphabet. This little half-code is popular with bikers, who often refer to Hells Angels as "81" since H is the eighth and A the first letters of the alphabet. M, in biker parlance, can stand for motorcyclist, marijuana or murder.

The post went on to say that Bandidos' Canadian website (which was created by Lenti and Raposo back in 2004) would stay up for a few weeks in honor of the Shedden Eight. Since then, things have been very quiet. A few media stories from Winnipeg and Edmonton have hinted that Bandidos are planning to return, but nothing concrete has emerged. An ad actually ran in a Winnipeg newspaper in early 2008 claiming that, of all things, a Rock Machine clubhouse would be opening soon. It hasn't yet.

There was another flicker of Bandidos' presence in February 2008. Bandidos' Canadian website was redesigned as a single page. "Big changes coming soon ... stay tuned," it read. It was signed by NSCC, likely an acronym for No Surrender Crew Canada. But whoever put it up remains anonymous. Within weeks it was down again and the site no longer exists.

The official Bandidos site lists 198 chapters in 16 countries, including Thailand, Singapore and Costa Rica, but not a single one in Canada. And most of the references to Canada in the guestbook have since been deleted. There are persistent posts supporting Bandidos from an Alberta man named Kevin who calls himself "Limey" (North American pejorative slang for an Englishman) and claims to represent the "Barbarians Nomads."

There are two fairly well known motorcycle gangs called the Barbarians. One is an all-black club based in Philadelphia, and the other is a relatively small British club. Neither is considered a player in the outlaw biker universe and neither wears the "1%" symbol on their patch. I asked the leadership of both clubs if "Limey" had any connection to them; they told me he didn't.

But that doesn't mean that Hells Angels have no opposition in Canada (other than law enforcement, naturally).

Consider this: when the Bandidos Canada website breathed its last, Lenti — or whomever he told to put it together — found the time and wherewithal to include an MP3 of the song "House of the Rising Sun." That might not seem like a big deal, but it is considered the anthem of yet another gang — the Mongols.

Founded in East Los Angeles in 1969 by Vietnam veterans who were denied membership in Hells Angels because of their Hispanic heritage, the Mongols grew rapidly. By collecting Hispanic and other disaffected would-be bikers, the Mongols soon outnumbered Hells Angels in their own place of origin — Southern California. Empowered and armed by close connections with local Hispanic gangs and Mexican drug cartels, the Mongols have basically pushed Hells Angels out of all but a few strongholds in Southern California. And they still hold a grudge against the club that wouldn't let their founders join.

A lot of other outlaw motorcycle gangs hate Hells Angels, but with the Mongols, it seems pathological.

But Hells Angels were forced to recognize the existence and power of the upstart Mongols in 1977. At that time, Hells Angels had a policy forbidding any other gang from wearing "California" as the bottom rocker of their patch. They would routinely beat up or, according to some sources, even kill those who defied this order.

They tried to do that with the Mongols, who they greatly outnumbered, but it didn't work. The Mongols fought back with an intensity and an efficiency Hells Angels had never seen before. Before long, Hells Angels conceded that the Mongols could wear the patch. It drew the attention of law enforcement and the respect of other gangs.

Later, rather than risk all-out war, they made a strategic deal for their home state. In exchange for allowing the existing Southern California Hells Angels chapters — Monterey, Orange County, Riverside, Fresno, Ventura, San Diego ("Dago") and the original in San Bernardino ("Berdoo") — to remain open and a promise not to invade the northern half of the state, the Mongols were given free run of the rest of Southern California — perhaps the most desirable spot in the world for organized crime and the birthplace of Hells Angels themselves.

But sometimes the Mongols test that treaty. They will taunt the Hells Angels, and often violence will break out. The best-known example came on April 26, 2002.

Everybody in Laughlin, Nevada, knew the Hells Angels were coming to town for the annual pan-biker get-together — the Laughlin River Run, which draws about 80,000 bikers of every stripe, from weekend wannabes to Outlaws to Bandidos to Hells Angels. The police — through a series of informants — knew the Mongols would be there with a plan to add more mystique to the gang's image. Police interpreted this as a plan to attack the Hells Angels.

The local police warned casino and hotel owners about what they thought was the Mongols' plan. Both law enforcement and local business owners did their best to increase security, but it couldn't prevent the two gangs from meeting up.

Early in the day, Hells Angel Christian H. Tate was riding back to his home in San Diego. But he didn't make it. His body was found by the California Highway Patrol just on their side of the state line. Tate had been shot in the back, and his body was thrown in a roadside ditch. His wallet was found some yards away, and his driver's license was placed on the seat of his Harley.

After they found out, the Hells Angels — who had taken up most of the Tropicana Hotel — were heard on police wiretaps discussing the use of night-vision goggles and sniper scopes that night.

Later that evening, 35 Hells Angels showed up at Harrah's, where they knew the Mongols were staying. They walked onto the casino floor, everything was caught on surveillance video. Security rushed in, but the Hells Angels assured them they were just there to have a good time.

Suddenly, they were spotted by a group of Mongols — maybe 40 in total — who were relaxing in Rosa's Cantina, a Mexican-themed bar on the other side of the nickel slots. They approached in full colors and armed with knives, wrenches, hammers and other makeshift weapons.

"Who's in charge here?" asked an unidentified Mongol. "We don't want any trouble."

"I am," replied a Hells Angel. They began to pass by each other, but there were some unintelligible shouts on the tape. The groups turned back to face each other.

"What's your problem?" asked a Mongol.

"You're my fuckin' problem!" shouted a Hells Angel.

An armed Mongol approached the front line of the Hells Angels. "We're gonna fuck you up," he promised. Then a Hells Angel — later identified as Raymond Foakes — delivered a martial arts–style front kick to the chest of a Mongol.

After that it was pandemonium. The tapes captured patrons and employees running for their lives as Hell Angels and Mongols clashed on the casino floor. Men were being hit with chairs, with wrenches, with anything bikers could put their hands on. It actually looks like a poorly shot movie; the action is so frantic, it almost seems like it's being shown at too fast a speed.

Suddenly, shots rang out. The tape captures a dark-haired Hells Angel — Calvin Brett Schaefer (also spelled "Schaffer" in some legal documents) — frantically trying to reload a handgun, while a Mongol named Kenneth Dysart appears to fire at him.

By this time, the Mohave County SWAT team had surrounded the Casino, and officials had closed every bridge and highway out of the city. Ambulances arrived. When the police finally gained control of the situation, three men were dead and 16 others were taken to nearby emergency rooms.

The dead men included one Mongol — Anthony "Bronson" Barrera, who succumbed to stab wounds to his heart — and two Hells Angels — Jeramie Bell and Robert Tumelty Jr., both of whom were shot. One other Hells Angel and an innocent bystander were shot, but not badly enough to warrant headlines. Many bikers were treated for stab wounds and blunt-force trauma. One Mongol suffered a fractured skull.

Schaefer was charged with murder, but bargained down to committing a violent crime in aid of racketeering. He received two years.

And the Mongols, who are generally seen as an up-and-coming power, have relished their higher profile since the Harrah's incident. They made even more headlines when Mark Guardado (himself of Hispanic descent, but considered white because of his appearance and manner of speaking), president of the San Francisco Hells Angels Chapter was assassinated. Police and media pointed their collective fingers at the Mongols. San Francisco is far on the Hells Angels' side of California's Northern/Southern divide.

Since the Harrah's fight, the Mongols have — according to U.S. law enforcement — forged alliances with the Outlaws, Bandidos, the Vagos and the Pagans to go along with the ones they already had with local Hispanic gangs and Mexican drug cartels, making a strong front of very anti–Hells Angels bikers and gangsters.

But that's south of the border. Although there is a Mongols MC Canada website that claims to represent chapters in Toronto and Niagara Falls, there's no hard evidence of any Mongols' presence in Canada. The site, police and other observers tell me, is either wishful thinking or a playful yank of the collective Hells Angels' chain. None of the cops and none of the bikers I spoke with could identify a single Mongols chapter they knew of in the country.

The fact is, Hells Angels have a stranglehold on organized crime in the country. Because of an expansionist philosophy started by Yves "Le Boss" Buteau and perfected by Walter "Nurget" Stadnick, every major Canadian center has become a Hells Angels stronghold. Hells Angels' official website lists 36 chapters, and unlike the Mongols' imaginary ones in Toronto and Niagara Falls, they are very real.

But due to mass arrests and other problems, many of them are weakened. And there's just no way to hold up an organized crime monopoly. Many of the factors that make them so strong also strengthens their enemies.

Their whites-only policy gave birth to the Mongols and has engendered animosity for many other gangs, like the powerful-in-Western-Canada Indian Posse. Hells Angels' habit of passing over candidates for various reasons created people like Frank Lenti and the Loners. Their demand to monopolize crime led to the emergence of gangs like the Rock Machine. Their penchant for strong-arm tactics led to animosity from people like Wayne Kellestine.

In short, there are always bikers and other gangsters who won't play ball with Hells Angels. Monopolies just can't hold, especially when it comes to organized crime. They tend to draw intensified efforts from law enforcement, they have every upstart wanting to make a name for themself wanting to take a shot at bringing them down, and they also fall victim to their own successes and excesses and to the weaknesses in their philosophies and strategies.

While it is true that Hells Angels have beaten or outlasted such capable competitors as Satan's Choice, the Rock Machine, the Outlaws and Bandidos, they should still be looking over their shoulders at other bikers.

Most Canadians know that what happens in the United States usually happens north of the border a short time later. And if you look at what's going on with Hells Angels in the U.S., you may get something of an accurate predictor of what is likely to happen in Canada.

Just as many rival biker gangs united in Ontario to keep Hells Angels out of Ontario, gangs like the Mongols, the Outlaws, the Pagans and the Vagos are working more or less in synch to protect their own areas from Hells Angels. If you took a map of the U.S., you could color Southern California black and white for the Mongols, almost all of Texas (and many neighboring states) would be covered in the familiar Bandidos red and yellow, while the upper Midwest (especially Chicago and Detroit) along with much of Florida would be black and white for the Outlaws. Maryland and many of the adjacent east coast states could be represented in the red, white and blue of the Pagans, who have recently had violent clashes with Hells Angels on Long Island and in Philadelphia. And while Hells Angels are present in Arizona and Nevada, you'd have to color big stretches of those states (and much of Mexico) in Vago green, and much of Oregon would be Free Souls blue.

Hells Angels red and white would cover the rest. They have some allies — notably the Sons of Silence in Colorado, the Iron Horsemen of the Ohio River Valley and the Highwaymen in Detroit — but none is that significant or growing. Another small gang called the Florida Warlocks — not to be confused with the bigger and more powerful Warlocks of Eastern Pennsylvania and New Jersey who are unaligned — are also said to have a deal with Hells Angels, but other sources have told me they also work with the Vagos. Either way, they are too small to tip the scales to either side.

One of the reasons those clubs have aligned with Hells Angels is that they share a whites-only rule. Others, like the Outlaws, started out all-white, but have adapted to keep up with the times. Of course, Hells Angels will work with non-whites, but — at least for now — would never accept one as a member.

Take, for example, Greg "Picasso" Wooley. His family immigrated to Montreal from Haiti when he was very young. He grew up as a friend and professional associate of Maurice "Mom" Boucher's. Wooley was tough, courageous, intelligent, charming and had a knack for making money. He used to take Hells Angels for rides on his luxurious speedboats all the time. But he could never become a member no matter how much cocaine he sold or how many witnesses he beat up. Instead, Boucher slipped him into the Rockers, the Laval, Quebec–based club that specialized in carrying out violent work for the Montreal Hells Angels. The bosses in Manhattan either didn't know about him or turned a blind eye.

But the whites-only rule doesn't just keep out prospective members, it also limits who can and will do business with you. Much of the Mongols' strength comes from its association with Mexican and other Hispanic street gangs. The Mongols — as well as Bandidos and the Vagos, both of which have strong Hispanic memberships — can recruit and employ these foot soldiers and street-level dealers almost at will.

Hells Angels will deal with Hispanic, black and other ethnic gangs — as with the West Toronto Chapter's gun- and drug-running relationship with the Mount Olive Crips or the Montreal Hells Angels' close association with the Master B street gang — but not nearly as easily. Shared languages, cultures and even friends and family give more diverse gangs an edge on the increasingly isolated Hells Angels.

This, of course, makes perfect sense in California (particularly in the south) and other southwestern regions where non-Hispanic whites are a minority. The same could be said of Toronto and many parts of Canada that are becoming increasingly diverse. And many of these immigrant communities — like those before them — have brought their own crime organizations with them.

A related reason why Hells Angels have ceded large areas of the United States to other biker gangs has to do with who their suppliers and employers are. Traditionally, bikers such as Hells Angels have depended on the traditional Italian Mafia to supply them with drugs and tasks like extortion, loan-sharking and protection rackets.

But the Mafia is shrinking both in size and scope. Law enforcement would like to take credit for this, but a big part of it has been demographics. As Italian and Irish families become further removed from the immigrant experience, the lure of organized crime has diminished.

Taking their place are gangs from other regions: East Asia, South Asia, Eastern Europe and, in particular, Latin America.

It's safe to say that the Latin American gangs — especially the Mexican drug cartels — are better armed, better trained and more determined than any other criminal organization before them. Among them, they have turned much of Mexico into a war zone, with government troops occupying many border towns, while violence — including the beheadings of rival gang members and those in law enforcement — rages. At the heart of the violence are a number of former special operations officers from police and the military who were taught about urban combat by American, Israeli and other experts but then left their employers for the higher pay and added prestige of the cartels.

As Mexico became increasingly lawless, U.S. authorities stepped up border security. The cartels adapted in a number of ways. Instead of sending large shipments over the border, they sent small shipments over with illegal immigrants — paid a pittance or forced to do it, and always sworn to secrecy — carrying small amounts of drugs or the basic ingredients of manufactured drugs over the border with instructions to collect on the other side.

Since importing finished products like methamphetamine is a felony, while smuggling key components like pseudoephedrine (the active ingredient in most decongestants) is a misdemeanor, the cartels have gradually moved their drug manufacturing over the border. Throughout the American West, there are secret drug-making factories staffed by illegal immigrants who manufacture methamphetamine quickly and efficiently.

This has become a huge problem for Hells Angels. They have been dealing meth on a large scale since the 1960s. But they and their increasingly small network of independent meth-making operations — what American cops often call "Beavis and Butthead labs" because of the kind of people who run them — simply can't compete with the volume, quality and prices offered by the Mexicans.

Nor can they compete with their ferocity. Despite their reputation for violence, Hells Angels are no match for the battle-hardened, well-armed soldiers and commandos the Mexican cartels have at their disposal. As one New Mexico–based agent with the Bureau of Alcohol, Tobacco and Firearms (ATF) told me: "Once the Mexicans show up, those guys [Hells Angels] scramble to get out of town."

But since much of the drug-buying public (and those involved with other vices like prostitution and illegal gambling) are English-speaking, the Mexican cartels usually rely upon bikers to serve as their retailers. Every once in a while, there will be a deal between the Hells Angels and Latin Americans (particularly in Canada), but the cartels are increasingly turning to gangs with Spanish-speaking members, including previously all-white organizations like the Outlaws and Bandidos.

Although the Latin American immigrant population of Canada is still relatively small, the country — especially British Columbia — has caught the attention of the Mexican cartels. The primary draw has been BC Bud, a particularly powerful strain of marijuana grown in the province. Through the use of such specialized farming technology as aeroponics and halogen daylight simulators, farmers in B.C. have been able to produce unprecedentedly huge crops of marijuana with a much higher THC content than ever seen before.

While it sells for a small premium on the domestic market, it sells for a much higher amount across the border and is even reported to be traded on a one-for-one basis for cocaine in Miami. Because of this, authorities have intercepted BC Bud traveling into the U.S. not just in the traditional ways, but in school kids' knapsacks, hot-air balloons, ocean-going kayaks and even purpose-built tunnels constructed under the border. That kind of profit margin has led to many different gangs attempting to get a piece of the pie (which authorities estimated to be worth $6.3 billion in 2008), and the Mexican cartels have moved in with force.

Not only has the volume and potency of BC Bud led to decreased sales of Mexican- and U.S.-grown marijuana, but the cartels have also found that it is actually much easier to move product over the Canadian-U.S. border than it is over the heavily defended U.S.-Mexican border.

So far, Hells Angels have managed to keep a lid on B.C. They have done so largely by staying off the front lines and dealing with smaller (often racially mixed) gangs like the United Nations and the Red Scorpions. But they are in a precarious position. In fact, it's a scenario not unlike the one that occurred in Montreal in the 1990s that gave birth to the Rock Machine because it pits an insular gang that makes rules against street-level dealers and smaller gangs who have their own ideas about how best to profit from the distribution of drugs.

Back then, a few dealers who did not want to deal with Hells Angels and their rules teamed with bar owners and disgruntled bikers like the Cazzetta brothers and Paul Porter and the Mafia to form an alliance that eventually fought a long and bloody war with Hells Angels for the streets of Montreal. The Mafia was Hells Angels' primary supplier, but they did not want to have one single avenue of sale; instead they played the Rock Machine against Hells Angels. By having them both sell drugs in direct competition with one another, it increased the Mafia's volume and selling price.

Currently in B.C., one can see the Mexican cartels eclipsing Hells Angels as the primary distributors and exporters of BC Bud and they are reported to be currently seeking other gangs to deal with. Complicating matters is the fact that until recently, Hells Angels practically had a monopoly on cocaine sales in B.C. But the Mexicans have more, better and cheaper cocaine. In fact, they have found it easier to barter cocaine for BC Bud instead of importing the large quantities of cash that would be necessary for such huge transactions. The effect has been to bring down the overall price of cocaine, putting a significant bump in Hells Angels' bottom line. And the bartering has brought cocaine — and its inherent problems — to parts of B.C. that had never seen that kind of thing before.

While the Mexican cartels already deal with a number of ethnic gangs in major Canadian centers, if they want to expand in Canada, it would make sense to employ outlaw biker gangs. While it is, of course, true that previous attempts by the Outlaws and Bandidos to establish themselves north of the border met with eventual failure, that doesn't mean they won't try again.

Keep in mind that Hells Angels were repeatedly rebuffed when they first tried to come to Canada, and, even under the masterful hand of Walter Stadnick, it took many years and some significant failures and some outside help before they could take Ontario.

For now, Hells Angels are pretty much it for bikers in Canada. But another group will almost certainly rise to challenge them. Maybe the Outlaws or Bandidos will take another shot. More likely, a gang who hasn't already been burned in this country will set up shop.

Until recently, my money would have been on the Mongols, but they have hit a massive roadblock. On October 21, 2008, 38 members were arrested after ATF agents infiltrated a chapter and became full-patch members. Two days later, U.S. District Court Judge Florence-Marie Cooper granted an injunction that prohibited club members, their family members and associates from wearing, licensing, selling or distributing the Mongols' logo. The reason she gave was that, according to police testimony, the Mongols had used the logo and names as an identity and as a form of intimidation to help them, among other things, commit crimes. Despite an outcry from the club and free-speech advocates, the injunction held for a year.

While the Mongols have slowly started to wear their patches around the U.S. and started to sell support wear again, their long-planned expansion east of the Mississippi and into Canada appears to have been indefinitely shelved. Still, the guestbook on the Mongols Canada website is peppered with posts from people claiming to be Canadian Mongols, including one who goes by "Irish" (there was a Bandido prospect by the same name) and another named "Red Power." Before the injunction, media reports as recent as 2007 claimed that the Mongols were setting up a loosely organized puppet gang in Winnipeg made up of former Bandidos associates — many of Aboriginal descent — called Red Power.

There are, of course, always the Outlaws. As the years have gone by, more and more of the original Outlaws have gotten out of prison and more and more of the court-ordered restrictions on the free ones expire. They have regrouped to some extent in Ottawa and Niagara (under the auspices of Mario Parente's old friend Richard "Dooker" Williams), but still appear too small to make a dent in the Hells Angels hegemony in the province. Some knowledgeable sources I've spoken with have speculated that Parente could rejoin his old mates and rally them back into a viable force. They point out that, back in 1988, he told a judge he had quit the Outlaws and had put them entirely out of his life. While it's true that he did do that, it appeared from speaking to him that this time he really meant it when he said he was through with the Outlaws. It was no ploy to get his stuff back from the government; he really was disgusted with the way the Outlaws behaved during his trial.

And in April 2008, another familiar name popped up in Ontario — the Rock Machine. According to media reports, the Rock Machine had re-formed in Winnipeg (there had been a few newspaper ads there that announced it was going to happen) and Edmonton, and that their recruiters had come to Toronto to drum up support.

The recruiter, who refused to be named, said that the Rock Machine had a small probationary chapter in Toronto and another one in Kingston that already had 12 members. The one in Toronto was called Rock Machine Ontario West and the one in Kingston was Ontario East. The recruiter admitted that some of the new Rock Machine had been associated in the past with Bandidos (by then a dirty word in Ontario because of the publicity of the Shedden Massacre), but that most of them were younger and had come from a small Woodbridge-based gang called The Crew or had never been in a motorcycle club before.

One of the more well-known members of the Rock Machine Winnipeg Chapter was a man named Ron Burling. He looked pretty much how you'd expect a biker to look these days. He had a shaved head and a bushy goatee. He was a physically huge man, one of those body-builder types who had grown so muscled that his arms were no longer able to touch his sides. And, except for his face, it looked like every square inch of him was covered in tattoos, even the top of his head. His Facebook profile (49 friends) listed him as a "member of the rock machine nomads," and he named his employer as "Edmonton Maximum Security Penitentiary General Population."

Ron Burling

He wasn't kidding. Burling was in prison (in part) for his contributions to a February 8, 2005 kidnapping and assault in Toronto. Burling (a full-patch in Sandham's prospective Bandidos chapter at the time) and Adam Curwin, Billy Joe Ducharme, Daniel Pereira and Jason Michel (all members of a local puppet gang called La Familia) forced a car driven by Adam Amundsen off the road and into a snowbank. Then they approached the car and smashed in its windows. As the 20-year-old Amundsen and his girlfriend attempted to escape, the bikers grabbed the pair and forced them into what some newspapers called a nearby apartment building and others called a crack house. They were held in separate rooms.

Amundsen, the court was told, was a street-level dealer for Bandidos and was also way behind in his drug debts. To encourage him to pay the $6,000 he owed, the bikers beat him with fists and wooden baseball bats for several hours, sliced off a tattoo on his left hand and broke the index finger of his right hand with a sledgehammer before cutting its tip off.

On the same day, a woman claimed to have been robbed of drugs and money by two armed men she identified as Burling and Pereira, but they were acquitted of that crime.

Although Amundsen endured the beatings in broad daylight and for a very long time, he claimed he could not identify his attackers. His testimony rarely ranged from anything other than "I don't know" or "I don't remember." Burling kept grinning at his responses, until his lawyer told him to stop.

Instead, Michel (who took no active part in the torture), spoke on his behalf. "He looked like a beach ball. He was all puffed up," Michel testified. "His finger was smashed; it was flat."

The bikers' defense attorney, Ian Garber, asked the jury to disregard the testimony from Michel and the robbed woman as he was an admitted drug dealer and had already made a plea deal that saw the Crown drop kidnapping charges against him in exchange for his testimony and she was an admitted crack addict. "If the Crown had a choice, they wouldn't be asking you to take [the two witnesses'] word for anything," he said "On cross-examination [Michel] admitted there is no reason for [the jury] to believe anything he told you. Mr. Michel would promise anyone anything he had to get out of the mess he was in."

But the jury did believe Michel and all four accused bikers were found guilty of kidnapping, aggravated assault and extortion. Burling was given an eight-year sentence, while Curwin, Ducharme and Pereira were given six each. A woman who lured Amundsen to the address and had some degree of knowledge of the plan, was given four years.

Burling appealed his sentence, believing it too harsh because he was already serving nine years for another crime, but lost. On hearing the verdict at his failed appeal, Burling stood up in court and started screaming. He began by telling the judge that "the Bandidos aren't fuckin' going anywhere! God forgives, the Bandidos doesn't!" Then he turned to the Crown attorneys, calling them "fucking clowns" and vowing "to see [them] in 10 years." As soon as the tirade began, he was rushed by court officers who started to drag him out of the room. As Burling attempted to overturn (or perhaps lift) a bench, the officers brought him to the ground. Moments later, Burling began clutching his chest and bellowing: "My heart! My heart!" He was removed from court on a stretcher, but never lost consciousness and asked his defense attorney for his sunglasses on the way out.

But the Rock Machine recruiter, a former Bandido himself, wanted to distance his new gang from the Rock Machine's first incarnation. "Obviously, we're keeping out of crime. We're going back to old-style biking and brotherhood of the '50s and '60s," he said. "We want to go back to the older ways, the way it was in the early '50s — when it was just a bunch of drunken toughs." He further denied that the new Rock Machine would be involved in crime, at least anything serious. "We're not going to throw a guy out for a bar brawl," he said. "But anything that we consider an assault on society will be immediate expulsion."

When asked about guys like Burling — who was still serving 17 years for a laundry list of violent crimes — being in the club, the recruiter demurred. "We believe everybody deserves a second chance," he said. "We won't throw our members out who are in jail. We don't abandon our brothers that are in jail."

He completely ignored the fact that this new version of the Rock Machine was actually formed when Burling was in prison for his crimes. In fact, they were not standing by him when he was put into prison, but actively recruited him *while* he was behind bars.

There's no irony here; or if there is, it's old and tired. Every outlaw motorcycle gang says the same thing about not being interested in crime. All they want to do, they say, is ride and drink and party and engage in "brotherhood." And, of course, a remarkable number of them are eventually arrested for crimes — often in conspiracy with their "brothers" — or killed.

But what is interesting is that the new club has chosen to call itself the Rock Machine, a name completely at odds with their self-stated philosophy of avoiding organized and violent crime. Those paying attention will remember that the Rock Machine was formed by a group of disgruntled drug dealers who recruited dozens of toughs and a few legitimate bikers — notably the old SS minus Maurice "Mom" Boucher. It existed for years before it even started calling itself a motorcycle club, let alone actually becoming a semblance of one. And even if the Rock Machine was ever a motorcycle club (and that is stretching the definition), it certainly wasn't an old-school '50s and '60s gang. In fact, no prominent gang was on the farther end of the spectrum. The Rock Machine were justifiably known not for riding and partying, but for trafficking drugs, shooting opposing dealers and setting bombs in public places.

But these guys aren't the Rock Machine. In fact, they have little to do with them. If you want a good idea of who these guys really are, take a look at their website. Then click on the link marked RIP. It's commonplace for outlaw biker gang websites to have a page dedicated to the memory of deceased members (although they normally call it GBNF, gone but not forgotten). For the Rock Machine, you'd expect to see the names of notable dead Rock Machine members like Johnny and Tony Plescio or

Richard "Bam Bam" Legace. But instead this is what you'd see at the time of this writing:

> Shedden 8 (? – April 8, 2006)
> Our fallen brothers will never be forgotten. Your memory will always live on with us.
>
> George (Pony) Jessome, 52
> George (Crash) Kriarakis, 28
> Luis Manny (Chopper) Raposo, 41
> Frank (Bam Bam) Salerno, 43
> Michael (Little Mikey) Trotta, 31
> Paul (Big Paul) Sinopoli, 30
> Jamie (Goldberg) Flanz, 37
> John (Boxer) Muscedere, 48

Clearly, these guys are the same guys that used to be the Canadian Bandidos. But they couldn't call themselves Bandidos because the club's international leadership in Texas wouldn't allow that crew ever to use their name again. Bandidos may eventually want to take another shot at Canada, but not with the same guys they worked with last time.

So when the old Canadian Bandidos got together to re-form, the guys needed to either come up with an original name or take an established one that wasn't being used. Of the established gang names no longer in use, the obvious choices were limited to Satan's Choice and the Rock Machine. Since Satan's Choice worked for Hells Angels for years before being absorbed by them, and the Rock Machine fought a bloody war against Hells Angels and almost toppled them from the top spot, the decision must have been easy. Since their raison d'être is to be in opposition to Hells Angels, what better name than the gang that killed more of them than any other?

While the reappearance of the Rock Machine name may instill fear in some, most law enforcement I spoke with aren't that impressed. One cop I know summed up his opinion of the new Rock Machine by telling me: "Internet bikers? LOL."

So that's how it stood in 2010 when it came to bikers in Canada who weren't Hells Angels, their allies or their servants.

The Outlaws existed, but were few in number and many are still limited by court-ordered restrictions. The men they had were mostly old, and they had a hard time recruiting new members as they were seen by many in their environment as the guys who always finish second. That, however, could change with the emergence of a charismatic leader. There appeared to be a few people identifying themselves as the Mongols in Canada, but they had no official presence, certainly no charter or clubhouse. And, because of judgements in the U.S., they were unlikely to change that status in the foreseeable future. Bandidos had officially ceased to exist in Canada, but what remained of their former membership had regrouped and renamed themselves the Rock Machine. They may not sound like much, but they actually had better numbers and better organization than what Hells Angels faced in Quebec until the Rock Machine began to coalesce in the 1990s.

Chapter 15
"I did not have anything to do with the murder ..."

Bang! The sound knocked Robert Parrish out of a deep sleep. "I thought my truck had blown up," he said, not explaining why. So he gathered himself up, and went out the front door of his one-story Hamilton Mountain bungalow to investigate. It was December 15, 2009 — a cold morning, but warmer than you'd expect considering the date — so he had to bundle up a little.

Once outside, the first thing — and only thing — he saw was about two dozen heavily armed and heavily armored cops. Some were from Hamilton — many of the locals still call them "regionals," a vestige of when they were called the Hamilton-Wentworth Regional Police Force — and some were from the Ontario Provincial Police (OPP).

Maybe it's a Hamilton thing, but Parrish instinctively surrendered. "I put my hands up, and they said, 'Please, go back inside your home,'" he said. "So I did." Before he left, one of the officers (a regional) told him not to worry, that they were only serving a warrant. Nothing terrible had happened there that night.

Parrish knew who they were after. Everyone in the neighborhood knew that his next-door neighbor, John Cane — the man who resided at 174 Duncairn Crescent, a pleasant home with a yard that backed onto Gourley Park — was a member of Hells Angels. He lived up in this nice, quiet neighborhood, but drove down the 300-foot hill Hamiltonians call "the Mountain" every day to the city's rough-and-tumble north end, where his very successful store, Darkside Tattoos, was located.

Another neighbor told me that everybody knew he was a biker — and they liked it. "Those guys ... they keep the neighborhood safe," she told me with the self-assurance I have often heard from the neighbors of bikers and other organized crime figures. "Nobody's gonna do anything wrong with one of them around."

It's a commonly held opinion, but one that's not necessarily true. Although they can intimidate other criminals — the Hells Angels in London became locally celebrated when they politely and effectively asked a crack dealer to move from their neighborhood — but bikers in the neighborhood can attract violent crime from other bikers. Just ask the people who lived in Montreal in the '80s and '90s when almost 200 people were killed because of a biker war. Or the neighbors of Thomas Hughes, the Outlaw who lived beside the Outlaws' London clubhouse, after his house was the scene of a shoot-out between Hells Angels supporter crew the Jackals and his own gang in January 2002. No matter where they live, the red-and-white Hells Angels face enemies in the black-and-white Outlaws, the red-and-yellow Bandidos and the biggest gang of all — the ones who wear blue.

And it was the cops who held sway on December 15, 2009. A joint-forces operation called Project Manchester made five forced entries in three cities and made seven arrests, laying a total 91 charges that day. And those 91 charges would increase as the police sifted through the arrestees' houses and businesses.

The cops made it abundantly clear who they were after. "They're all associated in one way or another with the Hells Angels," OPP Sergeant Dave Rektor said of the accused. "Some are full [-fledged members], some are associates, some are prospects."

Actually, most of them were small fry, but one was a truly big fish. In the Hammer, the joint-forces operation arrested Cane, Joseph Cafagna, David Behrens, Luis Barberiz and David Lachapelle. They also took in Cafagna's wife, Carmelina, for firearms violations, but I've since been told she was just taking the fall for her guy. They also took in a 26-year-old kid, Brandon Goodfellow, who lived in Nanticoke — a town on the shores of Lake Erie connected to Hamilton by an oil pipeline and an out-of-business steel company.

Altogether, they didn't add up to one-tenth of the value of the other arrest. In a quiet, suburban Waterloo neighborhood, the cops grabbed 56-year-old Andre Watteel. Charged with one count of being involved with a criminal organization, 28 counts of drug trafficking and 27 counts of possession of proceeds of crime, the former national president of Satan's Choice, former president of Hells Angels Kitchener and former secretary of Hells Angels Ontario, was quite a prize to law enforcement.

To be fair, he was also well known as a pillar of the community. Owner of the Barking Fish Café — described on a restaurant review site as "likely to be boarded up at any moment" — and several residential properties, Watteel was also locally noteworthy for sponsoring local kids' sports teams and being involved in turkey drives and other charities.

Using the power of all of the laws at their disposal, the police also confiscated one residence, three businesses — including Cane's burgeoning Darkside Tattoos — vehicles and motorcycles. They valued the total haul at $875,000.

• • •

Two days before the arrests of Project Manchester, I actually was in the Hammer. Since this book is the story of outlaw motorcycle gangs in Ontario — and every thread of every story about bikers in Ontario tends to lead back to Hamilton — I went to the source.

I went to the Hells Angels clubhouse. I'm pretty familiar with it from my research for my 2006 book, *Fallen Angel*, about Hamilton-born Hells Angels national president Walter Stadnick. But it's different now. While it's still a narrow, windowless block with barbed wire and cement barriers in front of it, I noticed two major changes.

The death's head logo has been removed. In fact, the windowless structure was just a concrete gray box trimmed with red.

Although there were video cameras and concrete barriers, it appeared as though the Hells Angels dared not speak their name even on their own clubhouse. Gone is the familiar illustration on the door (but you can still see it on Google Maps Street View if you look hard enough). It was the club's mascot, a nearly life-sized anthropomorphization of the Hells Angels' trademark death's head logo. In his hands, he wielded two hammers. While that's clearly a reference to the town's nickname, every time I saw it I couldn't help thinking about Scott Steinert and Donald Magnussen — enemies of Stadnick's who were beaten to death with hammers.

I asked the OPP's Sergeant Len Isnor about it later. "Sure, it's gone; I unscrewed it myself, took it off and left it just inside the door," he said, then chuckled. "That was the second time I've been in that building." He was referring to the time when the OPP seized the building in 1996 when it was the Satan's Choice clubhouse in Hamilton.

He described what it was like inside: "Not a single window. It was very neat; you could eat off the floors. There were pictures of other [Hells Angels] chapters from all over the world and plaques they had earned. You'd go in the back door and the first thing you'd see is a display case where they'd have support gear for sale. In the main room was an L-shaped bar with a dance floor. Behind the bar was a beer fridge and a shelf with a variety of liquor. The basement was more of a crawlspace, maybe six feet; I had to duck to walk around in there. On the second floor, there was a meeting room with a big-screen TV and a table with maybe ten seats. In the back was a small kitchen. There were cameras everywhere and you could see the monitors in the meeting room and behind the bar."

Then he drew me a floor plan that matched what he described. The arrests of Project Manchester may actually have killed off the Hamilton Chapter. On Hells Angels' official website — run by the original San Bernardino "Berdoo" Chapter in California — the list of official charters does not list Hamilton anymore. Likely it is at least on suspension due to a lack of active members.

After the raid, the closest remaining Hells Angels chapter was Niagara. Under the leadership of Stadnick's handpicked

ful, especially as the Outlaws were rounded up by police first in
Hamilton and then later in St. Catharines. But just before 8 a.m.
in the warm and clear morning daylight of June 1, 2009, 15 officers
in full riot gear from the OPP and Niagara Regional Police cut
the padlock off the gate of the chain-link fence surrounding the
clubhouse on secluded Darby Road in a rural part of Thorold.

Even though surveillance told them nobody was inside, they
stormed the clubhouse, knocking down the door violently. "You're
always going to assume the worst-case scenario," said Niagara
police spokeswoman Jacquie Forgeron. "We don't know if [the
Hells Angels] had been tipped off ... our members were dressed
in full emergency gear ... you take all precautions."

While the cops inside the clubhouse were still searching, a
truck pulled up. The driver, Timothy Panetta, stepped out and
approached the officers guarding the front door. He was wearing
a black Hells Angels Nomads T-shirt. When they wouldn't let
him in, he launched into a long, profanity-laden tirade, but did
not become physical. As he turned to leave, one of the officers, a
sergeant, handed him a box. Inside was a phonebook-thick pile
of warrants, subpoenas and charges. Panetta threw it in his truck
and drove off.

Just as he was leaving, the police moved in an unmarked SUV
and two rented cube vans to collect evidence. One cop climbed
a ladder to the roof and removed the bikers' surveillance equipment. It was the fourth Hells Angels clubhouse in Ontario to be
seized in less than a month, after seizures in Oshawa, Thunder
Bay and London. And, of course, the cops still had the Outlaws'
clubhouse in St. Catharines from Project Retire.

The Niagara clubhouse, like the others, was seized on an
exclusive possession warrant that was issued in Toronto because
it "was considered a place where illegal activities took place," said
Forgeron. "There are six members of the Hells Angels Niagara
Chapter and four known associates."

But Ward wasn't one of them, neither was his trusted No. 2,
Kenneth "Wags" Wagner. In fact, of the seven men who met with
Walter Stadnick back in 2001 to form the Hells Angels Niagara
Chapter, Panetta was the only one who was still in the club.

The others had been arrested in Project Tandem, a huge province-wide raid that involved 500 cops from 11 different services and took 18 months to put together. In total, 27 people were arrested, including 15 full-patch Hells Angels and a full-patch Vagabond. Billy Talbot, president of the Toronto East Chapter and arguably Ontario's (if not Canada's) top Hells Angel at the time was charged with six counts related to trafficking. From Windsor, the cops arrested full-patch Greg McIlquhan, prospect Giuliano Raimondo and his girlfriend Cathleen "Fawn" Meeking, associates Kevin Hurst, Jesse Thibert, Marc Rizek and Hamilton-resident Martin O'Boyle who was caught with three kilograms of cocaine in the parking lot of the Oakville Community Centre. Particularly hard hit was Niagara, with president Ward, full-patches Wagner and Richard Beaulieu, and associates Timothy Miuse, Alain Lacroix and Deborah Fetz all going down hard. Oshawa lost president Mark Stephenson and full-patches Ronald Zomok, Shawn Campbell and Sean West to a number of charges, including conspiracy to commit the murder of Francesco Lenti. Remond Akleh of the Ontario Nomads (Ottawa) Chapter also went down for that. Of course, Oshawa also lost Stephen Gault, who was paid $1 million to become an informant, and James Heickert, who went on the lam. Also arrested were Simcoe County full-patches Terry Pink and Brian Jeffrey, Keswick full-patch Luciano Capelli and associate Marco Freitas, Toronto East associates Ryan Kempton and Jim Spring, as well as Toronto Vagabond Peter J. Kennedy.

Also seized were $467,100 in Canadian currency, $6,914 in U.S. currency, about $60,000 in gang-related jewelry, $7,000 in surveillance gear, 10 cars and trucks ranging in value (according to the Biker Enforcement Unit) from $3,000 to $85,000, five Harley-Davidsons, six rifles, three handguns, something they called a machine gun and an estimated $2.9 million worth of drugs, including 13 kilograms of cocaine, 50,000 tablets of ecstasy, 50 pounds of marijuana, two kilograms of crystal meth and three pounds of hashish.

BEU chief Don Bell made it clear that his force had been targeting the Hells Angels in particular, had used informants to collect evidence and were intentionally trying to foment doubt and paranoia within the club. "We've taken down significant members within the hierarchy of the Hells Angels," he said. "We've also infiltrated them with one of their own and now they have to look over their shoulder because who's a member and who's working for the police?"

The last of the original Hells Angels Niagara Chapter were arrested on October 8, 2008. The others had either been arrested after Project Tandem, or had quit. In fact, other than Panetta, all the Hells Angels in the Niagara clubhouse were on loan from Hamilton or Kitchener. It was a situation not unlike when full-patch Hells Angels were shipped from British Columbia to keep the Halifax Chapter afloat.

Panetta, who lived in nearby Wainfleet, was the owner of Advantage Auto Sales and Leasing on Allanport Road in Thorhold. He was charged with 12 counts of fraud. The advantage he had in auto sales, police alleged, was that he would buy salvaged cars in the U.S. for almost nothing, then fudge the paperwork and sell them to the public in Canada as legitimate used cars. Of the five cars in question, two had already been sold and three — two gigantic Chevy Suburbans and a Porsche Carrera — were still on his lot. The Porsche, police found, also contained stolen parts.

Things did not go well for the Hells Angels arrested in Project Tandem. Ward and Pink were tried together. After the weight of evidence made it foolhardy for them to try to deny their drug dealing, they acknowledged it but claimed that it was their own enterprise, separate from the organization.

It didn't work. "The whole idea of a patch and being a full-patch member is that you can be 100-percent trusted," Gault testified. "And you can do business with anybody and they're to trust you 100 percent and that's meaning business as in illegal business — drugs, stolen property, anything — robberies." He also said that dealers would pay Ward $500 per week above and beyond the price of product for the right to sell drugs in his territory and that others would pay him "tribute" just to keep the Hells Angels at bay. Since Gault was the first full-patch Hells Angel in Canada to wear a wire, it changed the situation a great deal, amping up the paranoia many bikers already had about informants.

"I am satisfied beyond a reasonable doubt that one of the main purposes or activities of the Hells Angels Motorcycle Club in Canada is the facilitation or commission of serious offences including trafficking in cocaine and other drugs, extortion and trafficking in firearms," said Justice John McMahon at their trial in Toronto on December 11, 2008. His decision supported the earlier conviction of Steven "Tiger" Lindsay and Raymond Bonner in which the Barrie Chapter was named a criminal organization.

On March 25, 2009 — a remarkably short 30 months after the original arrests — those arrested in Project Tandem were sentenced. Ward received 14 years. Wagner got 11 and Jeffrey (also considered a big target) received nine. Charges were dropped against three of the accused, and Stephenson and Akleh were acquitted of attempted murder because the jury did not believe Gault's testimony was credible.

And Hamilton's most famous biker — after perhaps Stadnick and maybe Mario Parente — isn't in any position to help either. Things got pretty bad for Johnny K-9 after his fateful trip to Sudbury back in 1997. While the OPP were still gathering evidence against him for his involvement in the bombing, the Hamilton Chapter of Satan's Choice had its charter revoked. Some of them quit the life altogether, and a few were accepted by the Toronto Chapter. Johnny K-9 probably would have liked to have gone, too, but was stripped of his colors.

During this period — on January 13, 1998, a quiet Tuesday afternoon — it came out in court that a Hamilton patrol sergeant just happened to be driving down Park Row, a residential street where the northbound and southbound lanes are separated by a strip of greenery, when he saw a commotion. As he drew closer, he recognized Johnny K-9 and another man, Jimmy Rich, as former members of Satan's Choice. They were arguing. Suddenly, K-9 lunged at Rich and landed a vicious right cross to his mouth, knocking him to the ground. The sergeant stopped and arrested him on the spot. The victim, with a torn lip, declined to lay a complaint, but Johnny was charged with assault, possession of a concealed weapon and failing to comply with recognizance (cop-speak for violating court-ordered release conditions). And after Rich turned informant, they added extortion to the list of charges.

Johnny went on trial for those crimes and the Sudbury police station bombing in September 1998. After a long proceeding interrupted by Johnny's breaches of bail and Michael Dubé's suicide, Johnny pled guilty to conspiracy to bomb the Solid Gold. He received a 33-month sentence.

And 1998 was a busy year for organized crime in Hamilton. After the deaths of Papalia and Barillaro, the subsequent arrests of the Musitano brothers and the disbanding of the local Satan's Choice chapter (not to mention the Outlaw arrests in 1996), the resulting vacuum of drug sellers sucked all kinds of contenders into the city.

Among the most prominent were the east end–based Gravelle brothers. Led by the youngest of the four brothers, André (34 years old in 1998), they had a history of supplying hashish and hash oil to Hamilton from Jamaica through connections in the United States and Nova Scotia. In fact, they were implicated in the biggest hashish shipment ever intercepted by law enforcement at the time in 1992, when 450 kilograms of hashish (worth $14 million) was seized in Florida. André received a four-year sentence in the U.S. and his big brother Paul (17 years older) received two years.

Even during the heyday of the Mafia in Hamilton, the blond, rakish Gravelles operated with impunity — as long as they knew their place. Hashish is generally considered a more lowbrow drug than marijuana (with which it shares the same active ingredient), and sells for less, yielding a lower profit margin. It's not even in the same neighborhood as cocaine or ecstasy, both of which command astronomical profits. So while the Gravelle brothers sold enough volume of their bargain-basement drug to make themselves comfortable, the big boys — the Mafia and the bikers — tolerated them, rather than seeing them as competition.

So in 1998, with all the major sellers of more desirable drugs sidelined, the demand for (and retail price of) hashish and hash oil went through the roof. The Gravelles went into overdrive.

And like many burgeoning crime families, they felt they needed a bit of muscle. So they contracted the services of Johnny K-9. It was good timing. After he was stripped of his Satan's Choice patch and with the cops holding most of his cash and possessions as evidence and potentially proceeds-of-crime booty, he was desperate for work.

• • •

Lynne Gilbank was a very successful corporate lawyer who lived in Ancaster, Hamilton's nicest suburb. But at the age of 49, she decided to give more back to the community and switched to criminal law. She was interested, in fact, in becoming a public defender. One of her first clients was a man named Bill Smith who was being held in the Maplehurst Detention Centre in nearby Milton.

André Gravelle

He told her quite a story. He was a contractor living on Manitoulin Island with his fiancée when he was approached by Denis Gravelle, to spruce up his cottage there. Denis was so impressed with his work that he asked Smith to come to Hamilton to install a sauna in his brother Paul's house. The Gravelles set Smith and his new wife up with an apartment and he went to work.

Right away, Smith realized the Gravelles were not ordinary businessmen. Hash and hash oil was everywhere, and so was cash. And Smith reported seeing Johnny K-9 at Paul's house regularly. On one occasion, one of Paul's "runners" (drug deliverymen, usually area teenagers) made a very bad choice and "mouthed off" to him. Smith testified that he had witnessed Johnny brutally beat the young man in Paul's basement. According to Smith, the runner's face was "smeared all over the wall" and there was blood from one end of the room to the other. The runner suffered a broken orbital bone, nose and jaw.

When Smith finished the sauna, he had planned to take his wife on vacation in Niagara Falls, less than an hour's drive from Hamilton. But Paul said he'd pay their way to a fancy resort in

Jamaica — and pay him a little extra — if he'd just do him a little favor. He also told him: "If you get caught, just plead guilty; we have lawyers who'll take care of you."

He did get caught. After a week in Ocho Rios, a tanned Smith and his wife were arrested in Toronto's Pearson International Airport on February 11, 1997 with $500,000 worth of hash oil hidden in their double-locked Samsonite hard-sided bags. Smith called Paul. The gangster laughed and told him not to worry, he'd get him a lawyer, they'd plead guilty and get 18 months, probably serve less than a year.

But Smith wasn't interested in playing the good soldier. He got his own attorney. Out of the Yellow Pages, he hired Gilbank. She did her research. She found that the Gravelles had been arrested many times, but had spent little time behind bars through fancy legal work and by offloading the blame to inferiors. She was outraged. She told everyone who would listen about what monsters the Gravelles were, how she was sure they were capable of murder. Smith was surprised that a defense attorney would be so interested in prosecuting bad guys, but admitted she had "a real hard-on for these people; and she definitely was gonna step on some toes."

Police stepped up their investigations of the Gravelles' activities. One of the brothers, 37-year-old Danny, was stopped on the 401 while driving his truck from Halifax back to his home in Burlington. The police found 314 kilograms of hash ($12 million worth) hidden in the tubing of the boat trailer he was pulling. He received 15 months of house arrest after pleading guilty. Denis was caught with $20,000 worth of hash oil on his way to Manitoulin Island.

Smith was leaving the Hamilton courthouse when he was approached by a man later identified in court as Denis's lawyer. Smith told Gilbank the man said to him: "You're the one that ratted out Denis." She put him in the witness protection program that day.

The arrests didn't stop. Danny and André were implicated in a scheme to import $12.5 million worth of hash oil in May 1998, and Paul's son Christian was caught with $160,000 worth of marijuana and hash oil on him in October.

Realizing things were heating up, Gilbank told her daughter, Kristen, who worked in her law office, to be careful.

Fred and Lynn Gilbank

Somewhere between 5:15 and 5:30 on the chilly morning of November 16, 1998, the residents of Ancaster's exclusive Postans Path neighborhood heard loud blasts and then the sound of a car's doors slamming and of it peeling rubber to get away in a hurry.

Someone had broken into the Gilbanks' home and killed Lynn and her husband, software consultant Fred, with close-range volleys from a large-barrelled shotgun.

What followed was one of the longest and costliest murder investigations in Canadian history. In 2004, police offered absolute immunity to anyone who would talk. Nobody came forward. Finally, on January 6, 2005, Johnny K-9 was charged with two counts of first-degree murder for the killing of the Gilbanks. At the end of March, André Gravelle was also charged with two counts of first-degree murder, and Johnny's friend Jack Howard was charged with being an accessory after the fact. The police admitted they didn't believe either André or Johnny actually pulled the triggers on the gun or guns that killed the Gilbanks, just that they ordered the hit in an attempt to stop her from continuing to investigate and prosecute the Gravelles.

When the charges were made public, the media tracked down Paul Gravelle, who had retired to a luxurious home on Mexico's Pacific Coast. He was asked if he was, as the prosecution alleged, the kingpin of the Gravelle brothers crime family. "There's 12 in our family and only the boys have a criminal record. And not all of them. That's just pure fabrication," he said, smiling. "I've just gone out of it altogether now. I've retired. It's no secret, yes, I was a drug importer. Mostly hash oil and marijuana." Then the reporter asked if he gave the order to have Lynn and Fred Gilbank killed. "No. That's not true," he said. "Our family is not killers ... That's beyond us to do a thing like that. That's a despicable act. That's a cowardly act."

It was an ugly trial. Even the lead investigator, Steve Hrab, admitted much of the evidence was circumstantial. Despite six years' worth of evidence, including thousands of wiretaps, the Crown didn't have much against the pair. And they lost a great deal of their ammo when the testimony of a lip-reader (who had been paid more than $20,000 to tell them what Johnny was saying in a videotape of a meeting in a restaurant) was thrown out because she had been found guilty of perjury in a trial in England and because, when tested for her ability, she was only able to decipher 55 percent of the words spoken by people right in front of her.

At the summary of the original bail hearing — André was released on $2 million bail — Justice Donald Gordon told the Crown that their case was "less than strong" and that "I am satisfied the issue of an alternate suspect is very real." On June 12, 2006, the Crown dropped all charges against André, Johnny and Howard and announced they were re-opening the case.

The Gilbanks' children — both adults — went on CTV's W5 newsmagazine and blamed the collapse of the case on corruption within the Hamilton police and the Ontario justice system. They claimed that someone was leaking evidence to the Gravelles from the police force. Hamilton police chief Brian Mullan went on the show and denied their claims and pointed out that the OPP had already spent months investigating the Gilbanks' claims and found no evidence to move forward. Ontario Attorney General Michael Bryant — now more famous for his fatal run-in with a drunken bicyclist than anything he ever did in office — called the claims "false, baseless, scurrilous and potentially libelous and defamatory."

Johnny was asked to be on the show, but declined. Instead, he sent the following message via e-mail:

> I am suing for what happened to me so I cannot provide an interview for your program. I do want to say that what hap-pened to me was wrong. I did not have anything to do with the murder of Mr. and Mrs. Gilbank and do not know who did. It

is wrong that after six years of investigation — they watched everything I did and wiretapped all my calls — after six years of investigating me, the police did not find any evidence I committed this crime — everything showed that I'm innocent, but they charged me with two murders I did not commit — I sat in jail for months when there was no case, no evidence that I was guilty. What happened to me was not right, it should not happen to anyone.

André filed a $25 million lawsuit against 20 officers (including Chief Mullan), Bryant and the lip-reader. "I was wrongfully charged for the murders of the Gilbanks," he said. "I want the truth to come out and for the record to be set straight for myself and my family." Johnny — who, unlike André, logged some serious jail time because he didn't make bail — launched a similar suit for $15 million.

And the case brought down the career of Inspector Rick Wills, Hamilton's top drug cop. Wills had arrested André Gravelle a few times, and had alleged that he'd heard that André had hired Johnny to kill him, but that after talking with André, things cooled down. Wills — who once dined and chatted with Prince Charles as a representative of the Hamilton police — retired abruptly. The investigation of him that began with his part in the handling of the Gilbanks netted even more charges of corruption, including the alleged theft of $57,000 from the police evidence locker.

André went back to business and was arrested a couple more times, but received only probation.

Johnny — the failed minor-league hockey player, failed wrestler, failed biker and allegedly successful hitman — left Hamilton for the west coast. He reunited with his common-law wife and their two sons (then aged five and eight) and told a wrestling fan magazine that he was having the time of his life in Vancouver. "It's beautiful out here, oh my God; the ocean, the mountains," he said. "Hamilton makes me puke now when I think about it; all those years wasted sitting there in that garbage, you know what I mean?"

And he had a new job. Johnny had done plenty of work as a bouncer in the Hammer, but in Vancouver he rented himself out as a celebrity bodyguard, counting Jack Nicholson and Cyndi Lauper among his clients. "I love it!" he said of his new profession. "I dress up nice, eat the best food, just hang around and make sure nobody screws with these people."

And like so many Canadian bikers, he said he planned to write a book about his experiences. "This will be a bestseller," he predicted. "I've been on every extreme in the world — the bikers, I was a wrestler, Major Junior A hockey player for the Kitchener Rangers — I've done a lot of things people can only dream about." He forgot to mention that he also had a part in the low-budget comedy-action movie *Oklahoma Smugglers* as "Wrestler No. 1."

Things looked good for Johnny, but once again he picked his friends poorly.

Chapter 16
Dead, in Prison or On the Run

It's ironic that the United Nations gang, like so many others, was founded specifically to be in opposition to Hells Angels. It started with two young men, James Coulter and Clayton Roueche from Abbotsford, B.C., who hung out and went to raves together in the late '90s.

"It started slowly. I started using E — ecstasy — just to stay awake and stay balanced because when you take ecstasy and you drink, it sort of counterbalances, you don't get high from ecstasy and you don't get drunk from drinking. But as soon as the ecstasy wears off, you are super, super drunk," Coulter said. "Then I just started using crack, just for an extra high. Maybe it was just to take stress away, I don't know." Like many young men who like to take drugs, they started selling them in order to pay for more.

The two of them had many Asian friends who, since many of them were physically quite small,

Clayton Roueche

were often bullied by white kids. This offended Coulter and Roueche and they began to look out for their friends. For mutual protection, their crew started going out to bars in increasingly greater numbers. That confidence led more than a few of their guys to start picking fights.

One night in 2000, the group ran into some Hells Angels associates at a since-closed Abbotsford nightclub called Animals. It was pretty obvious who they were because they were wearing "Support 81" T-shirts, which Hells Angels supporters wear because they are not allowed to wear the Hells Angels name. The Hells Angels associates, as usual, started pushing other guys around, especially the Asians.

But much to the would-be bikers' surprise, they fought back. "I remember back in the day, everyone and their dog used to be afraid of anyone who had a Hells Angels [support] shirt," said Coulter years later, "and you would tread lightly, you would tiptoe around those people and we were just a bunch of kids and thought, you don't have to be afraid of people. Right? You don't want to be bullied around. Numbers rule. We had a lot of numbers."

As the cops were breaking it all up, the Hells Angels supporters threatened Coulter and his friends. They told them they were "dead" and that they were coming back next weekend.

The crew started calling themselves the "United Nations" to reflect their ethnically diverse membership and as a subtle jab at the Hells Angels' whites-only membership rule. They went back to Animals, about 70 of them. The Hells Angels supporters showed as well, maybe two dozen. They saw the United Nations crowd and called for reinforcements, boosting their number to about 40 guys.

Coulter later recalled that evening: "I'll never forget. There was the big fight inside. It lasted maybe five minutes. Then everyone started running outside. I remember I came out the front doors and there were probably about five or six different fights happening out on the street and I seen an Abbotsford police officer pull up and he gets out of his car and he's on his walkie-talkie and he's like, 'There's H.A.! There are fights everywhere!' It was like he had never seen anything like this before. Nor had I. That was one of the bigger fights I had ever been in."

It put the United Nations on the map, and more and more young men wanted to join up. Roueche emerged as the club's president and established its structure. Members were expected to learn and practice martial arts and get the words "honor, loyalty, respect" tattooed on their bodies, often in Chinese characters rather than Western text. Members usually wore hoodies with metallic embellishments, often depicting dragons.

They started to make a lot of money. Expanding from their base of selling ecstasy, crack and meth to ravers, they began to export the super powerful BC Bud to the U.S. — often using helicopters — for incredibly large profits.

And they made enemies. In the clubs, the white and East Asian United Nations started stepping on the feet of the more established mainly Indian and Pakistani members of Independent Soldiers. As the United Nations matured as a gang, a number of crimes committed against members of the gang and the Independent Soldiers occurred and went unsolved. In 2008, there were more than 100 gang-related shootings in Vancouver, with 20 fatalities. It was a gang war not unlike Quebec's in that young men were shooting at each other to maintain and expand drug-selling territory, but instead of the combatants being two easily identifiable groups, it was a number of small, unfamiliar factions. None of the victims or accused belonged to Hells Angels.

As the United Nations grew more ambitious, they decided there was only one place to go in order to raise themselves above the mass of small gangs vying for space in the Vancouver area — and this is where the irony kicks in — so they formed a working relationship with Hells Angels. They weren't a puppet gang in the traditional sense, but allied independent contractors.

It had been going on for years, but only came to police attention when they were investigating Hells Angels and a United Nations member named Omid Bayani kept showing up in taped conversations. Bayani's an interesting guy. He was born in Iran and raised in the Baha'i faith — a religion whose adherents have sworn off violence, even in cases of self-defense. His father was murdered just before his family moved to Canada, and his family (when Omid was 16) moved to Turkey, then later to the desolate streets of Red Deer, Alberta.

Bored and out of both work and school, Bayani started robbing convenience stores for cash and cigarettes. A disgruntled ex-girlfriend ratted on him and he found himself in court. His lawyer called him "really just some sort of young puppy out on the lot." The judge disagreed, and sentenced him to five years.

At the Bowden Institution, a medium-security prison just outside Red Deer, Bayani's personality came out. He found his calling in life. Almost as soon as he arrived, he got in trouble for beating a fellow prisoner with a homemade club that had the words "goof beater" carved into it. While he served his sentence, Bayani had 21 new charges leveled against him, including threats and assaults against guards. His official report said: "The subject has a history of being sullen and defiant of officers."

He was transferred to the Kent Institution, a maximum security prison in Agassiz, B.C., about an hour away from Abbotsford. The reports on him did not improve:

> While incarcerated he has on a number of occasions tried to provoke staff members into fights with him. It was noted that Bayani's actions during one of the offences caused a female victim to suffer serious psychological trauma. It appears that Bayani does not have a full understanding of this.

His case was brought to the attention of the people at immigration, and an order signed by the federal immigration minister called for Bayani's deportation because his presence "constitutes a danger to the public of Canada."

But they never got around to getting rid of him. The official story is that the people at immigration just lost track of him.

They should have asked the police where he was. The cops saw him in a car in Abbotsford and stopped it. A search yielded a loaded .38-caliber handgun, a machete, a hunting knife, a piece of a wooden chair that police thought would be used as a club, some marijuana and cocaine. And he was arrested — along with his partner, full-patch Hells Angel Vincenzo Sansalone from the Haney Chapter — on April 4, 2007 for trafficking 600 liters of GHB, better known as "roofies" or the "date-rape drug."

After his arrest, his connections with Hells Angels became clear. "Mr. Bayani, although he is a UN gang member, was known to work and associate criminally with other gangs," RCMP biker specialist Inspector Gary Shinkaruk said. "The fact that he is charged jointly with a member of the Hells Angels is not a surprise to us and it is really indicative of the networking and the relationships that now exist in the Lower Mainland and throughout Canada where these criminal organizations are working cooperatively with each other."

And it's not like Bayani was a maverick member of the United Nations who dealt with the Hells Angels against club wishes. The cops realized that when they watched the May 15, 2008 funeral of Duane "D.W." Meyer, who was shot on the front porch of his friends' house in Abbotsford by some men in a silver Mercedes-Benz SUV. Meyer had been a prominent member of the United Nations. His funeral was attended not just by all the important members of the United Nations, but also all the local Hells Angels, including full-patches. Clearly, the United Nations — which had actually been incorporated in opposition to Hells Angels — were now working for them.

But the United Nations ran into a far bigger opponent than Hells Angels. American authorities caught Roueche on a stopover in Texas while he was flying to Mexico. He was arrested for conspiring to possess cocaine, conspiring to export cocaine, conspiring to import marijuana and conspiring to launder money. The prosecution wanted Roueche to get 220 years in prison. They didn't get it, but they weren't exactly disappointed. He was sentenced to 30 years and fined $8 million.

That did not leave the United Nations leaderless. Barzan Tilli-Choli, born in Iraq, took over and moved the United Nations' focus onto another group, Red Scorpions.

Red Scorpions were very much like the United Nations. They were a multi-racial gang who dealt drugs through nightclubs and had generally white leadership. Tilli-Choli decided that the best way to cripple Red Scorpions was to target their leaders, the Bacon brothers. The

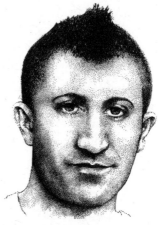

Barzan Tilli-Choli

Bacons — Jonathan, Jarrod and Jamie — had been dealing drugs for years out of their mom's Surrey apartment. They were so successful that their gang became the United Nations' primary opponents in the South Vancouver area.

So it was decided among the United Nations leadership that they would assassinate the Bacon Brothers. Using taped phone conversations and evidence gained from other listening devices that had been ordered as part of the Roueche investigation, the police arrested the conspirators before they could act. In all, eight men were arrested in connection with the assassination plot, and one name in particular stands out. They were: United Nations leader Tilli-Choli, 26; his second-in-command Daniel Ronald Russell, 27; members Karwan Saed, 32, Soroush Ansari, 28, Dilun Heng, 25, and Yong Sung, 27; and associate Aram Ali, 23; and Ion William Croitoru, 43.

The last guy is, of course, Johnny K-9. It is entirely possible that Johnny could have fallen in with these much younger, mostly Asian gangsters naturally, as he did with the Gravelle brothers in Hamilton, but my sources in the city tell me a much more likely story. Johnny, looking for work, approached the Hells Angels and they put him in contact with the United Nations for the Bacon Brothers hit.

While it led to a number of arrests in the end, the relationship between Hells Angels and the United Nations in British Columbia looks like the template for their continued success in Canada. The Hells Angels in British Columbia are generally an older group. They own bars and other legitimate businesses, and are not the type to get their hands dirty by handling drugs or anything else that could get them into trouble.

Traditionally — as under the Nomads model established by Stadnick — the Hells Angels would rely on associates in support organizations and puppet clubs to work for them and potentially take the fall. But the Animals nightclub incident in Abbotsford proved that wasn't going to work anymore. They were just too few in number to compete on the streets of Vancouver.

So Hells Angels employed a more diverse gang with much bigger numbers. It wasn't unprecedented; Stadnick himself used the Zig Zag Crew in Winnipeg with its many Iranian and

Aboriginal members; even the mighty Rockers of Laval had a black president in Greg Wooley.

The difference between these new allied gangs and the traditional puppet gangs is motivation. The members of puppet gangs and support crews work for the Hells Angels — even put their lives on the line for them, often for meager rewards — in the hopes of becoming Hells Angels down the road. But the members of these new, more diverse gangs (at least the non-white ones) don't have that option.

Instead, they work with the Hells Angels because it's in their best interest to do so. The Hells Angels have access to drugs and weapons and other resources that the individual gang members could never get without them. For many, the quickest road to wealth involves working with the Hells Angels, like it or not. And, of course, the white ones — for a perfect example, look at former Crip turned full-patch Hells Angel David "White Dread" Buchanan — still get the chance to become a Hells Angel.

There are all-white puppet gangs and support groups, especially in suburban and rural areas. In the area around Toronto alone, Hells Angels can expect help and support (and potentially new members) from Aces & Eights, Iron Horse, the Rangers, Redline, the Brotherhood and perhaps also the Comrades and the North Wall.

Their existence (and the willingness of the more diverse gangs to work with them) is testimony to the Hells Angels' strength in Canada. In fact, Hells Angels are so strong in Canada, they can make national headlines simply by being mentioned in a scandal.

• • •

Early in 2008, they returned to national consciousness in a big way because a high-ranking member of the federal government's cabinet irresponsibly left some classified documents at his girlfriend's house. The story would have appeared on page B16 of your local newspaper if the girlfriend in question hadn't been married to a prominent biker, and to have had a common-law relationship with another. That guaranteed the front page.

Maxime Bernier was a career politician and the son of a career politician. He was elected to federal parliament in 2006 as a Conservative for the riding of Beauce, a semi-rural but very industrious district just south of Quebec City, even though he lived in Montreal. His father, Gilles, had represented the same riding from 1984 to 1997.

The Conservatives were a bit surprised by their minority victory in the federal election and scrambled to find suitable ministers for their cabinet. Despite being new to Parliament, Bernier was appointed Minister of Industry and Registrar General. No more than 18 months later, he was anointed Foreign Affairs Minister, one of the most important and powerful posts in the Canadian government.

It did not always go well. On a trip to Afghanistan, he told a group of reporters that Kandahar Provincial Governor Asadullah Khalid should be replaced, even though Khalid had been democratically elected, had a long and distinguished career fighting the Taliban and had survived a number of suicide attacks. Immediately, Afghan President Hamid Karzai, Canadian Prime Minister Stephen Harper and the rest of the Canadian government rushed to criticize Bernier, and claim that Canada did not actively interfere in Afghan politics.

Less than a month later, when Cyclone Nargis devastated Burma (also known as Myanmar), Bernier promised that a Canadian Forces CC-177 transport aircraft (usually referred to in the media by its American designation, C-17 Globemaster) would be dedicated to the relief effort. But he didn't realize that all four of Canada's CC-177s were busy in Afghanistan at the time. In order to fulfill his hasty promise, the Forces were obliged to rent an identical C-17 from the American Army for just over $1.1 million for the weekend.

As bad as the start of his parliamentary career was, it got far, far worse. Even at the start of his political career, questions had been raised in the media about Bernier's girlfriend. Julie Couillard was younger than him and pretty; and the media focused primarily on her habit of wearing revealing, even risqué clothing.

They should have dug a little deeper. After a failed common-law relationship with a real estate developer when they were both teenagers, Couillard became a waitress at a Montreal strip bar. There she met and later lived with a man she called Norman, one of the bar's bouncers, but left him after he grabbed her by the throat in what she described as a "'roid rage."

On her own, but very active in the bar scene, she became close friends with Tony Volpato. Born in Italy, Volpato was a cocaine importer, high-ranking member of the Cotroni Mafia family and close friend of Frank Cotroni's. She told him she was worried about Norman, who she believed was stalking her. Volpato said he'd take care of it. Couillard didn't ask him how he would, but felt confident he would be successful and stopped worrying about Norman.

She soon met another man (she called him Steve) who was an American playing for the Montreal Machine, a short-lived franchise with the World League of American Football, the National Football League's unsuccessful attempt to export its product outside the United States. She was quite taken with Steve, and went to California with him, but returned to Montreal when she found him too aggressive.

And then, while eating a hot dog in a crowded restaurant, she met the man she would befriend and then eventually move in with, Gilles Giguère. She said it was his eyes that caught her attention. "All I could focus on was those eyes, brimming with gentleness and goodness and wielding a strange power over me," she wrote. He introduced himself as a construction worker, but she soon found out that he was actually, in her words, a "moneylender." In fact, he was a notorious loan shark with a close association with the Montreal Hells Angels and had spent time in prison for robbery.

Their relationship helped in her new ambition to become an actress. She appeared in small roles in a variety of movies and TV shows including *Highlander III: the Sorcerer* and even appeared topless in a TVA miniseries documenting the life and times of former Quebec premier René Lévesque. She was so taken with Giguère, in fact, that she claimed to have turned down repeated romantic advances by Quebecois pop star and heartthrob Roch Voisine to stay with him.

Couillard later acknowledged that she knew what Giguère did for a living, but she never saw the violent side of it. They would dine at a restaurant and someone would hand Giguère an envelope full of cash. In her own telling of the story, she admitted to not allowing herself to think about what would happen to debtors should they fall behind on a payment.

They had been together for years when Giguère told Couillard that a friend of his was getting out of prison and needed some help getting back on his feet, perhaps with some construction work. The guy who was looking for a few bucks hammering nails just happened to be the notorious Maurice "Mom" Boucher. Couillard later said that she was scared of Boucher the moment she saw his eyes, that she felt they revealed he had no conscience. She warned Giguère that she wanted to see as little of Boucher as possible, and that she considered all of his biker friends to be too vulgar for them to see often.

Couillard particularly disliked one of her boyfriend's biker pals. She described Léo Lemieux as a "motormouth" and admitted she warned Giguère that he was probably a police informant and that he shouldn't say anything in front of him. He didn't follow her advice, and Lemieux informed on him.

At 6 a.m. on December 5, 1996, a SWAT team from the multi-force Carcajou (Wolverine) unit broke into their condo. Couillard claimed they beat Giguère brutally and unnecessarily, and accused them of trying to see her naked. She sold the story to *Allô Police*, Montreal's lurid tabloid that focused on the city's crime. They ran it under a headline with bold, inch-tall, all-capital type that read: "Arrested In the Bedroom! The Spouse of the Mobster Gilles Giguère, the Actress Julie Couillard Condemns the Wolverine!" In her autobiography, *My Story*, she made it very clear she has a low opinion of police, and frequently referred to them as "animals." Both Giguère and Couillard were soon released, but she said that their relationship started to turn sour. He admitted that he had made some statements to police — who, he said, threatened to "get" her if he didn't — but did not make clear what he'd said. Giguère was later charged with conspiracy to commit murder because of his association with the Hells Angels management team, but police withdrew the charge due to lack of evidence two months later.

Although they were both very shaken from their experiences, the couple decided to get married, but put off setting a date because Giguère was still facing charges related to drugs and weapons found in his possession. He assured her they belonged to Lemieux, and she believed him.

On the morning of April 26, 1996, Couillard recalled that she went downstairs to say good-bye to Giguère on his way to work only to see his truck leaving. She never saw him alive again.

After two days of looking for him, Couillard received a call from police telling her that Giguère's body had been found, that he had been shot six times and left in a rain-filled ditch by the side of a rural highway. She didn't believe it, but later that day saw his body on a TV news report while visiting with family members at her brother Patrick's house.

Couillard later said that she was shocked and even sickened by the fact that Boucher attended Giguère's funeral. Desperate to make sure Giguère's name was clear and to help secure her own safety, she assured Boucher that Giguère would never have turned informant. "Don't worry about it," Boucher told her, smiling. "There's people who think *I'm* a snitch."

Fearing not only that the Hells Angels had killed her boyfriend, but were planning to kill her, Couillard tried to distance herself from them. She took what money they had saved up and, with some of Giguère's non-biker contacts, set up a contracting company.

Her tenure away from the bikers did not last long. At a bar, she met up-and-coming Rockers full-patch Stéphane Sirois, a good friend of Boucher's who had also worked with Stadnick. It didn't take long before she found out he was a biker, but instead of running away, she rationalized her attraction to him:

> In those days, I was going through survivor's guilt. I was finding it very difficult to accept the fact that I hadn't seen Gilles's murder coming. At that point, I thought to myself, 'If I hadn't been able to save Gilles, maybe I could at least save this guy Stéphane.'

And to her credit, she saw some success in her plan to "save" Sirois. At the height of the Hells Angels-Rock Machine war (in which the Rockers were primary combatants), Sirois was asked to turn in his patch because the Rockers found out that he was living with Couillard. As the ex-girlfriend of a man they considered to be an informant, she was certainly too dangerous to have around. Faced with choosing between his girlfriend and his gang, Sirois chose Couillard. Surprisingly, the Rockers accepted his resignation and stayed on generally positive terms with him.

He asked her to marry him and she accepted. But Sirois had a hard time finding legitimate work, and the couple began to get encumbered with massive debts from wild spending. He started borrowing money from her and convinced her to pay $12,000 for her own wedding ring. Their wedding was a massive, lavish — and by most accounts garish — affair that saw the couple leave in the same Rolls-Royce limo Celine Dion had rented for her wedding. On his way to the ceremony, Sirois was stopped by a Rocker who asked him for the $5,000 he owed him. Sirois begged off, citing the fact it was his wedding day.

Their honeymoon was a disaster as their credit cards were declined in the Bahamas and they had to pay cash for a flight home. Sirois then revealed that he was in much more financial trouble than he had let on, and he pushed her to lend him more money, intimating that his old biker friends might kill him if she didn't.

Couillard decided to divorce him. Knowing he would refuse, she took matters into her own hands and had an affair with one of her contracting clients, a real estate developer she identified as Bruno. Before she could tell Sirois that she had cheated on him, he left her. But not for another woman. In fact, he turned informant and entered the witness protection program. Since he had been the Rockers' de facto bookkeeper, he had a great deal of information to pass along. The day after Couillard found out about Sirois, she discovered she was pregnant. Since she decided Bruno was almost certainly the father, she had an abortion. Sirois later testified that it was Boucher who ordered the hit on Giguère, and described Couillard as being "close to getting it" as well.

While starting her life over again as a bartender, she ran into another old real estate contact — she identified him as Sylvain — and began to work for him. They started an affair, but she broke it off because he was married and refused to leave his wife.

She then rebounded into another relationship with a man named Robert Pépin. Within days, he offered her a managing partnership in his security firm. Pépin was good friends with Jacques Duchesneau, president of the Canadian Air Transport Security Authority (CATSA), and the two of them were putting together a deal that would have put Pépin's systems into airports all around the country. Pépin eventually lost the contract, and then lost Couillard when she found out that the shares in his firm that he promised her were instead given to a man to whom he owed money. They parted, she said, on pleasant terms, but Pépin later committed suicide.

At that point, she entered into yet another relationship with a married man; this one was Phillippe Morin, who owned a Quebec City–based construction company named Kevlar. Couillard and her friend, Bernard Coté, were anxious to sell some real estate in the Turks and Caicos Islands. Luckily for her, Coté worked for Michael Fortier, the federal Minister of Public Works, who happened to be looking for property in Quebec City for federal government projects. Coté and Morin convinced Couillard to represent both of them to the federal government.

Morin took Couillard to a meeting at Montreal's upscale Ristorante Cavalli. Along with his business partner René Bellerive, political fundraiser Eric Boyko and five attractive young ladies, Morin's guest of honor was Bernier, who was then Minister of Industry and Boyko's boss at the federal government's Business Development Bank. Bernier, Couillard later said, had had a few drinks, sat next to her and even kissed her on the cheek.

Although somewhat offended at the time, Couillard started to communicate with Bernier and, after realizing that they were likely to hook up soon, she decided to reveal the details of her past in case it would jeopardize his career. "It was obvious to me if I became his partner, I would surely be subjected to background checks," she wrote. " ... if I'm wrong, then Canada's national security is truly in jeopardy."

They started dating and took trips together. Couillard said that Bernier made staying together at least a year a condition of their relationship, in part, she maintained, to silence persistent rumors that he was gay. He designated her as his personal companion on official trips and referred to her conversationally as "my spouse." And it was at that time she attended his swearing-in ceremony as Foreign Minister in a dress that sent tongues wagging and camera flashes popping.

Bernier's staff quickly grew tired of the demanding and sharp-edged Couillard and tried to keep them apart. One particularly persistent staffer stood up to her and Couillard admitted that she first considered slapping "the little bitch" but changed her mind and ordered Bernier to choose between the two of them. The staffer, who was still recuperating from a major car accident, was fired.

Soon after, Couillard accompanied Bernier to a meeting at the United Nations headquarters in New York City. She was introduced to and photographed with American President George W. Bush. Things were going well for the couple until Bernier took her to Paris in December 2007, where Couillard claimed to have caught him making out with an old girlfriend of his at the Canadian ambassador's residence. At that point, she said, she ended their romantic relationship, but agreed to continue to appear in public with him for the rest of their one-year agreement.

What happened next is not entirely clear, with only Couillard's often-contradictory recollections to go by because nobody else involved will comment. In April 2008, Couillard said she discovered a file with Bernier's name on it in her house. Too afraid, she said, to open it, let alone read it, she instead took it to a lawyer she knew.

"Maxime came to my house," she told reporters at the time, "and the document in question was left at my house. For now, what I can tell you is that the document made me feel very uncomfortable. I was panicked by the fact that I had it."

But a year later, she told a different story in her book, saying that Bernier directed her as follows: "Can you put this in the garbage for me? I would prefer that you wait for garbage day to do it, after all they are confidential documents."

Couillard went on to add: "I can't help but smile when I think that, in the eyes of some observers, I supposedly constituted a threat to national security and state secrets! I could have wallpapered my house in confidential documents."

The lawyer then returned the file in question (which happened to be his notes from a NATO briefing) to Bernier. I'm not sure what the lawyer said to him, but Bernier resigned from his cabinet post immediately. Only then did the media finally dig into Couillard's past, making an instant celebrity of her and pointing out how closely entwined she was not just with the federal government, but the Hells Angels as well.

Bernier was cleared of any wrongdoing and won his re-election bid in Beauce. Harper did not assign him a cabinet post.

Of course, neither Couillard nor Bernier were proven to have done anything against the law. He obviously could have been much more responsible with his documents and could have picked his friends in the real estate business better, and she could have at least worked less hard at drawing attention to herself and stayed away from married men. But what drew the attention of the nation was the fact that one of the most powerful members of the federal government had left classified documents at the house of someone who had been married to one notorious Hells Angels associate and had had an earlier common-law relationship with yet another. Perhaps she did not look at the documents, and perhaps she no longer had ties with the Hells Angels, but it could just as easily gone another way. If, for example, she owed a great deal of money to a member or associate, such documents could easily have been used in an extortion attempt. Keep in mind that Boucher had indicated that intimidating the members of government that opposed him were an active part of his master plan.

The close call that was the Couillard-Bernier Affair is a chilling reminder of the amazing reach and infiltration the Hells Angels have in all parts of Canadian society.

• • •

To get an accurate perspective on the outlaw biker scene in Ontario now, consider that virtually every single one of the Hells Angels mentioned in this book is dead, in prison, on the run from the law or handcuffed by legal restrictions. The most notable exceptions are former Para-Dice Rider Donny Petersen and Satan's Choice founder Bernie Guindon.

Petersen still works at Heavy-Duty Cycles in Toronto where he is described as a "master builder." The business is now officially owned by a friend who goes by the name Tattoo Tony. Petersen also writes articles and books about Harley-Davidsons and even appears on TV to share his extensive expertise on motorcycle mechanics. But, much to the chagrin of many reporters, doesn't act as a spokesman for Hells Angels anymore.

Guindon — despite his lofty position in the history of biker gangs in Canada — has escaped prosecution for decades. His son, Harley Davidson Guindon, wasn't so lucky. He was one of 65 people arrested in November 2005's Project Superman. He was charged with sexual assault with a weapon, forcible confinement, extortion using a firearm, assault with a weapon, assault causing bodily harm and aggravated assault.

Bernie Guindon has since founded and is still the honorary chairman of the Ontario Confederation of Clubs (OCC), an advocacy group for motorcycle enthusiast organizations. All of the member organizations are — with the possible exception of the famously neutral Red Devils — decidedly pro–Hells Angels. The Outlaws, Bandidos, the Mongols, Black Pistons and other anti–Hells Angels groups don't belong. In January 2010, the OCC announced the addition of the 55 V-Twin Cruisers, Cinco Chagas, Iron Dragons, Iron Horse and Messiahs Creed as new members. Of course, that doesn't mean they are puppet clubs. In fact, the Cinco Chagas (Spanish for "five wounds," a reference to Jesus Christ's suffering) and the Messiahs Creed profess to be non-violent, Christian-based clubs. But it does indicate that there are lots of clubs out there who wouldn't mind getting a little closer to Hells Angels.

And Guindon, like Parente and Johnny K-9, is trying to get somebody to write his life story. And he, too, has a title picked out: *From Satan to an Angel, Your Side, My Side and the Truth.* Knowing what I know about bikers, I'm sure Guindon's book would reflect "his side" as the unalloyed "truth."

But bikers like Petersen and Guindon are very rare.

Over the last decade Hells Angels have suffered more arrests and about as many casualties as the other biker gangs in Canada. But while the Outlaws had been essentially reduced to a disparate band of gray-bearded men waiting for their court-ordered restrictions to expire and the amorphous Loners/Rock Machine/Bandidos entity seems to be a club on the Internet only, Hells Angels continue to groom new members and employ gangs of many different stripes all over the country.

It's all about the branding. It comes down to the logo. As Isnor told me: "Nobody makes movies about the Outlaws."

• • •

But the Outlaws are still there. I'd finished the book. Had sent it off to the editor and thought I was done with it when I got a call from a well-placed biker cop I trust. "You know Parente's back with the Outlaws; back in charge," he said. I told him that I had heard that, but not from a reliable source. And that despite all his assurances of the opposite, I had a feeling Parente couldn't stay away. "Looks like there could be some violence ahead for the HA," the cop added. I told him I wouldn't be too surprised.

I asked another biker cop what he thought. "There's a chance Stadnick could be out next year," he told me. "If he wants to re-establish himself, he'll have to do something big ... and if the other side wants to establish themselves, they're going to have to do something big."

So while both sides have been weakened by arrests, court-ordered restrictions, internal dissent and age, it would appear that Hells Angels and the Outlaws are once again sizing each other up and preparing to do whatever they have to to come out on top of the organized crime world in Ontario.

And if they can settle a few old scores in the process, I'm sure that would be just part of doing business.

Acknowledgments

Like all books, *Showdown* was a truly collaborative effort. My name might be on it, but the work of many is in it. Many people deserve to be thanked.

First and foremost is Don Loney, the greatest editor on the face of the earth. That's not just my opinion, it's a well-known fact.

I am equally indebted to my outstanding illustrator, Tonia Cowan. Her work is always spot-on. Readers who want to see more of her talent can visit squeakymarker.blogspot.com.

I also have to thank Don's team at John Wiley & Sons, especially production editor Pauline Ricablanca, marketing whiz Robin Dutta-Roy, publicity specialist Erika Zupko, do-everything-guy Brian Will, designers Michael Chan and Diana Sullada, copy editor Andrew Borkowski and proofreader Eleanor Gasparik.

And, of course, I have to thank the sources, especially Mario Parente. We didn't talk that much and, in the end, didn't really accomplish what he wanted, but I have to commend him on his honesty and courage. I also have to thank Luther, who brought us together. My other sources — notably John Harris and Len Isnor — were excellent, providing wit and wisdom along with information.

As always, I have to thank Leta Potter because I'd be in trouble if I forgot; and I have to thank my wife and children for their nearly infinite patience and kindness.

Index